THE FODDER GRASSES OF NORTHERN INDIA

THE FODDER GRASSES OF NORTHERN INDIA

J. F. DUTHIE, B. A., F. L. S.

GYAN

Published by

Gyan Publishing House
5, Ansari Road
Daryaganj, New Delhi-110002
Phone: 011-47034999, 9811692060
E-mail: books@gyanbooks.com

Distribution Network
gyanbooks.com
India, USA, Canada, UK, Australia, France

ISBN: 978-81-212-8348-9 (PB)
First Published, 1888

2nd Impression 2023

Printed at: Gyan Press, Delhi.

THE FODDER GRASSES OF NORTHERN INDIA
Author: J. F. DUTHIE

THE

FODDER GRASSES

OF

NORTHERN INDIA.

BY

J. F. DUTHIE, B.A., F.L.S.,

DIRECTOR, BOTANICAL DEPARTMENT OF NORTHERN INDIA.

ROORKEE:

PRINTED AT THE THOMASON CIVIL ENGINEERING COLLEGE PRESS.

1888.

PREFACE.

I HAVE attempted in the following pages to give a short account of the more important kinds of grasses that are used in the plains of Northern India, either for fodder or forage. Several of the plains species extend up to considerable elevations on the Himalaya, but I have omitted all mention of those which are exclusively Himalayan.

The area of country to which this report refers, and which coincides with that over which my botanical investigations generally will in future be conducted, extends from the North-West frontier, and includes the Punjab, the North-West Provinces and Oudh, Sindh, Rájputána, Central India, and the Central Provinces.

The books and pamphlets which have been specially consulted in the preparation of this work are:—

Aitchison, Catalogue of Punjab and Sindh Plants.
Atkinson, Economic Products of the N.-W. Provinces, Part VI.
Baden Powell, Handbook of the Economic Products of the Punjab.
Baker, Flora of the Mauritius and the Seychelles.
Bentham, Flora Australiensis, Vol. VII.
,, Flora Hongkongensis.
,, Handbook of the British Flora.
,, in Journ. Linn. Soc. Vol. XIX. (1882).
Bentham and Hooker, f., Genera Plantarum, Vol. III.
Bentley and Trimen, Medicinal Plants.
Boissier, Flora Orientalis, Vol. V.
Brandis, Forest Flora of North-West and Central India.
Cosson and Durieu, Flore d'Algerie.
De Candolle, L'Origine des Plantes Cultivées.
Edgeworth, Catalogue of Plants found in the Banda District.
,, Botanico-Agricultural account of the protected Sikh States.
Hooker, Student's Flora of the British Islands.
Jaub. and Spach, Icones Plantarum Orientalium.

King, List of Plants in the Plains of the N.-W. Provinces.
Kunth, Enumeratio Plantarum.
Lindley and Moore, Treasury of Botany.
Mueller, Select Plants for Extra-tropical Countries.
Munro, Monograph of the Bambusaceæ in Trans. Linn. Soc. Vol. XXVI.
Oliver, First Book of Indian Botany.
Palisot de Beauvois, Agrostographie.
Parlatore, Flora Italiana, Vol. I.
Reichenbach, Icones Floræ Germanicæ.
Roxburgh, Flora Indica.
Royle, Fibrous Plants of India.
,, Illustrations of the Botany of the Himalaya.
Settlement Reports of districts in the Punjab.
Simmonds, Tropical Agriculture.
Steudel, Synopsis Plantarum Glumacearum.
Stewart, Punjab Plants.
Symonds, Indian Grasses.
Thwaites, Enumeratio Plantarum Zeylaniæ.
Trinius, Species Graminum.
Vasey, The Agricultural Grasses of the United States (1884).
,, Report on the Investigation of the Grasses of the Arid Districts of Kansas, Nebraska, and Colorado, 1886.
,, A Report on certain Grasses and Forage Plants for Cultivation in the South and South-West, 1887.

My annual visits to the Royal Botanical Gardens, near Calcutta, have been of much advantage, more particularly in connection with the strictly botanical portions of this work. In addition to an excellent library, there is the splendid herbarium in which grasses from all parts of India are largely represented. I wish to take this opportunity of expressing my gratitude to Dr. King, the Director, for his generous help on every occasion of my visiting the garden.

The Sahâranpur herbarium now contains a very fair representative collection of Indian grasses. I have myself collected largely in the N.-W. Provinces, in Râjputâna, and Bundelkhand. I am also very greatly indebted to many contributors for valuable collections obtained from districts that I have not yet had opportunities of visiting. In this way some very useful collections have recently been procured for me through the kindness of the Conservators of Forests of the Punjab, Oudh, the Central Provinces, and Hyderabad.

Separate collections were received from each of the following divisions :—

Central Provinces,	Punjab,	Oudh,
Chánda.*	Lahore.	Pilibhit.
Balaghát.	Ráwalpindi.	Kheri.
Nagpur.	Mooltan.	Bhira.
Seoni.	Jhelum.	

To Mr. J. R. Drummond, B.A., C.S., I owe special thanks, not only for large donations of specimens, but for many notes and suggestions rendered all the more valuable by his sound knowledge of botany, and his intimate acquaintance with the vernacular dialects of the Punjab.

To Mr. W. Coldstream, C.S., I am much indebted for kindly allowing me to make use of his valuable notes on the grasses of Hissar.

From the Rev. A. Campbell of Manbhum, I have received valuable collections of Chutia Nagpur grasses, together with a list of their vernacular names, many of which are in the Santáli dialect.

Mr. A. E. Lowrie, the officer in charge of the Ajmere and Merwára forests, has sent me a very complete collection of the grasses of that part of Rájputána, together with vernacular names and many useful notes.

From Capt. G. Wingate, Assistant Commissary General, I have frequently received grasses to be named ; and, as the specimens were mostly accompanied with their vernacular names, together with various notes, of which I have freely made use, these communications usually resulted to our mutual advantage.

I profited in like manner by correspondence with Mr. J. McC. Douie, C.S., a few years ago when he was engaged in settlement work in the Karnál district.

Col. D. M. Strong has also sent me for botanical identification sets of grasses from Beluchistan, Simla, and Allahabad. I am also indebted to this gentleman for some interesting notes on Australian pasture grasses.

* This was a very fine collection, and appears to have been personally superintended during its preparation by Mr. G. Foster, the Deputy Conservator, to whom I am also indebted for additional notes subsequently contributed.

Mr. A. Wingate, C.S., C.I.E., late of Udaipur, sent me a large and valuable collection of native-named fodder grasses from that district.

I have received an interesting collection of grasses from the Salt Range, prepared by Dr. Warth, who has recently been investigating the coal resources of that district.

Bhai Sádhu Singh, and Pundit Sundar Lál, forest officers attached respectively to the Jeypur and Patiála States, have each contributed useful collections accompanied with vernacular names.

From the Commissariat Department, in addition to Capt. Wingate's contributions, I have received native-named sets from Allahabad, Bareilly and Ráwalpindi.

Professor Hackel of St. Pölten, Hungary, who is at present engaged in the preparation of a monograph of the grass family for the new edition of DeCandolle's "Prodromus," has recently favoured me with many valuable notes on some specimens of Indian grasses despatched to him from the Saháranpur herbarium. I have by this means been able to give greater accuracy to the nomenclature of many of the species enumerated in the following pages.

I wish also to acknowledge with gratitude the kind assistance rendered by Sir W. Davies, K.C.S.I., late Financial Commissioner of the Punjab, Mr. R. S. Whiteway, C.S. and Mr. C. G. Palmer, C.E., in the way of additions and corrections in the alphabetical list of vernacular names. This list, together with the equivalent botanical names, will, it is hoped, prove useful in facilitating the identification of many of the Indian grasses.

Concerning the material which constitutes the main portion of the book, it will be found that the genera are arranged strictly in accordance with the "Genera Plantarum" of Bentham and Hooker, the species being placed alphabetically under each genus.

The analytical table given on page xiii is intended for the use of those persons who may wish to follow up the subject for themselves, and to acquire a more intimate knowledge of the genera of Indian grasses.

A short glossary of the technical terms which occur in the descriptive portions of this work is given on page ix.

There are many jungle plants not belonging to the grass family, which are readily eaten by cattle, and some of them are without doubt more nutritious than a large number of the grasses enumerated in this work. They include trees, shrubs and herbs. The fodder-yielding trees and shrubs are especially useful during seasons of drought when herbaceous vegetation becomes scanty. Sufficient attention has not hitherto been given to this source of fodder supply, which is capable of being greatly developed. The economic value of trees and shrubs so far as they contribute towards the value of forests in the way of fuel, &c., has been to a great extent recognized, but no special measures have been undertaken to develop their capabilities for fodder purposes. Of the herbaceous vegetation a large number of plants belonging to other natural orders besides the Gramineæ are eaten by horses and cattle promiscuously along with the ordinary grasses. Those which are known to possess nutritious qualities should be encouraged; for, in addition to their value as forage, they no doubt, in many cases, serve to protect the roots of the grasses amongst which they grow, as well as to fill up what would be bare spaces if the ground supported only grass. Considering the importance of many of these non-gramineous fodder plants, *e.g.*, babul (*Acacia arabica*), jhand (*Prosopis spicigera*), ber (*Zizyphus nummularia*), and a host of annuals, the subject is worthy, I think, of being specially investigated.

The two parts of nature-printed illustrations will together form a convenient companion volume to this book. I am glad of another opportunity of congratulating Mr. T. D. Bona, the able Superintendent of the Thomason College Press, Roorkee, for the skill with which he has succeeded in producing so many faithful portraits.

The six plates included in this work were lithographed at the Thomason College Press from drawings copied by my draftsman, H. Hormusji, from figures in the "Agrostographie" of Palisot de Beauvois, from Reichenbach's "Icones Floræ Germanicæ," and a few from Bentley's and Trimen's "Medicinal Plants."

J. F. DUTHIE.

CONTENTS.

INTRODUCTION.

The family Gramineæ, to which every kind of grass in the botanical sense belongs, is a very natural one; that is to say, the structural characters which distinguish it from other families are clearly defined. They also possess a superficial resemblance in common by which they can at once be identified as members of one family.

Amongst the characters by which the various grasses may be distinguished, the one from the other, are many which are sufficiently obvious to any observant person, and do not require any very special knowledge of botany to be recognized. Some, for instance, such as bamboos, have thick woody stems, and grow to the size of trees, whilst others are small and succulent, lasting only for one year or less from germination to the ripening of the grain. The habit of growth is often a sufficiently distinguishing character; the long creeping stems of dúb (*Cynodon Dactylon*), for instance; and the tendency to climb which is the normal condition of *Anthistiria scandens*, *Apluda aristata*, and some others. The arrangement of the flowers, known technically as the inflorescence, offers many conspicuous distinctions which characterize genera, or groups of species. The presence or absence of hairs, bristles, or spines on or around the florets are superficial characters and easily recognized, as also the colour of the pubescence whether white, reddish, or golden. Some species emit a sweet aromatic perfume; others are highly scented during the process of drying. Some kinds grow in isolated clumps, whilst others are gregarious, extending over large areas in the form of pasture. Some grasses are found only near water; others appear to prefer dry sandy ground. Clay soils and calcareous soils have each their characteristic species; and certain kinds appear to flourish better in shady places.

The distribution of particular species over wide areas of country is largely due to agricultural extension, for certain kinds are nearly always to be found associated with cultivated crops. A knowledge of the habitat of a plant is very frequently of great assistance towards its identification.

The occurrence of certain kinds of grasses in particular localities is determined to a great extent by climate; some species, and often entire genera, being restricted to the plains, whilst others cannot exist below certain elevations on the hills. Excessive moisture influences to a great extent localization of certain species; thus, the majority of the grasses inhabiting the damper eastern parts of Northern India are not to be found in the comparatively rainless tracts to the west, where the climate on the other hand appears to determine the existence of certain species characteristic of desert countries.

As regards the grasses of the plains, it will be found that those inhabiting North-Western and Central India, are more nutritious than those of Bengal and Burma. Excessive and continuous moisture, combined with a high temperature, tends to increase luxuriant growth, but the nutritive properties are expended in the formation of rankness. It may be stated in a general way that the best fodder grasses are to be found, and occur in greater abundance, where the climate approaches most to that of a temperate one. There is nothing in the plains of India, for instance, to compare with the richness of the pasture land which exists on the higher slopes of the Himalaya. The vast stretches of undulating meadows, known as "maidáns,"* and which extend from the upper limits of the forests to the snow line, are composed of many of the most nutritious grasses of the world, some of them belonging to species well-known in Europe for their good grazing qualities.

In order to acquire a sufficient knowledge so as to be able to distinguish one species of grass from another it will be necessary to learn something about the structure of the flowers, the minuteness of which, in many instances, constitutes the main difficulties of the study, considerable patience and close observation being required.

The following is a brief general description of the grass family:—Roots fibrous. Stems herbaceous, annual or perennial, round or compressed, erect, decumbent, or creeping and rooting at the nodes, hollow except at the joints. Leaves alternate, usually long and narrow, parallel-veined and entire, the lower portion embracing the stem in the form of a sheath which is split down on the side opposite to that where the free portion, or blade of the leaf, is given off. At the top of the sheath, and within the base of the blade, is a small scarious or hairy appendage called the ligule. The arrangement of the flowers, or inflorescence, is nearly always terminal, and the spikelets composing the inflorescence are variously arranged in panicles, racemes, spikes, or heads. Each spikelet (*see* adjoining figure)†

* These maidáns support the life of vast numbers of wild grass-eating animals, such as the burrel, for instance, whose flesh at the proper season of the year is equal to, if not better than, the finest mutton. They are also largely made use of by the Himalayan villagers, who annually, during the summer months, drive their cattle to these high pastures.

† Copied from Oliver's First Book of Indian Botany.

consists of three or more chaff-like scales, called glumes, of which the two

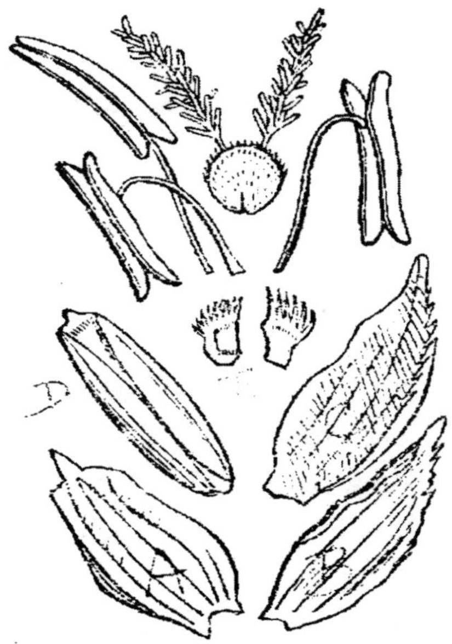

outer, or lowest, are usually empty, and are differently shaped from the others. The third and succeeding glumes, if there be more than three, are the flowering glumes, each of which normally contains a small scale, usually transparent and with two lateral nerves; this is called the pale. Within the pale is the real flower consisting of minute scales, usually only two, called lodicules, and three stamens, rarely more or less, with long filaments, supporting anthers which are attached by their middle (versatile). In the centre, surrounded by the stamens and lodicules, is the ovary, 1-celled, and containing a single ovule. At the top of the ovary are the two feathery styles. The grain, *i.e.*, the matured ovary, contains a single seed consolidated with the pericarp, or outer skin of the grain. The embryo lies at one side at the base of the seed, and is surrounded by a thick farinaceous substance known as albumen or perisperm.

The above are some of the prevailing characters of the family, but there are many exceptions; for instance, the stems of some of the perennial kinds become woody, as in bamboos, many of which attain to the size of trees, and their stems are frequently solid throughout. The greatest variation occurs in the structure of the spikelets. They are sometimes monœcious, as in Indian corn, which bears male and female clusters of spikelets on different portions of the plant. The spikelets may be 1-flowered (*Plate* E., *Fig.* 27), or 2-or more-flowered (*Plate* E., *Fig.* 26*a*, and *Plate* F., *Fig.* 29*a*). The florets of each spikelet may be perfect (*Plate* A., *Fig.* 1*c*), *i.e.*, with both stamens and pistil, or with only one set of organs (unisexual) (*Plate* A., *Fig.* 6*a*), or without either stamens or pistil (neuter); and sometimes without even the pale, in which case the floret is represented by a single scale or glume. In the same spikelet there may be both perfect and imperfect florets (*Plate* A., *Fig.* 5, *b*). In rice the lower empty glumes are minute, or reduced to bristles. In Panicum the outer empty glume is usually very much smaller than the other (*Plate* A., *Fig.* 4), whilst in Paspalum it is wanting altogether. The midrib of some of the glumes, usually the flowering one, is often furnished with a bristle, extending either from the tip or from its back; this when of a certain length is called an awn (*Plate* E., *Figs.* 25 and 26). These awns must be carefully distinguished from other bristles which often occur at the base of the spikelets in the form of an involucre. The true awn is represented in many species of Andropogon, in barley, oats, and in the bearded varieties of wheat. Examples of the involucral bristles occur in the genera Pennisetum, and Setaria, to which bájra and kangni respectively belong. The stamens, which are normally three in number, are sometimes reduced to two (*Plate* B., *Fig*. 10, *Plate* D., *Fig*. 21, *Plate* E., *Fig*. 23), or one, whilst in rice there are as many as six (*Plate* B., *Fig*. 7, *b*).

THE NUTRITIVE VALUE OF INDIAN GRASSES.—Very little is known regarding the actual feeding value of our commonest fodder grasses. What we do know is chiefly of a relative nature. Close enquiry amongst graziers and intelligent zamindars indicates in a general kind of way what are the best available grasses in any one district, but the opinions obtained from different districts are often very contradictory. For instance, a particular kind of grass may be highly valued in one part of India and despised elsewhere. Many widely distributed species do, no doubt, vary in actual nutritive value according to the climate. It may also happen, that the actual value of any particular grass remaining constant, its relative value varies in proportion to the general standard of excellence attained by the grasses of different districts. In these and many other cases the only sure method of ascertaining the true value of grasses is by chemical analysis. A large portion of an analyst's work would tend to confirm by rational methods, the facts which had been empirically ascertained. His original investigations would lead him to discover to what extent the variations of climate and soil tend to alter the nutritive value of certain grasses. There are many grasses in India, which, on account of their being sparingly distributed, have hitherto been more or less overlooked. By chemical analysis the intrinsic nutritive value of many of these rarer species might very possibly be found equal to that of the best known fodder grasses. Such kinds, however, to be rendered practically useful, would have to be encouraged by cultivation, or by special means of protection; for the value of any particular grass for fodder or forage purposes does not, after all, depend so much on its nutritive qualities as on its being available in sufficient quantity. The prevailing spontaneous species of a district will, as a rule, therefore, be found to head the list in regard to utility.

GRASS RESERVES.—In a general way it is found that the periodical protection of grass lands has a direct advantage. Many of our most nutritious perennial grasses manage to exist on ground which presents a most unpromising appearance. They seem to have acquired the power of adapting themselves to withstand the trying effects of long-continued droughts, and the unrestricted cropping by goats and other animals. Nevertheless, they possess capabilities of vigorous growth, and respond immediately under the influence of favouring conditions, whether natural or artificial. Of the natural incentives to recuperative growth the most beneficial is seasonable rainfall. In the case of large areas of grass land, the only way in which we can assist nature during the critical periods of deficient rainfall, is by preventing indiscriminate grazing. The effects of over-grazing are not only directly injurious to grass vegetation, but indirectly in consequence of the destruction of young trees and shrubs, under the shade of which many kinds of grasses find sufficient protection to be available as fodder long after every blade, not so protected, is shrivelled up and destroyed. Before proceeding to make arrangements for the formation of grass reserves, it should first of all be ascertained whether the existing grasses are of sufficient value as fodder or forage to justify the cost of such protection. Every grass reserve should contain a large percentage of the best of the prevailing indigenous species of the district, rather than be stocked with introduced kinds, however superior they may prove to be in other localities. Attention should also be directed to the extension of all the really good local kinds in the place of useless or noxious weeds. There are certain tracts of country, however, where the natural or indigenous grasses are found to be very deficient in nutritive value, and which can be advantageously replaced by superior kinds introduced from other countries. In New Zealand, for instance, I am told that an acre of land, where only the indigenous grasses exist, will support only one sheep; whereas three to six, or more, can be maintained on an acre which has been sown with grass seed introduced from Europe.

THE PRESERVATION OF FODDER.—During ordinary seasons, when the rainfall is up to the average, the yield of fodder throughout Northern India, in the form of grass alone, must be very largely in excess of actual requirements. A very large portion, however, of the spontaneous or indigenous fodder supply is practically unavailable for the same reason that the value of the produce of some forests diminishes according to the distance to the nearest suitable market. Nevertheless, many outlying grass tracts can be utilized to some extent by driving the cattle to such places for grazing purposes; in fact there are certain classes of graziers, who both in the plains and on the hills habitually migrate with their herds to distant localities during the different seasons of the year. Notwithstanding this, there must be a very large quantity of good grass which is never grazed nor cut for fodder. During seasons of long continued drought the whole of the spontaneous growth of grass within the area affected is suddenly checked, and the supply of fodder from this source becoming reduced to a minimum the usual results take place, *viz.*, the loss or impoverishment of an immense number of cattle. The custom of migrating from one part of the country to another in search of fodder is a remnant of primitive times, when whole tribes of people, and even nations, led a nomadic life for the purpose of obtaining food and fodder for themselves and their beasts. The adoption of agricultural pursuits gradually led to the establishment of permanent settlements, and to the localization of agricultural produce by cultivation. The advantages acquired by civilized nations after generations of cumulative experience ought in these days to be applied, as far as can be, towards regulating the supply of fodder in India, and to secure its being continuously available during good and bad seasons alike. The condition of grass lands which are protected merely to prevent destructive grazing is, during exceptionally severe droughts, very little better than that of the open and unprotected tracts, the only difference being that the evil effects of the drought are not so soon apparent in the case of the protected reserves owing to the more luxuriant growth of the vegetation. What is really required, and more particularly in those districts which are subject to periodical droughts, is the adoption of an extensive system of preservation of grass in the form of compressed fodder or silage; and, where irrigation can be secured, the cultivation of suitable fodder plants, either indigenous or introduced, would yield a valuable reserve during times of scarcity. The stacking of hay, which is a form of compressed fodder, is undertaken more or less in certain parts of Northern India, but the object in most instances is merely to prepare a sufficient quantity for use during the cold weather months. Many of the Indian grasses when stacked will retain their nutritive properties for several years; encouragement should, therefore, be given to bring about a much more extensive system of stacking, so that the excess of fodder yielded during good seasons may be rendered available during times of scarcity. There is one drawback to the production of really good hay in this country, and that is, the difficulty of drying the various grasses at the time when they ought to be cut. The majority of the indigenous species of Indian grasses flourish during the rainy season, and some of the best kinds have flowered and are ripening their seed by the time that the rains are well over; and as it is well known that the stems and leaves of grasses attain their maximum nutritive value during the period of flowering, it would appear to be greater economy to cut the rainy season grasses at that time, and to preserve it as silage.

There are a few indigenous grasses, and many other kinds might be introduced from other countries, which would thrive under cultivation in the climate of Northern India as winter grasses. These would come to the flowering stage at a time when the weather would admit of their being made into excellent hay, and a certain amount of valuable fodder would thus be rendered available throughout the hot weather months. In the United States, the climate of the southern parts of which is somewhat similar to that of Northern India, these winter grasses are very advantageously made use of. In the introduction to my "List of the Grasses of North-Western India," published in 1883, I remarked:—"Necessity in future years will no doubt bring about a more careful consideration of what is now being adopted with so much success in Europe and America, *viz.*, the preservation of fodder by the process of ensilage. The art of preserving fodder is capable of much development, and when brought more into practice, new processes, will no doubt be discovered, which will render its application more simple, and with certain modifications, more suitable for its adoption in this country." Within the last few years ensilage operations have been extensively undertaken all over India, and with so much success, that silage may now be considered as a safe and valuable form of food for cattle. The last sentence of the above quotation reads almost like a prophecy in the light of Mr. Arthur Rogers' happy idea of utilizing the cotton presses of the country for compressing fodder. The many advantages which this process possesses in the direction both of economy and efficiency have been so recently made public, that it is needless to recapitulate them here. For military purposes, especially in war time, fodder prepared in this way will no doubt be largely used in future; and the difficulties which have hitherto been experienced in procuring at certain seasons of the year a sufficient quantity of cut grass for cavalry horses should now be very considerably lessened.

I have not alluded to the interesting experiments which, within the last few years, have been undertaken with the object of utilizing the grass of cantonment lands. Operations were first commenced in 1883 at Allahabad under the direction of the late General Sir Herbert Macpherson, and, the results proving so satisfactory, the system was extended to Cawnpore. Sir H. Macpherson was assisted by Capt. G. Wingate, Assistant Commissary General, who has submitted detailed reports of the operations at both these military stations. Important and interesting results have also been obtained by General Wilkinson at Calcutta, more especially as regards the preservation of fodder. Capt. Wingate has again, I believe, been placed on special duty in connection with Grass Farms, and reports indicating further progress will no doubt be forthcoming.

EXPLANATION OF SOME OF THE TECHNICAL TERMS AS APPLIED TO THE STRUCTURE OF GRASSES.

Acuminate.—Tapering gradually to a point.

Adnate.—Partially or wholly united.

Amplexicaul.—Applied to sessile leaves, bracts or glumes, which clasp the stem or rachis at their base.

Androgynous.—Composed of both male and female florets.

Appressed.—Lying flat against or together for the whole length.

Articulate.—Jointed.

Auricled.—With rounded ear-like projections.

Awn.—A bristle-like hair proceeding either from the summit or from the back of a glume.

Bract.—Applied usually to leaf-like organs situated between the foliage leaves and the flowers. In grasses they are usually the uppermost leaves surrounding the clusters of spikelets or each separate spikelet, and are either spathe-like, as in *Apluda* and *Anthistiria*, or setiform, as *Setaria* and *Pennisetum*.

Cleft.—Cut about half way down.

Collateral.—Standing side by side.

Confluent.—Blended into one, or passing by degrees the one into the other.

Connate.—Applied to pairs of leaves or bracts which are opposite and amplexicaul.

Dichotomous.—Forked in pairs.

Digitate.—Applied to two or more terminal spikes radiating from one point.

Distichous.—Disposed in two vertical ranks.

Dorsal.—Referring to the back or outer side of a glume.

Fasciculate.—In clusters.

Flowering glume.—The glume opposite to the pale, and which with it encloses the true floret.

Glumes.—Chaff-like bracts enclosing the florets of a spikelet.

D

Grain.—The mature fruit.

Hermaphrodite.—Applied to a floret which has both stamens and pistil.

Heterogamous.—Bearing two kinds of florets.

Homogamous.—Applied to a spikelet containing one kind of floret, either male or female.

Hyaline.—Thin and transparent.

Imbricate.—Overlapping like the tiles on a roof.

Inflorescence.—The arrangement of the spikelets on the flowering stem.

Internodes.—Portions of the stem or rachis between each node or joint.

Involucre.—A collection of two or more bracts surrounding the base of a spikelet.

Lanceolate.—Shaped like a lance.

Ligule.—A thin scarious projection from the summit of the sheath of a leaf.

Lodicules.—Minute scales situated outside the stamens, usually 2-3 in number, but sometimes wanting.

Membranous.—Thin and soft.

Mucronate.—Abruptly tipped with a short point.

Nodes.—The thick solid part of the stem from which the leaves take their rise; also applied to the joints of a rachis.

Ovoid.—Egg-shaped, but with the broad end downwards.

Pale.—Usually a thin almost transparent scale opposite to and a little higher on the axis than the flowering glume.

Panicle.—Like a raceme, but the pedicels are branched.

Pedicel.—The ultimate branch of an inflorescence supporting a spikelet.

Peduncle.—The main stem of an inflorescence up to the first or lowest branch. Beyond this is the main rachis.

Pericarp.—The fructified ovary.

Perennial.—Lasting year after year.

Raceme.—Like a spike, but with pedicelled or stalked florets.

Rachilla.—The axis of a spikelet.

Rachis.—The main axis of an inflorescence.

Rudimentary.—Undeveloped or abortive.

Secund.—Directed to or facing one side.

Sessile.—Without a stalk.

Spicate.—Arranged in a spike.

Spike.—A collection of sessile spikelets on a common rachis.

Spikelet.—One or more florets enclosed within one or more pairs of empty glumes.

Stipe.—A stalk.

Stipiform.—Stalk-like.

Subulate.—Awl-shaped.

Terete.— Cylindrical.

Thyrsus.—An ovate panicle.

Unisexual.—Having flowers of one sex only.

Verticillate.—When the spikelets are in whorls or verticils.

A SYNOPSIS OF THE GENERA OCCURRING IN THE PLAINS OF NORTH-WESTERN INDIA.

SERIES A. **Panicaceæ.**—Pedicel jointed below the spikelet or cluster of spikelets. Fertile floret solitary (except in *Isachne*) and terminal, with sometimes a single male or sterile one below it.

TRIBE I. **Paniceæ.**—Spikelets hermaphrodite, in spikes or panicles; rachis of inflorescence not jointed; flowering glume not awned, becoming hard as the grain ripens.

* Panicle spike-like, spikes simple or digitate or more or less scattered along a common peduncle. Pedicels not jointed.

Spikelets in one or two rows on one side of the flattened rachis of each spike. Each spikelet consists of one perfect flower enclosed within the two membranous outer glumes. Flowering glume hard and thick embracing the hard and thick pale. (*Kodon*, &c.).

PASPALUM, *p.* 1.

Inflorescence paniculate, branches simple and spike-like. Glumes as in *Paspalum*, but attached to a thickening of the pedicel above the joint.

ERIOCHLOA, *p.* 2.

Panicle spreading. Spikelets 2-flowered, small. Glumes 4, the two lower empty ones nearly equal and usually persistent below the joint, the two upper fruiting ones equal and hardening.

ISACHNE, *p.* 2.

Inflorescence usually paniculate, simple or compound, rarely reduced to a simple spike. Spikelets small, 1-flowered or with a male floret below it. Outer glumes 2, of which one is usually much smaller or even wanting. Grain enclosed in the hardened glume and pale. (*Sáṅwak*, *china*, *Guinea grass*, &c.). (*Vide Plate* A., *Figs.* 1 to 4).

PANICUM, *p.* 3.

Panicle branches simple, scattered, secund. Spikelets

clustered, on one side of the rachis. Glumes 4, the two lower empty ones awned.

OPLISMENUS, *p.* 13.

Spikelets in a dense cylindrical spike or narrow thyrsus, furnished with stiff persistent bristles (sterile branchlets) on the pedicels below the joint. *(Kangni, &c.).*

SETARIA, *p.* 14.

** Inflorescence spicate. Pedicels jointed below a bristly or scaly involucre which encloses 1—3 spikelets.

Involucre double, the outer whorl composed of stiff bristles, the inner of hard scales connate at the base.

CENCHRUS, *p.* 15.

Involucre composed of weak simple or feathery bristles. *(Dhâman* or *anjan, bâjra, &c.).* (*Vide Plate* A., *Fig.* 5).

PENNISETUM, *p.* 16.

TRIBE II. **Maydeæ.**—Spikelets unisexual. Male florets in terminal spikes. Female florets in spikes at the lower nodes, or in a separate inflorescence, ultimately breaking up at the jointed nodes (except in *Zea*).

* Spikes with the male spikelets attached to the upper nodes, and the female spikelets solitary or in pairs at the base of the spike.

Spikes stalked, female spikelets 1—2 at the base of the spike. Bract, sheathing, ultimately enclosing the grain and becoming globose and stone-like. Tall perennial grasses, usually growing in or near water. (*Vide Plate* A., *Fig.* 6).

COIX, *p.* 18.

Spikes projecting from a sheathing bract. Female spikelets 1-flowered, at the base of the spike. Outer empty glume globose or ovoid, thick and stony, enclosing the spikelet. Habit similar to that of *Coix*.

CHIONACHNE, *p.* 19.

** Male spikes many, in a terminal panicle; female axillary and sessile.

Female spikes fasciculate within the sheaths of the leaves, each spike partially enclosed within a large bract. Spikelets in a single row. A tall succulent annual introduced from Mexico. *(Téosinté).*

EUCHLÆNA, *p.* 19.

Female spikes axillary, very large, and enveloped in leafy

bracts; the spikelets densely packed in many rows on a thick spongy rachis. (*Indian corn*).

ZEA, *p.* 19.

TRIBE III. **Oryzeæ.**—Spikelets in panicles, not articulated with the rachis. Pales 0.

Glumes 2, lower one awned. Stamens 6. An aquatic species, often floating on the surface of the water.

HYGRORHIZA, *p.* 20.

Glumes 4, the two outer minute or setiform, the upper inner ones (the pales of some authors) rigid, the outer of which is sometimes awned. Stamens 6. (*Rice*). (*Vide Plate* B., *Fig.* 7).

ORYZA, *p.* 20.

Glumes 2, membranous, not awned. Stamens 6 or fewer.

LEERSIA, *p.* 21.

TRIBE IV. **Tristegineæ.**—Spikelets jointed with the pedicel, hermaphrodite, solitary, in pairs, or fasciculate. Flowering glumes hyaline or membranous, awnless or with a bent awn.

Spikelets crowded or in fascicles along the branchlets of the panicle, 1-flowered. Glumes 4, the two lowest empty, pointed; the third one empty or enclosing a male floret. Glume of fertile floret with a twisted awn bent near the middle.

ARUNDINELLA, *p.* 21.

Panicle loose, branches and pedicels slender. Glumes 4, the outer one with a ring of hairs at its base, second silky hairy on the back and with a long slender awn between the teeth, terminal one much shorter and awnless.

RHYNCHELYTRUM, *p.* 21.

Spikelets very small, arranged in fascicles on the numerous long branchlets of the large panicle. Glumes 4, not awned. A tall handsome grass with broad leaves.

THYSANOLÆNA, *p.* 21.

TRIBE V. **Zoysieæ.**—Spikelets hermaphrodite, or a few of them imperfect. Pedicels singly scattered or alternate along the inarticulate rachis of the spike.

Spikelets in clusters of 3—5, arranged all round the axis of the simple compact spike, the terminal one sterile. Glumes 2—3, lowest one very small or wanting; upper larger, stiff, and covered on the back with hooked bristles. A small erect annual. (*Vide Plate* B., *Fig.* 8).

TRAGUS, *p.* 21.

Spikelets in a lax raceme, solitary or rarely in pairs on each pedicel, small, and stalked. Glumes 3, lowest stiff, deeply concave and muricate on the back. A small rigid annual.

LATIPES, *p.* 22.

Spikelets in a long slender spike-like raceme, nearly sessile. Glumes 3, the two lower ones linear, stiff, with slender terminal awns. (*Vide Plate* B., *Fig.* 9).

PEROTIS, *p.* 22.

TRIBE VI. **Andropogoneæ.**—Spikelets in pairs at each node of the articulate rachis of the spike or of the panicle branches, or in triplets at the end of each branch, more or less surrounded by long silky hairs. Inner glume under the fertile floret smaller and thinner than the lower or outer empty ones.

* The two spikelets of each pair hermaphrodite. Inflorescence paniculate.

† Panicle branches not jointed. Spikelets of each pair unequally pedicelled.

Spikelets in a dense cylindrical spike-like panicle clothed with silvery white hairs. None of the glumes awned. Stamens 2. A perennial occurring usually on wet or undrained soil. (*Vide Plate* B., *Fig.* 10).

IMPERATA, *p.* 22.

Spikelets in a loose panicle. Flowering glume awned. Stamens 3. A tall perennial grass.

MISCANTHUS, *p.* 23.

†† Panicle branches jointed. Spikelets of each pair the one sessile and the other stalked.

Spikelets small in a dense compound usually large panicle. Glumes without awns. Tall grasses with thick woody stems, and panicles densely clothed with silky hairs. (*Sugarcane, munj grass, &c.*).

SACCHARUM, *p.* 23.

Inflorescence as in *Saccharum*. Flowering glume awned. (*Vide Plate* B., *Fig.* 11).

ERIANTHUS, *p.* 26.

Panicle loose; branches short, ending in 3 spikelets, with occasionally one or two pairs below, as in *Chry-*

sopogon. Third glume sometimes enclosing a male floret. Terminal fertile glume awned.

SPODIOPOGON, *p.* 26.

Spikelets in pairs on the simple panicle branches. Branches of panicle spike-like, 2 or more, digitate or scattered along the main rachis. (*Bhábar grass*, &c.).

POLLINIA, *p.* 26.

Spikelets on a single spike. Second empty glume and flowering glume awned. A slender much branched ornamental grass, common on rocks.

POGONATHERUM, *p.* 27.

Spikes slender, solitary or in clusters. Glumes 4, the two lower ones narrow and rigid. Flowering glume awned. Stamens 2.

DIMERIA, *p.* 27.

** The second spikelet of each pair reduced to a stipiform rudiment. Inflorescence as in *Pollinia.*

Spikelets usually subdigitate, slender. Flowering glume with a dorsal awn from near the base. Leaf blades cordate lanceolate.

ARTHRAXON, *p.* 27.

*** Spikelets in simple spikes, in pairs at each notch or excavation of the rachis, the one sessile and the other stalked. Flowering glume not awned.

Spike densely clothed with long silky hairs, otherwise as in *Rottbœllia.*

ELIONURUS, *p.* 28.

Spike terete. Spikelets smooth, one sessile and fertile, the other stalked and sterile.

ROTTBŒLLIA, *p.* 28.

Spike terete. Spikelets all sessile, solitary, or in pairs at the lower part of the spike.

OPHIURUS, *p.* 29.

Spike subterete. Spikelets in pairs, one sessile fertile and globose, the other stalked and sterile. A much branched usually hairy annual. (*Vide Plate* B., *Fig.* 12).

MANISURIS, *p.* 29.

Spike compressed, imperfectly jointed. Spikelets in pairs, one sessile and fertile, the other stalked and sterile. Pedicels usually adnate to the rachis. (*Vide Plate* C., *Fig*. 13).

HEMARTHRIA, *p*. 30.

**** Spikelets of each pair bearing two kinds of florets. Flowering glume of the fertile one usually awned.

† Spikelets in many pairs along the rachis of the simple spikes or panicle branches.

Spikes 2—3, rarely solitary. The sessile spikelets have a male floret below the terminal fertile one.

ISCHÆMUM, *p*. 30.

Spike solitary. Spikelets 1-flowered, appressed, imbricate. Sessile florets of each pair fertile, all facing one side, their flowering glumes with a long twisted awn. Stalked florets male or sterile, not awned. (*Spear grass*).

HETEROPOGON, *p*. 32.

Spikes solitary, in pairs, or several. Sessile spikelet of each pair fertile and with a long twisted awn; the stalked spikelets sterile, not awned. Pale small or none. (*Khas-khas*, *palwa*, &c.) (*Vide Plate* C., *Figs*. 14 to 16).

ANDROPOGON, *p*. 33.

†† Spikelets in triplets at the ends of the panicle branches, or in dense clusters.

Spikelets in triplets on the jointed branchlets of the panicle; central one sessile and fertile, the two lateral ones stalked and sterile with occasionally 1—3 additional pairs below. (*Vide Plate* D., *Fig*. 17).

CHRYSOPOGON, *p*. 39.

Spikelets as in *Chrysopogon*, but the panicle branches are scarcely jointed, and the ovate outer glume of the fertile spikelet becomes hard. (*Judr*). (*Vide Plate* D., *Fig*. 18).

SORGHUM, *p*. 40.

Spikes or clusters arranged on a leafy panicle, and composed of seven or more spikelets, four of these, *i.e.*, two pairs, which are either empty or contain male florets, surround the three terminal spikelets in the form of an involucre. Terminal spikelets stalked, the central one fertile, the two lateral ones usually sterile. (*Vide Plate* D., *Fig*. 19).

ANTHISTIRIA, *p*. 42.

Clusters small glabrous. Spikelets more or less stalked and, as well as the clusters, enclosed within sheathing bracts.

ISEILEMA, *p.* 43.

Spikelets with one fertile floret and a male one below it, sessile between two flattened pedicels each bearing a rudimentary or barren spikelet, the whole embraced by a sheathing bract, the bracts clustered on the branches of a leafy panicle. Terminal glume of fertile floret usually awned. (*Vide Plate* D., *Fig.* 20).

APLUDA, *p.* 44.

SERIES B. **Poaceæ.**—Pedicel continuous below the glumes (except in *Crypsis* and *Alopecurus*). Rachilla often jointed above the persistent lower glumes, and sometimes produced beyond the fertile florets in the form of a stipe. Male or rudimentary florets, when present, above the fertile one.

TRIBE VII. **Phalarideæ.**—Each spikelet contains one terminal hermaphrodite floret. Glumes 6 (or 5 and a pale); lowest pair empty, usually persistent below the joint; second pair (above the joint) usually empty and small, and often reduced to a bristle; upper pair, enclosing the terminal fertile floret and grain, without any continuation of the rachilla above it.

* Two empty glumes below the joint.

Spikelets in a dense spike-like panicle or thyrsus. The two inferior glumes largest, flat, and often with a winged keel; second pair narrow or reduced to bristles; upper pair thin and transparent. (*Canary grass*, &c.)

PHALARIS, *p.* 45.

** No glumes under the joint.

Spikelets in a dense head surrounded by 2—3 sheathing bracts. Receptacle broadly convex. Glumes 4, not awned. Stamens 2. A small diffuse grass with short stiff leaves. (*Vide Plate* D., *Fig.* 21).

CRYPSIS, *p.* 45.

Spikelets in a dense cylindrical spike-like panicle; receptacle linear. Glumes 3 or 4, the outer ones larger, boat-shaped and keeled on the back. Pale and lodicules none. Stamens 3. (*Vide Plate* D., *Fig.* 22).

ALOPECURUS, *p.* 46.

TRIBE VIII. **Agrostideæ.**—Spikelets 1-flowered. Rachilla jointed above the lower empty glumes, often produced beyond the floret. Flowering glume with or without an awn. Pales 2-nerved, usually thin and transparent.

Panicle lax. Spikelets cylindrical. Flowering glume with a terminal 3-fid awn, rigid, and closely investing the grain when mature. Slender feather-like grasses with very narrow leaves.

ARISTIDA, *p.* 46.

Panicle spike-like, densely cylindrical or ovoid, stalked or sessile within the upper sheaths. Flowering glume blunt, loosely covering the grain. Habit of *Crypsis*. (*Vide Plate* E., *Fig.* 23).

HELEOCHLOA, *p.* 48.

Spikelets in lax or in spike-like panicles, minute. Flowering glumes not awned. Grain usually exposed and falling readily from the glumes. Pericarp often quite loose. (*Usar grass*, &c.) (*Vide Plate* E., *Fig.* 24).

SPOROBOLUS, *p.* 48.

Spikelets in a dense spike-like panicle. Outer empty glumes narrow, keeled, and ending in a fine straight awn. Flowering glumes shorter, with or without an awn. Grain enclosed within the fruiting glume. (*Vide Plate* E., *Fig.* 25).

POLYPOGON, *p.* 50.

TRIBE IX. **Aveneæ.**—Inflorescence loosely paniculate. Spikelets with two or more perfect florets. Rachilla produced beyond the upper floret. Flowering glume with a twisted or bent awn, which is either dorsal, or terminal between two teeth.

Florets hermaphrodite, or the upper one male. Awn of flowering glume dorsal. Flowering glume rounded on the back, many-nerved. Ripe grain furrowed in front, more or less adhering to the pale. (*Oats*). (*Vide Plate* E., *Fig.* 26).

AVENA, *p.* 51.

Spikelets in threes at the ends of the panicle branches, 2-flowered. Lower floret male, upper hermaphrodite or female. Awn of flowering glume terminal between the two lobes.

TRISTACHYA, *p.* 51.

TRIBE X. **Chlorideæ.**—Spikelets 1—many-flowered, sessile, arranged in two rows along the rachis of the unilateral spike. Rachis neither jointed nor notched (as in tribe *Hordeæ*). Inflorescence similar to that of *Paspalum*. Lowest or single perfect floret hermaphrodite. Awn when present terminal and straight, not dorsal or twisted as in *Aveneæ*. Rachilla usually produced beyond the florets.

* One fertile floret in each spikelet, rarely two.

Spikes at the summit of the peduncle, 1—4. Spikelets with long capillary awns. Rachilla not produced beyond the florets. Flowering glume much shorter than the empty ones.

SCHŒNEFELDIA, *p*. 52.

Spikes 2—6 slender, digitate at the summit of the peduncle. Spikelets small, 1-flowered, without awns. Rachilla produced beyond the floret into a small point or bristle. (*Dúb grass*). (*Vide Plate* E., *Fig*. 27).

CYNODON, *p*. 52.

Spikes usually crowded at the summit of the peduncle, or in verticils. Flowering glume with a few empty glumes above it, usually awned, 1—3-nerved.

CHLORIS, *p*. 53.

Spikelets forming numerous short scattered clusters which fall off at the joints. The two lower empty glumes are clothed with long feathery hairs. Flowering glume with three awns. Upper empty glumes decreasing in size upwards. A small elegant annual.

MELANOCENCHRIS, *p*. 54.

** Two or more fertile florets in each spikelet.

Spikes 1—3, at the top of the peduncle, erect, covered with long silky hairs. Spikelets crowded, 3—4-flowered. Flowering glume awned.

TETRAPOGON, *p*. 55.

Spikes scattered along the peduncle. Spikelets 1—3-flowered. Flowering glumes bluntish, much shorter than the somewhat awned lower empty glumes. (*Vide Plate* F., *Fig*. 28).

DINEBRA, *p*. 55.

Spikes digitate or verticillate. Spikelets many flowered, sessile, crowded, flattened, unilateral. Flowering glumes without awns, longer than the unequally obtuse inferior empty ones. Seed transversely wrinkled, usually loose within the pericarp. (*Makra, mandua, chhimbar*, &c.) (*Vide Plate* F., *Fig*. 29).

ELEUSINE, *p*. 56.

Spikelets small, flat, sessile or nearly so, arranged on one side of the slender spike-like branches of a long panicle. Flowering glumes without awns, longer than the lower empty ones.

LEPTOCHLOA, *p*. 59.

TRIBE XI. **Festuceæ.**—Spikelets with two or more perfect florets, rarely only 1-flowered, panicled, rarely in racemes or clusters. Flowering glumes usually without awns, which when present are terminal and straight.

Spikelets 1—2 rarely 3-flowered, in dense spike-like panicles. Flowering glumes with nine awns. In India confined to Northern Punjab.

PAPPOPHORUM, *p*. 59.

Panicle branches long, slender, and spike-like as in *Leptochloa*. Spikelets many-flowered, narrow. Flowering glumes 3-toothed, the central one mucriform.

DIPLACHNE, *p*. 59.

Spikelets 2—4-flowered, arranged in large branching panicles Axis of spikelets silky hairy. Flowering glumes clothed with silky hairs, 3-nerved, 2-toothed and mucronate between the teeth. (*Tall reeds*).

ARUNDO, *p*. 60.

Lowest floret of spikelets male or sterile. Flowering glumes without hairs. Otherwise as in Arundo. (*Vide Plate* F., *Fig*. 30).

PHRAGMITES, *p*. 60.

Spikelets many-flowered, minute, crowded into compound subglobose clusters, the whole forming an interrupted spike. Flowering glumes 3-nerved, mucronate, acuminate or almost awned. Pales keeled on both sides, one or both keels broadly winged. A very distinct looking annual, usually occurring on a moist clayey soil. (*Vide Plate* F., *Fig*. 31).

ELYTROPHORUS, *p*. 60.

Spikelets dimorphic, in a dense unilateral panicle; terminal one of each branchlet 1-flowered. Flowering glume and upper empty one awned. Glumes of lower barren spikelets many, blunt, and bifariously imbricate. A small annual with handsome golden coloured inflorescence.

LAMARCKIA, *p*. 61.

Panicle spreading or compact. Spikelets numerous, usually many-flowered, more or less compressed. Outer glumes shorter than the distichously imbricate flowering ones. Flowering glumes 3-nerved, not awned, keel prominent. Rachilla usually persistent, rarely jointed as in *Poa*. (*Dâb*, &c.)

ERAGROSTIS, *p*. 61.

Panicle spikelike, densely cylindrical, or more or less interrupted towards the base. Margins of flowering glumes transparent.

KŒLERIA, *p*. 61.

Spikelets many-flowered, arranged in dense spike-like clusters. Flowering glumes broad at the apex and mucronate, 5- or more-nerved. Small prostrate grasses with short stiff almost prickly leaves. In India confined to the Punjab.

ÆLUROPUS, *p*. 66.

Panicle various, usually lax. Spikelets few-flowered. Rachilla jointed between the florets. Flowering glumes 5- or more-nerved, membranous, keeled, not awned.

POA, *p*. 67.

Spikelets rather large, subterete or compressed, many-flowered. Outer glumes shorter than the florets. Flowering glumes 5- or more-nerved, rounded on the back, and usually awned from a little below the 2-cleft apex. Pale shorter than the flowering glume, with two rigid ciliate keels, adherent to the grain.

BROMUS, *p*. 67.

TRIBE XII. **Hordeæ.**—Spikelets 1-many-flowered, sessile at the teeth or excavations on the rachis of a simple spike.

* Spikelets solitary at the nodes, 3- or more-flowered.

Spikelets many-flowered, alternate, distichous, compressed, placed edgeways on the rachis. (*Rye grass*).

LOLIUM, *p*. 68.

Spikelets 3-5-flowered, somewhat compressed. Margins of glumes facing the main rachis. Flowering glumes rounded on the back or keeled above, 5—9-nerved, lateral nerves not confluent, short, or produced into teeth or distinct awns. (*Wheat*).

TRITICUM, *p.* 68.

** Spikelets solitary at the nodes, 1-flowered, forming a slender spike.

Spikelets completely immersed at the nodes of the slender spike, as in *Rottbœllia*. A very diminutive grass found on sandy waste land.

OROPETIUM, *p.* 69.

*** Spikelets 2 or more, collateral at the nodes. Spikelets usually in threes, 1-flowered.

Empty glumes subulate, rigid and resembling an involucre. Lateral spikelets imperfect (in 2-rowed barley) or perfect (in 6-rowed barley). (*Vide Plate* F., *Fig.* 32).

HORDEUM, *p.* 69.

TRIBE XIII. **Bambuseæ.**—Tall perennial aborescent grasses. Leaves flat, often disarticulating from the sheath. Spikelets 2-many-flowered, arranged in clusters on the panicle branches. Empty glumes 3—6. Stamens 3 or 6.

Stamens 6. Lodicules 3, large. Pericarp thin, adnate to the seed.

BAMBUSA, *p.* 70.

Stamens 6. Lodicules 0. Pericarp crustaceous, free from the seed.

DENDROCALAMUS, *p.* 71.

EXPLANATION OF PLATES.

Figures 10, 14, 17, 18, 21 and 30 were copied from Reichenbach's "Icones Floræ Germanicæ"; Figures 26 and 32 from Bentley's and Trimen's "Medicinal Plants"; and the rest are from the "Agrostographie" of Palisot de Beauvois.

PLATE A.

Fig. 1. Panicum Crus-Galli, Linn.

a. Spikelet.

b. Male floret.

c. Hermaphrodite floret with the flowering glume and pale removed.

Fig. 2. Panicum miliaceum, Linn.

Spikelet with one hermaphrodite and one male floret.

Fig. 3. Panicum Myurus, Lamk.

a. Spikelet.

b. Pistil with lodicule.

Fig. 4. Panicum sanguinale, Linn.

Spikelet, showing the unequal outer glumes.

Fig. 5. Pennisetum cenchroides, Rich.

a. Spikelet surrounded by an involucre of bristles.

b. Spikelet containing one hermaphrodite and one male floret.

Fig. 6. Coix Lachryma, Linn.

a. Spikelet of male florets.

b. Involucre enclosing a female spikelet.

c. Grain.

PLATE A.

FIG. 1.

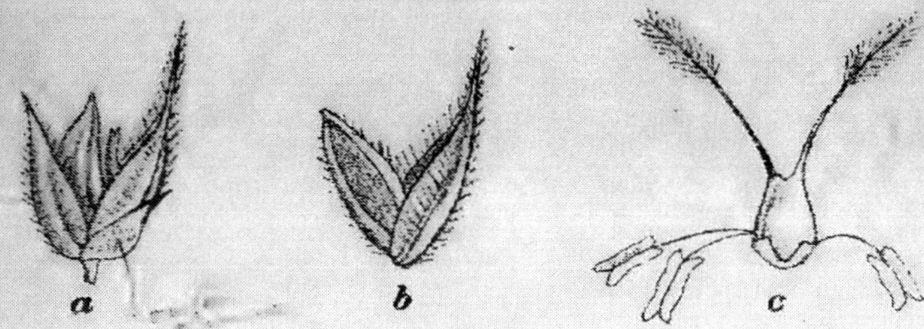

Panicum Crus-Galli.

FIG. 2.

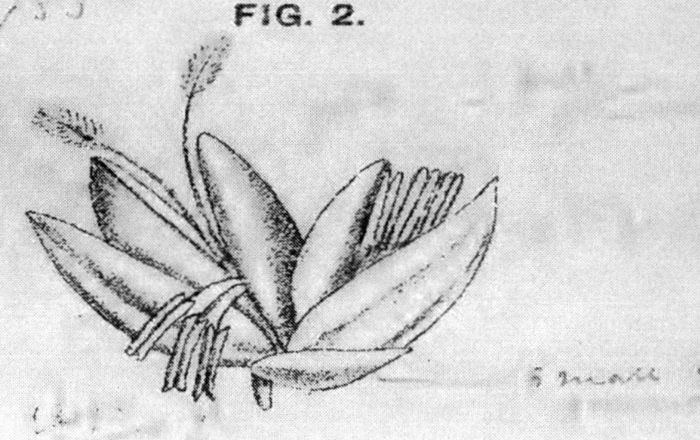

Panicum miliaceum.

FIG. 3.

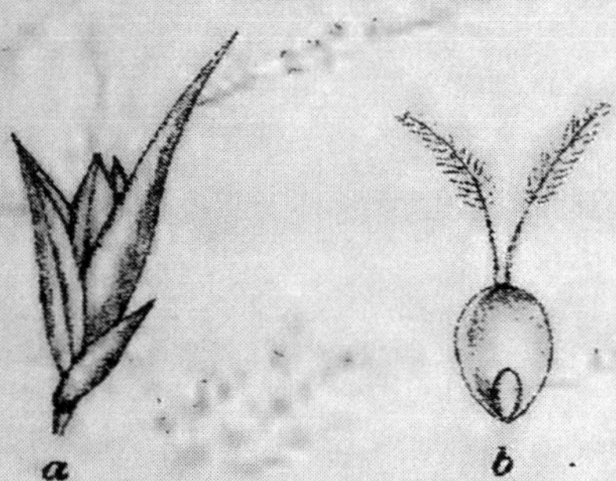

Panicum Myurus.

FIG. 4.

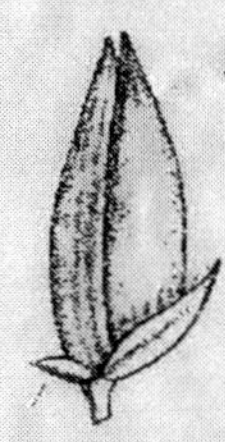

Panicum sanguinale.

FIG. 5.

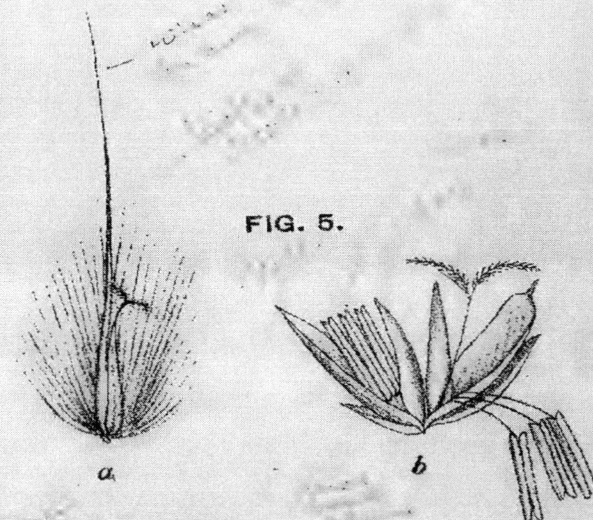

Pennisetum cenchroides.

FIG. 6.

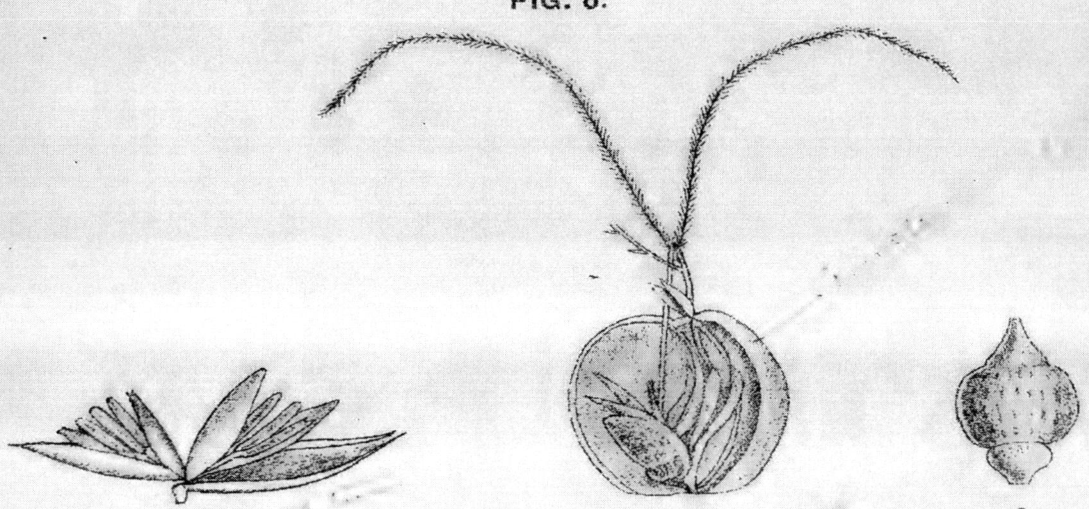

Coix Lachryma.

Litho. T. C. Press, Roorkee.

THOS D. BONA, *Supdt.*

PLATE B.

Fig. 7. Oryza sativa, Linn.

a. Closed spikelet showing the two inner glumes, and at their base the two minute outer glumes.

b. Spikelet open showing the two inner glumes, the absence of pales, and the six stamens.

Fig. 8. Tragus racemosus, Hall.

a. Cluster of three florets, of which the central one is sterile.

b. Pistil with lodicules.

Fig. 9. Perotis latifolia, Ait.

Spikelet. The two outer glumes are awned.

Fig. 10. Imperata arundinacea, Cyrill.

Hermaphrodite spikelet, stamens reduced to two.

Fig. 11. Erianthus Ravennæ, Beauv.

a. Cluster of spikelets with detached bract.

b. A single spikelet.

Fig. 12. Manisuris granularis, Swartz.

a. Cluster of spikelets, two fertile and one male.

b. Polygamous spikelets.

c. Male floret.

PLATE B.

FIG. 7.

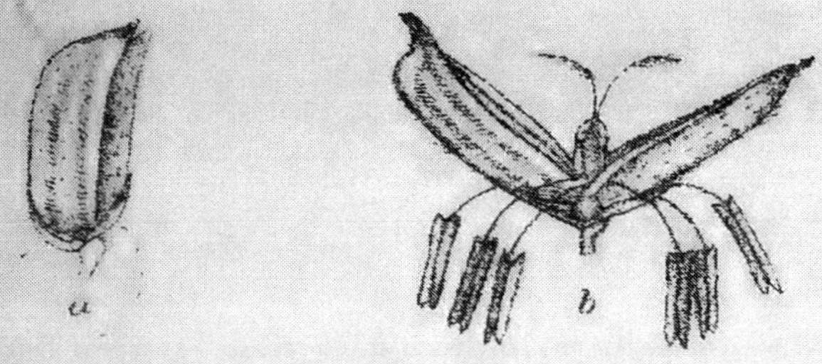

Oryza sativa.

FIG. 8.

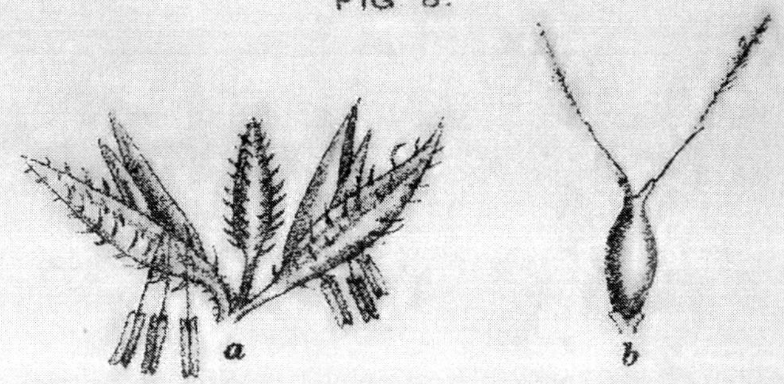

Tragus racemosus.

FIG. 9.

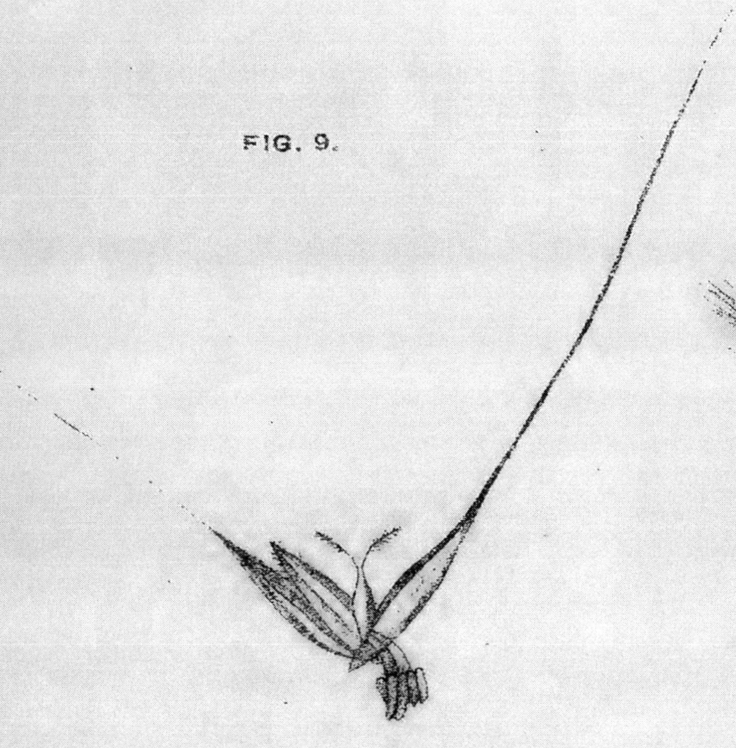

Perotis latifolia.

FIG. 10.

Imperata arundinacea.

FIG. 11.

Eriaathus Ravennæ

FIG. 12.

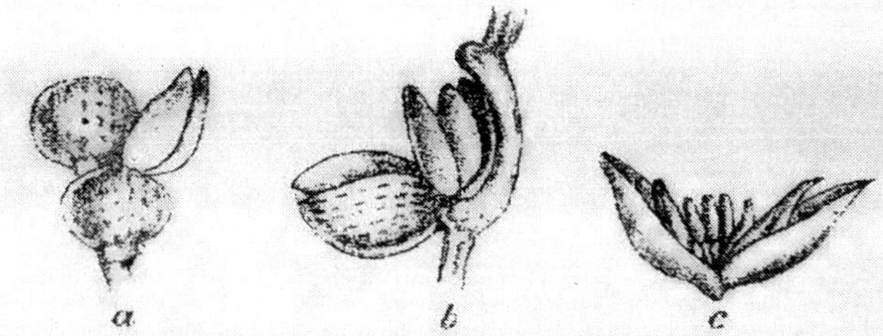

Manisuris granularis.

Litho. T. C. Press, Roorkee. THOS. D. BONA, *Supdt.*

PLATE C.

Fig. 13. Hemarthria compressa, R. Br.

a. Portion of rachis showing the embedded spikelets.
b. Single spikelet.
c. Male floret.
d. Female floret.

Fig. 14. Andropogon Ischœmum, Linn.

a. Cluster of spikelets, the lower sessile one fertile and awned, the upper stalked one sterile and without an awn.
b. Fertile floret, flowering glume reduced to a slender awn.
c. Male floret.

Fig. 15. Andropogon muricatus, Retz.

a. Pair of spikelets, one sessile and fertile, the other stalked and sterile.
b. Male spikelet.
c. Polygamous spikelet.

Fig. 16. Andropogon pertusus, Willd.

A pair of spikelets showing the pit on the back of the outer glume, and the long twisted awn of the fertile spikelet.

PLATE C.

FIG 13.

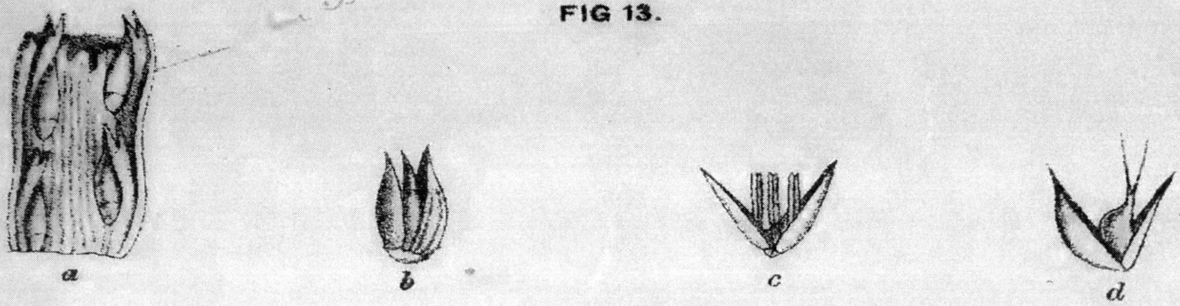

Hemarthria compressa.

FIG. 14

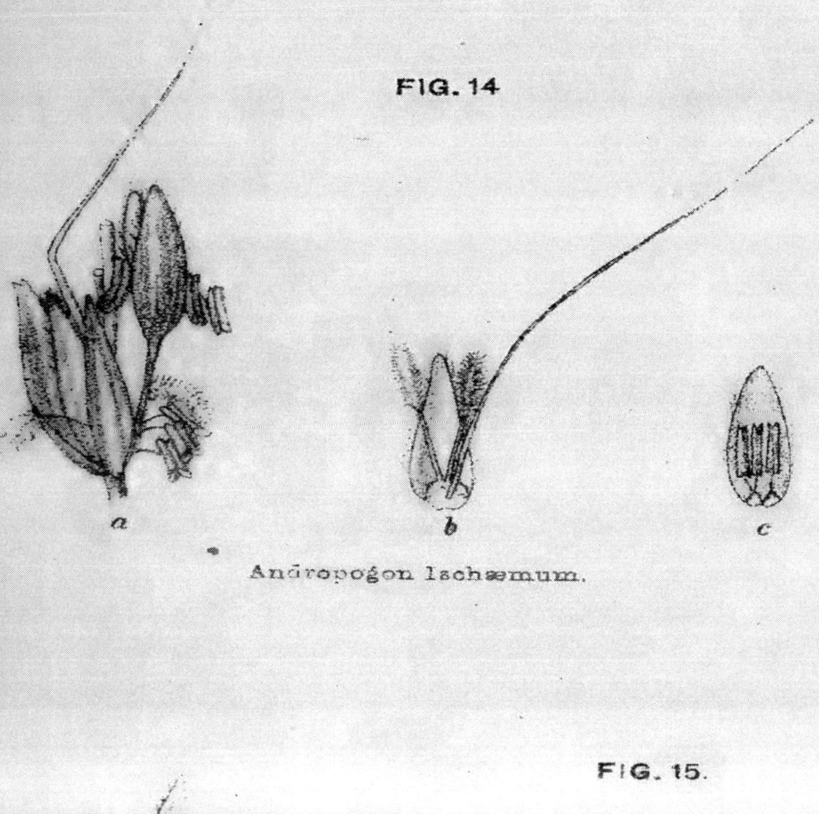

Andropogon Ischæmum.

FIG. 16.

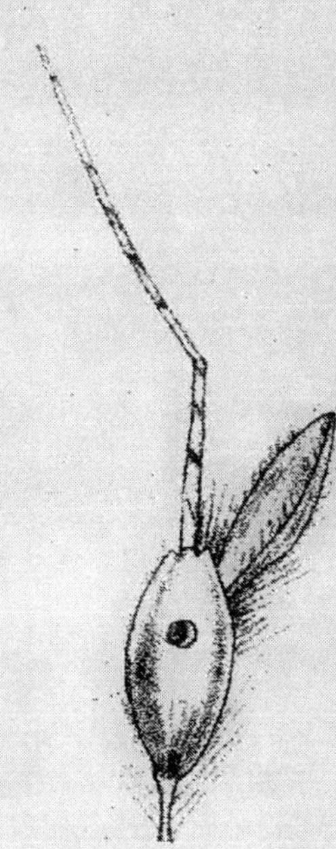

Andropogon pertusus.

FIG. 15.

Andropogon muricatus.

Litho. T. C. Press, Roorkee. THOS D. BONA, *Supdt.*

PLATE D.

Fig. 17. Chrysopogon Gryllus, Trin.

a. Cluster of three spikelets, the central one sessile and hermaphrodite, the two lateral stalked and sterile.

Fig. 18. Sorghum halepense, Pers.

a. Cluster of three spikelets, the central sessile one hermaphrodite, the two lateral stalked and sterile.

b. Hermaphrodite awned floret.

c. Male floret.

Fig. 19. Anthistiria ciliata, Linn. f.

a. Four sterile florets each composed of a single pale.

b. Polygamous spikelet.

c. Flowering glume and pale of male floret.

Fig. 20. Apluda mutica, Linn.

A cluster of spikelets with its spathe-like bract.

Fig. 21. Crypsis aculeata, Ait.

a. Single floret deprived of its coverings. Stamens reduced to two.

b. A Spikelet.

Fig. 22. Alopecurus agrestis, Linn.

a. Flowering glume showing the dorsal awn.

b. Pistil.

PLATE D.

FIG. 17.

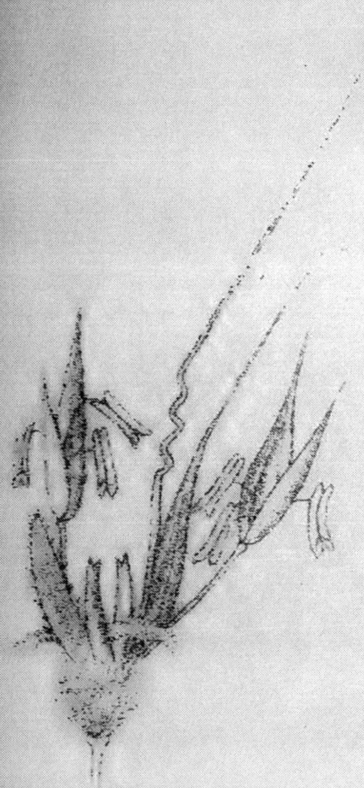

Chrysopogon Gryllus.

FIG. 18.

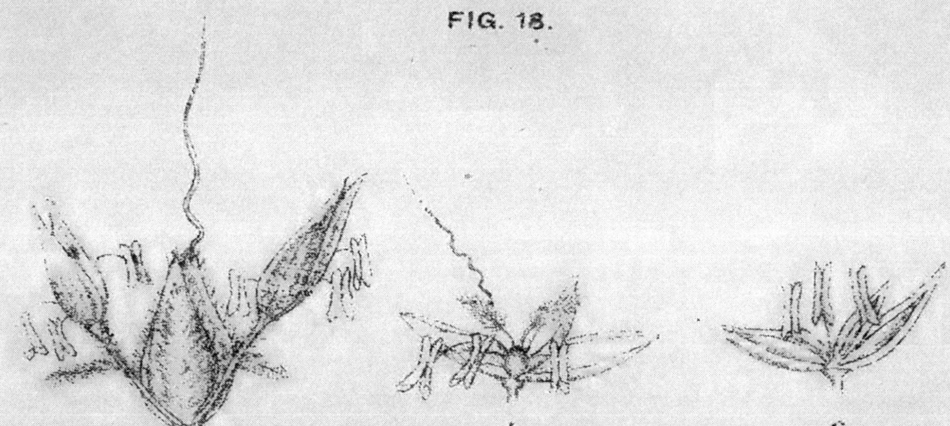

a b c

Sorghum halepense.

FIG. 19.

a b c

Anthistiria ciliata.

FIG. 29.

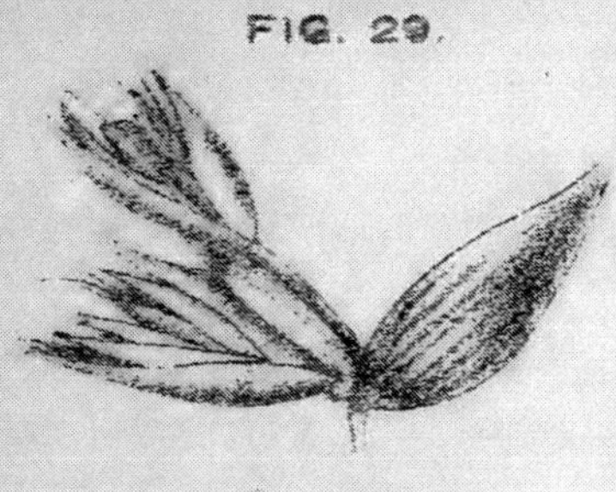

Apluda mutica.

FIG. 21.

a b

Crypsis aculeata.

FIG. 22.

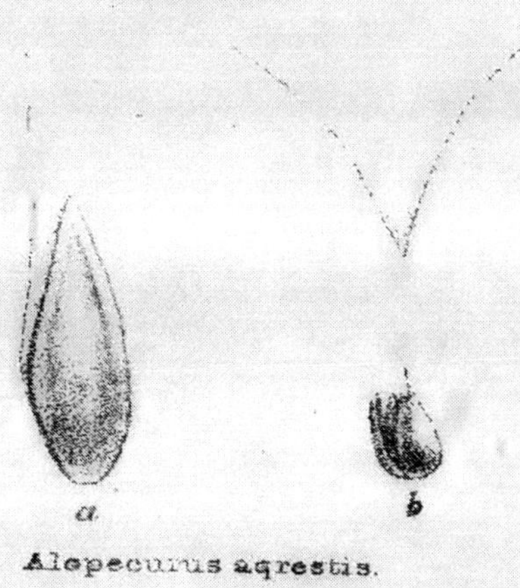

a b

Alopecurus agrestis.

Litho. T. C. Press, Roorkee. THOS D. RONA, *Supdt.*

PLATE E.

Fig. 23. Heleochloa schœnoides, Host.

A single floret showing the two stamens.

Fig. 24. Sporobolus indicus, R. Br.

a. A closed spikelet.

b. Ditto open.

Fig. 25. Polypogon monspeliensis, Desf.

a. Spikelet showing the long awns to the outer glumes.

b. Single floret showing the short awn on the back of the flowering glume.

Fig. 26. Avena sativa, Linn.

a. Single spikelet.

b. Hermaphrodite floret showing the long twisted dorsal awn to the flowering glume.

c. Ditto without the flowering glume and pale. *N.B.*—The ovary is erroneously shown as if it were composed of two distinct carpels, and the feathery stigma on the left is a little out of place.

Fig. 27. Cynodon Dactylon, Pers.

A single spikelet.

PLATE E.

FIG. 23.

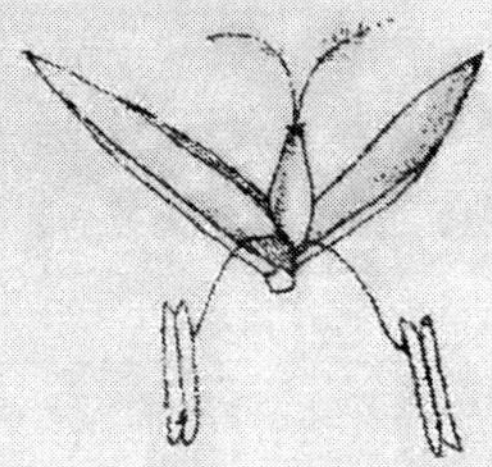

Heleochloa schænoides.

FIG. 24.

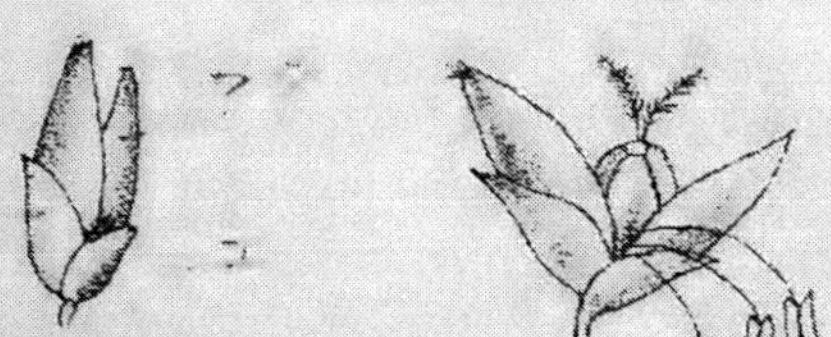

a *b*

Sporobolus indicus.

FIG. 25.

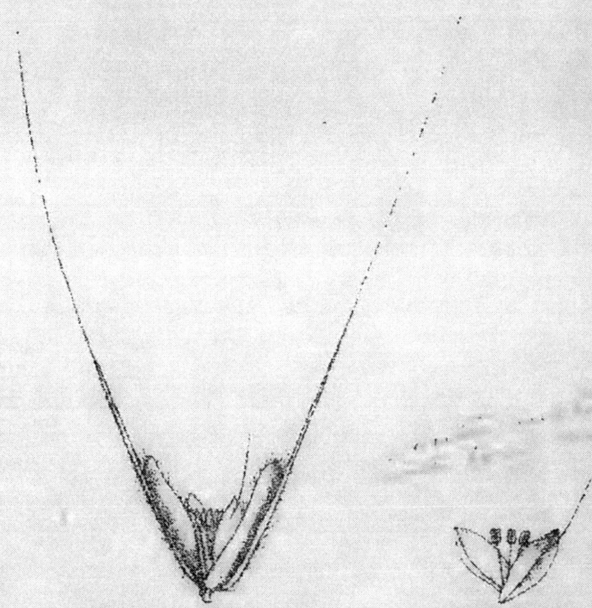

a *b*

Polypogon monspeliensis.

FIG. 27.

Cynodon Dactylon.

FIG. 26.

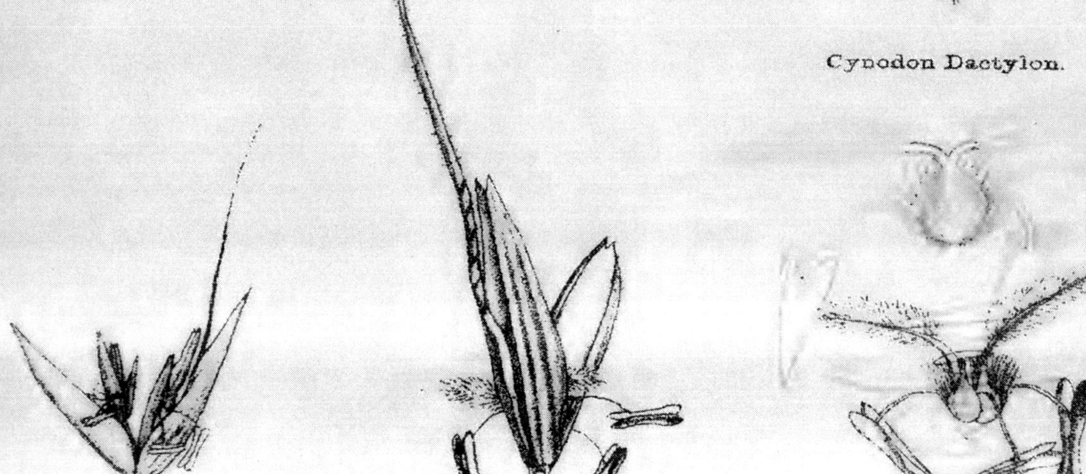

a *b* *c*

Avena sativa.

Litho. T. C. Press, Roorkee. THOS D. BONA, *Supdt.*

PLATE F.

Fig. 28. Dinebra arabica, Beauv.

a. A spikelet containing three florets.

b. The flowering glume.

c. The pale.

d. A floret deprived of its coverings.

Fig. 29. Eleusine ægyptiaca, Pers.

a. A single spikelet.

b. Flowering glume and pale.

c. Pale enclosing the young fruit.

Fig. 30. Phragmites communis, Trin.

a. Spikelet, of which the lowest floret is male.

b. Hermaphrodite floret.

Fig. 31. Elytrophorus articulatus, Beauv.

a. A cluster of spikelets.

b. A single spikelet.

c. Flowering glume and pale.

d. Pistil.

Fig. 32. Hordeum vulgare, Linn.

a. A single floret (terminal portion of flowering glume not shown here).

b. Ditto with the flowering glume and pale removed.

PLATE F.

FIG. 28.

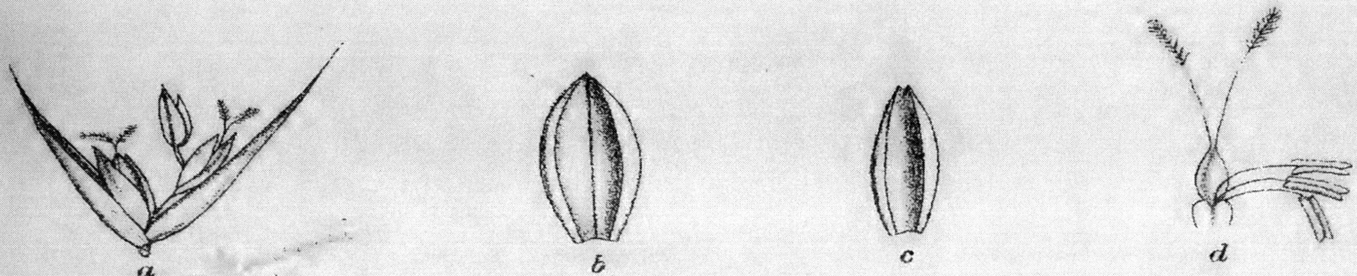

Dinebra arabica.

FIG. 29.

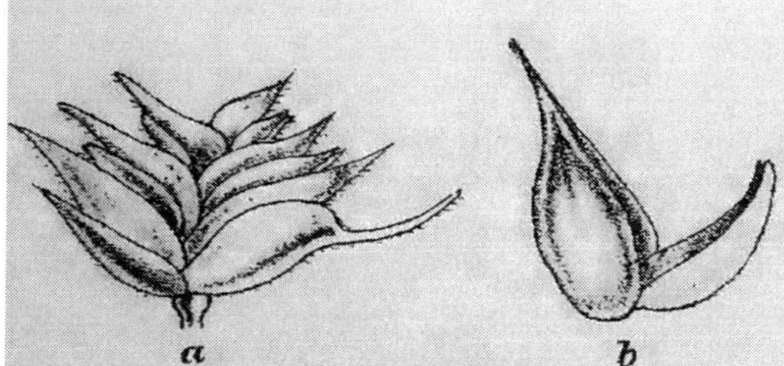

Eleusine ægyptiaca.

FIG. 30.

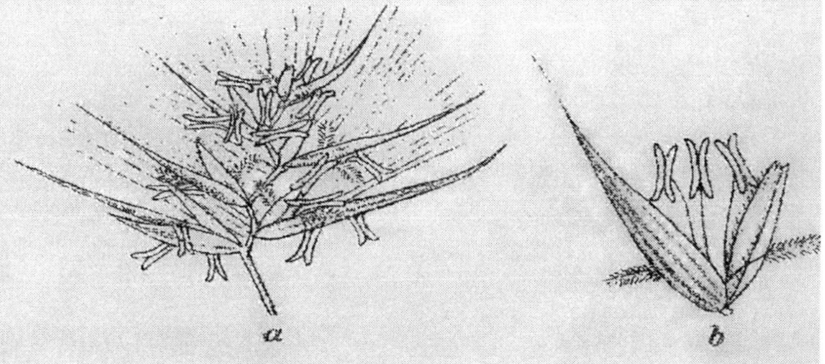

Phragmites communis.

FIG. 31.

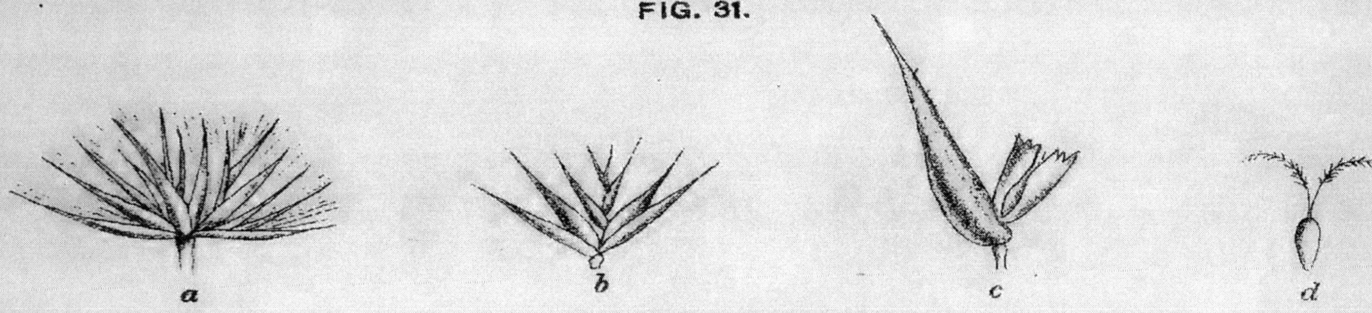

Elytrophorus articulatus.

FIG. 32.

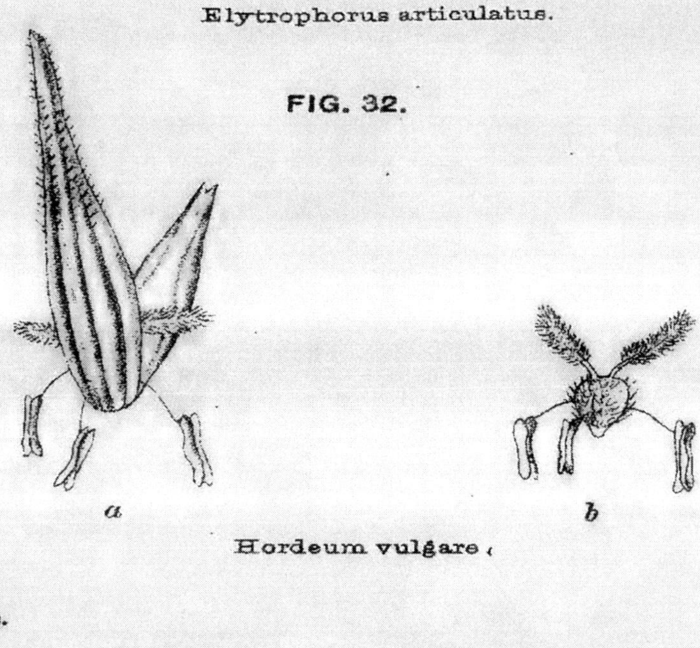

Hordeum vulgare.

Litho. T. C. Press, Roorkee. THOS D. BONA. *Supdt.*

SERIES A. PANICACEÆ.

TRIBE I. PANICEÆ.

1. PASPALUM, *Linn.* A large genus confined chiefly to tropical and sub-tropical regions, and abundantly represented in America. It is superficially distinguished from all other genera by the inflorescence, though a few of the *Panicums* are very similar in this respect. The small empty outer glume characteristic of *Panicum* is altogether wanting. Out of 160 known species about five only occur in North-West India.

P. scrobiculatum, *Linn.* (*Plate* I.) *Vern.*—GENERAL : *Koda, kodoṅ;* PUNJAB : *Kodra ;* N.-W. PROV. : *Kodrám* (Bijnor), *mársi* (Muttra) ; TELING : *Aruga* (Roxb.).

Annual, glabrous. Stems many, 2 feet or more, branching, erect or ascending, compressed. Leaves narrow, gradually tapering to a fine point; sheaths long, the upper ones spathe-like, often embracing and partially concealing the spikes. Spikes 2-5, terminal and axillary, sessile, erect or spreading, 1-3 inches long. Spikelets 1-flowered, sessile, arranged in two rows on one side of a broad membranous flattened rachis. (In cultivated specimens there are sometimes three or four rows on portions of the rachis). Outer glumes nearly equal, thin, and with a prominent midrib. Fruiting glume hard and brittle. Pale rather thinner, with auricle-like projecting edges embracing the stamens and pistil. Grain enclosed by, and adhering to, the pale, smooth and roundish, about the size of a hemp seed.

Cultivated as a rainy season crop throughout the plains, and at low elevations on the Himalaya. It is usually sown on the poorer kinds of soil, the grain being chiefly consumed by the lower classes. The straw is used as fodder. It is figured in Church's "Food Grains of India," also in Part II. of "Field and Garden Crops, N.-W. Provinces and Oudh."

P. Kora, *Willd.* (*Plate* II.) *Vern.*—HIND : *Kodu;* PUNJAB : *Kora ;* N.-W. PROV. and OUDH : *Kodela* and *kodeli* (Pilibhit and Kheri), *kudpal* and *pankhágar* (Bhira); RAJPUTANA : *Chinke* (Merwára), *sáwan duṅgarko* (Jeypur); CENT. PROV. : *Kudda jári* and *kodda gadi* (Chánda), *kodda jari* (Seoni), *ban kodo* (Balaghát); CHUTIA NAGPUR: *Kodo; SANTALI*: *Janhe;* TELING: *Aruga* and *neer* (Roxb.).

This is possibly the wild state of *P. scrobiculatum,* from which it differs by its decumbent stems usually rooting from the lower nodes, and by its shorter leaves. It is a common weed on low-lying marshy ground, and on river banks. Cattle, and especially buffaloes, eat it readily when it is young. Growing naturally in moist soils, its value as forage is largely increased during seasons of drought.

Of other Indian species of *Paspalum* the following are occasionally met with during the rainy season:—*P. filiculme,* Nees; *P. Royleanum,* Nees; and *P. pedicellatum,* Nees. In habit they are more closely related to some of the *Panicums* of the *Digitaria* section.

Some of the American species are highly valued both for grazing and stacking. Prof. Phares of Mississippi, quoted by Dr. Vasey in his "Report on the Agricultural Grasses of the United States," says with reference to the American *Paspalums*:— "They are all succulent, tender, nutritious, hardy, thrifty, and relished by all grass-eating animals. They fill the soil with a matting of roots, and cover the surface densely with luxuriant foliage from early spring till autumnal frosts."

2. ERIOCHLOA, *H. B. & K.* A genus of 5 species widely spread over the warmer parts of the globe. It agrees with *Paspalum* in having only three empty glumes, and with *Panicum* as to its inflorescence; but it differs from both in the presence of a hard cup-like disc at the top of the pedicel. One species is found in Northern India, and extends as far as Queensland.

E. polystachya, *H. B. & K.* (*Plate* XLI.) *Syn.*—*E. annulata,* Kunth; *Paspalum annulatum,* Flügge.

Perennial, erect, 2-3 feet high. Stems and leaves glabrous except at the nodes and mouth of sheaths. Leaf blades flat, dark green; sheaths paler, almost glaucous, somewhat inflated. Panicle narrow, 2-3 inches long; branches simple. Spikes slender, 1-1½ inches long. Spikelets narrow, tapering at the end. Flowering glume much shorter than the empty ones, coriaceous, the midrib produced into a point or short awn resembling those of the outer glumes of *Panicum helopus.*

A quick growing succulent grass, usually occurring on damp low-lying ground, but not common.

In Australia it affords fodder all the year round, and is said to be highly relished by stock.

3. ISACHNE, *R. Br.* A genus of about 20 species, two of which occur in the plains of North-West India. It has very much the habit of *Panicum,* but the two lower glumes, which are nearly equal, are persistent below the joint of the pedicel, a character which gives this genus an exceptional position amongst the *Panicaceæ.*

I. australis, *R. Br.* *Syn.—Panicum antipodum,* Spreng.; *P. atrovirens,* Trin. *Vern.*—RAJPUTANA: *Mez* (Mount Abu).

Stems 1 foot or more, slender, decumbent, rooting at the lower nodes. Leaves lanceolate, rough. Panicle loose, spreading, ovoid; branches numerous filiform. Spikelets stalked. Outer glumes glabrous. Lower floret usually male, and with a glabrous glume; upper one female, shortly stalked, and with its glume minutely pubescent. Rachis with a swollen joint under the upper glume.

Plains of Northern India and up to 5,000 feet on the Himalaya, usually in wet places. Symonds ("Indian Grasses," p. 33) says that horses and cattle are very fond of it.

I. albens, *Trin.* (*Panicum bellum,* Steud.) is a taller species with larger and looser panicles. It is found occasionally in the plains, and up to 6,000 feet on the Himalaya.

4. PANICUM, *Linn.* This is the largest genus of the grass family, containing upwards of 280 species. It is represented in all tropical parts of the globe, some few extending also into temperate regions. As a genus it has no very distinctive characters in regard to habit and inflorescence, and the safest single character by which it may generally be recognized, *viz.*, the inequality in size between the two lowest glumes, fails in the case of a few species, whilst in others the lower of these two outer glumes is altogether wanting, as in *Paspalum.* Of the Indian species several are much valued as fodder grasses owing to their abundant yield of grain, and the relatively large size of their grains. On this account we find so many species of this genus in cultivation, *e.g.*, *P. frumentaceum* (*sanwák* or *sánwan*), *P. miliaceum* (*chena*) and *P. miliare* (*kutki*). Guinea grass, an introduced fodder grass of great value, also belongs to this genus.

Mr. Bentham divides the genus into eleven sections, of which the following are more or less largely represented in Northern India:—

Digitaria. Spikelets usually small, in alternate pairs or clusters along one side of the simple spike-like branches of the panicle; those of each pair or cluster unequally stalked, or one of them almost sessile. The lowest glume is often very minute or deficient. Example.—*P. sanguinale.*

Brachiaria. Panicle of spike-like simple branches on a simple common peduncle. Examples.—*P. flavidum, fluitans,* and *erucæforme.*

Echinochloa. Inflorescence somewhat similar to that of the preceding section, but coarse plants with densely crowded spikelets on the partial spikes or branches of the panicle, the second and third empty glumes very generally terminating in long awns. Examples.—*P. colonum,* and *Crus-galli.*

Hymenachne. Spikelets small, numerous, crowded in a long cylindrical spike-like panicle. In the typical species, *P. Myurus,* the spikelets are rather acuminate, and the fruiting glume scarcely hardens.

Eupanicum. Spikelets awnless, collected together in a more or less spreading panicle, clustered or scattered along its simple or divided branches. Examples.—*P. miliaceum*, and *jumentorum*.

Tricholæna. Panicle loose as in *Eupanicum*, but fruiting glumes not much hardened, inflorescence ciliate with long hairs. Example.—*P. Teneriffæ*.

P. antidotale, *Retz.* (*Plate* III.) *Syn.*—*P. subalbidum*, Kunth. *Vern.*—TRANS-INDUS: *Male* and *shamukha* (Stewart); PUNJAB: *Gharam* (N.-West and Central), *ghamur* (E.), *girui* and *mangrur* (Stewart), *baru* and *ghamrur* (Simla and Kangra), *ghirri* (Hissar); RAJPUTANA: *Barwári* and *bari gagli* (Udaipur); SANTALI: *Layo-gundli.*

A tall glabrous perennial grass with erect stems thickened at the joints. Leaves long, linear, acuminate; ligule short and jagged. Panicle rather narrow, but loose, the lower branches in clusters, the upper usually solitary. Spikelets in sessile clusters or short spikes. Outer glume acute, less than half the length of the spikelet; second and third glumes about equal, prominently nerved, the latter enclosing a male flower; fruiting glume coriaceous, acute, smooth and shining. In general appearance it resembles Guinea grass.

Common all over the plains in hedges and amongst bushes. Opinions differ as to the quality of this grass as fodder. It is a tall coarse-looking species, and its real value commences probably at those periods when the better class of fodder grasses fails. Mr. Coldstream, writing from Hissar, says that it is grazed only when quite young, as it afterwards acquires a bitter or saltish taste. In the Sirsa Settlement Report it is mentioned that cattle eat it when dry; if they eat it green and young they are apt to swell, sometimes with fatal results. Dr. Stewart says that the smoke from this grass is used for fumigating wounds, also as a disinfectant in small-pox. In Madras it is said to be used medicinally in throat affections. It extends to N. Australia.

P. cimicinum, *Retz.* *Syn.*—*Coridochloa fimbriata*, Nees; *Milium cimicinum*, Linn. *Vern.*—*Siuri* (Dehra Dún).

Annual. Stems erect, 1-2 feet, sulcate, beset with bulbous-based hairs. Leaves short, broadly lanceolate, acute, base cordate, margin fringed with hairs. Spikelets rather large, two or three together on long slender terminal racemes; second glume with a thick fringe of reddish hairs along the margin.

Plains of N.-W. India, and on the hills at low elevations. I have no information regarding its nutritive value.

P. colonum, *Linn.* (*Plate* IV.)* *Syn.*—*P. brizoides*, Linn.; *Oplismenus colonus*, Kunth; *Echinochloa colona*, Kunth. *Vern.*—GENERAL: *Sawánk*; TRANS-INDUS: *Sirmakar* (Col. Strong); PUNJAB: *Sáñwak* (general), *jangli sámak* or *sáñwak*, *sámak* (Hissar), *chatta* (Simla Hills);

---

* *See* also Church's "Food Grains of India," *Fig.* 5.

BANDA: *sivaen;* OUDH: *Jharai* (Bhira), *oyia* (Kheri); CENT. PROV.: *Chichohi* (Balaghát), *gáwa* (Nagpur); CHUTIA NAGPUR: *Sama-ghás;* BERAR: *Saweli;* BENGAL: *Shama* (Roxb.); TELING: *Woodoo gaddi* (Roxb.).

Annual. Stems erect, 2 feet or more in height, or decumbent and rooting from the lower nodes. Leaves glabrous, flat, linear, acuminate. Panicle composed of several secund erect distant spikes. Spikelets sessile, in four rows on one side of the spikes. Rachis with sometimes a few empty scales (abortive spikelets ?) at the base of the spike. Glumes generally with rough hairs on the nerves, often pointed, but not awned; the lower outer glume nearly half as long as the second and third, which are about equal. Flowering glume and pale coriaceous and white.

Generally considered to be one of the best kinds of fodder grass. It is abundant all over the plains, and ascends to some few thousand feet on the Himalaya. It prefers a rich soil, and is often commonly met with as a weed on cultivated ground. It is greedily eaten by all kinds of cattle both before and after it has flowered, the abundant crop of grain yielded by it adding materially to its nutritive value. The grain, which is a saleable article in the bazars, is made into "khir" by the Hindus, to be used on their fast days. Dr. Aitchison states that it is cultivated in the Jhelum District. It extends to Australia, where, it is reported, its very succulent stems grow from 2-8 feet in height.

P. Crus-Galli, *Linn.* (*Plate* V.)* *Syn.*—*P. Crus-corvi,* Linn.; *Oplismenus Crus-Galli,* Kunth; *Echinochloa Crus-Galli,* Beauv; *Orthopogon Crus-Galli,* Spreng. *Vern.*—GENERAL: *Sánwak;* PUNJAB: *Bara sánwak* (Multan), *jarotha* (Sabáthu Hills), *bharti* (Hissar); RAJPUTANA: *Sama, horma* (Mount Abu); DOAB: *Dhand* (Royle); CENT. PROV.: *Bari bhodore* (Seoni), *bharta* and *datia* (Balaghát), *kunda buttam gadi* (Chánda); BENGAL: *Bura shama* and *dul* (Roxb.); TELING: *Pedda woondoo* (Roxb.).

Rather a coarse decumbent annual with stems ascending 2-3 feet. Leaves broad and flat, without any ligule. Panicle irregularly pyramidal, usually dense, and composed of short spikes diminishing in size upwards and directed to one side. Spikelets more or less hispid hairy; rachis ciliate or bristly. Outer glume very short and broad, second and third nearly equal, the second shortly awned, and the third with long awns sometimes an inch in length. Fruiting glume smooth and polished. A very variable species as to the length of the awns, the shorter awned forms approaching *P. colonum,* which Cosson and Durieu, in their work on the flora of Algeria, describe as a variety of this species.

---

* *See* also *Plate* A., *Fig.* 1, in present Volume.

Though similar in habit to *P. colonum*, it is usually a much coarser plant, and is nearly always found in or near water. The grain is eaten by the poorer classes, and is also used for making into "khir." I am told that it is frequently sown in the Lahore District for the sake of its grain. In Rájputána it is considered to be a good fodder, though not plentiful. It extends to Australia, where it affords a large amount of feed to cattle, and is much improved by cultivation. In America, where it is known under the name of "Barn-yard grass," it appears to be highly valued. The following quotations are from Dr. Vasey's "Report on the Agricultural Grasses of the United States":—

"It is greedily eaten (at Mobille, U. S.) by horses and cattle, and makes a hay of good quality. It is justly regarded as an excellent grass, particularly before it ripens its seeds.

"In Louisiana, Mississippi, and other States, it is mowed annually, and yields as much as four or five tons of hay per acre. Two cuttings are procurable each season when mowed as soon as it begins to bloom. It re-seeds the ground, and requires no care save protection from live stock. Cows and horses are very fond of it green or dry."

P. distachyum, *Linn.* (*Plate* XLII.) *Syn.—Digitaria distachya*, Pers. *Vern.—Motia* (Doáb).

Stems slender, usually creeping and rooting at the lower nodes, ascending to 1 foot or more. Leaves flat, smooth, or hairy at the mouth of the sheath. Panicle of 2-4 distant simple secund branches 1-2 inches long, at first erect, afterwards spreading or reflexed; rachis with a few scattered hairs. Spikelets loosely alternate, or sometimes more numerous and arranged in two rows, ovoid, acute, glabrous. Outer glume about half the length of the spikelet, broad and with the edges overlapping each other; second and third glumes prominently 3-nerved; fruiting glume a little shorter, obtuse, hardened, and with three distinct nerves.

Not uncommon on the plains. I have received no information as to its value for fodder in Northern India, though it has all the appearance of a good fodder grass. It occurs in Australia, where it is said to be grown for hay, and is an immense yielder.

P. erucæforme, *Sibth.* and *Sm.* (*Plate* XLIII.) *Syn.—P. caucasicum*, Trin. *Vern.*—Bundelkhand: *Tiliya, chinwári* (Lalitpur); Cent. Prov.: *Guhria* (Seoni), *loidan siput* and *sarpot* (Nagpur), *sarput* (Chánda).

Annual, cæspitose; culms branching and bent below. Leaves and sheaths softly hairy; leaves shortly spreading, broadly lanceolate; ligule ciliate. Spikes linear, solitary, shortly peduncled, arranged along a slender hairy rachis, close together and adpressed to the axis, sometimes compound at the base. Spikelets in two rows, short, hairy, ovate; lower glume very small or wanting; flowering glume and pale shorter than the glume of the elliptic obtuse hermaphrodite floret, coriaceous, shining, glabrous.

Common on cultivated ground in black and sandy soil in Bundelkhand and Central India. It is reckoned as a fodder grass, but its relative value is not known.

P. flavidum, *Retz.* (*Plate* VI.) *Syn.*—*P. brizoides,* Jacq. *Vern.*—PUNJAB: *Kangna* (Kángra), *pálon* (Patiála), *bharti* (Eastern Punjab and Doáb); RAJPUTANA: *Homa* (Mount Abu); N.-W. PROV.: *Sânka* (Dehra Dún), *dhanera* (Royle), *baunri* (Allahabad); OUDH: *Sathiya* and *sitiya* (Bhira); CENT. PROV.: *Paddatunga gadi* and *kura-tuka gadi* (Chánda), *chichwi* and *sama jodi* (Seoni); TELING: *Oda* and *woodoo gaddi* (Roxb.).

Annual. Stems erect, rigid, 1-2 feet high, branching below. Leaves rather broad, acute, glabrous except some hairs at the top of the sheath. Panicle of several erect distant branches or sessile spikes. Spikelets sessile, in two rows, ovoid, oblique; outer glume very short, broad and blunt; second glume the largest; upper floret usually without stamens. Grain short, oval, pointed, slightly rugose.

Common throughout the plains, and up to moderate elevations on the hills. It is considered to be a good fodder grass both for horses and bullocks. It produces a large quantity of grain, which is collected and eaten by the poorer classes in times of scarcity. It is indigenous also in Australia, and it is said that when growing on alluvial flats the panicles are often prostrate from the weight of the seed. An analysis lately made by Professor Church shows that the grain of this species contains much more indigestible fibre than any species yet examined, but is exceptionally rich in oil or fat, containing nearly twice as much of this constituent as any other kind (Bulletin of Miscellaneous Information, Royal Gardens, Kew, No. 12, 1887).

P. fluitans, *Retz.* (*Plate* XLIV.) *Syn.*—*P. brizoides,* Retz. (non Linn.) *Vern.*—BENGAL: *Peti-nar* (Roxb.); TELING: *Doosa* (Roxb.).

Perennial, floating, glabrous. Stems rooting at the lower nodes. Leaves elongate, linear, acuminate; lower sheaths inflated. Racemes often several on each stem, elongate. Spikes linear, sessile, adpressed, lower distant. Spikelets imbricate along the flattened smooth rachis of the spike, sessile, ovate oblong, acute, sub-compressed; glumes membranous, the lower one very short and truncate; the upper one not much larger, orbicular, ovate, obtuse; lower floret reduced to a membranous ovate acute prominently 3-nerved glume; flowering glume and pale of hermaphrodite floret coriaceous, ovate oblong, acute, and wrinkled.

Plains of North-West India, but not very common. It is strictly a water grass, and is usually found with a considerable portion of its stems under water. It produces an abundance of grain.

P. frumentaceum, *Roxb.* *Syn.—Oplismenus frumentaceus,* Kunth; *Echinochloa frumentacea,* Link. *Vern.*—GENERAL: *Sáńwan* and *sáwan;* PUNJAB: *Sama* and *sáńwak* (Plains), *sámuka* (Sutlej basin); N.-W. PROV. and OUDH: *Sáma* and *samei* (Bijnor), *sáwan-bhedeha* (Bara Banki), *jhangora* and *jhungara* (Him.); BENGAL: *Shama* (Roxb.); TELING: *Bonta-shama* (Roxb.).

An annual, 2-4 feet high. Leaves large, often over-topping the panicles, margins hispid. Panicle erect, composed of numerous secund usually incurved spikes entirely surrounding the common rachis, and frequently forming verticels. Spikelets in threes, the one sessile, the other two on pedicels of unequal length. Outer glumes very unequal, pubescent, cuspidate.

Largely cultivated in Northern India as a rainy season crop, but chiefly near and at low elevations on the hills. It is a rapid grower, coming to maturity within six weeks after sowing. The grain is not considered of a high class, and is mostly consumed by the poorer people. The stalks are given as fodder to cattle. It is figured in Part II. of "Field and Garden Crops, N.-W. Provinces and Oudh," and in Prof. Church's "Food Grains of India," *Fig.* 4.

P. helopus, *Trin.* (*Plate* VII.) *Syn.—P. setigerum,* Retz; *P. hirsutum,* Kœn.; *P. Kœnigii,* Spreng; *Urochloa pubescens,* Beauv. *Vern.*—GENERAL: *Kuri* and *kuriya;* PUNJAB: *Chatta* and *kowain* (Sabáthu Hills), *thun* (Kángra); N.-W. PROV.: *Basaunta* (Dehra Dún), *chapraila* and *semai* (Allahabad), *motia* (Mainpuri); BUNDELKHAND: *Galphula, basaunta,* and *samwán* (Banda); BENGAL: *Jal-ganti* (Roxb.); TELING: *Salla-woodoo* (Roxb.).

Stems usually tall, creeping and rooting at the base. Leaves rather broad lanceolate, with wavy margins, and cordate at the base, hirsute or glabrous; sheaths loose and hairy. Panicle branches 3-7, sessile above the upper leaf or on a long peduncle. Spikelets arranged irregularly in two rows, or in clusters at the base of the branches, ovoid acute, glabrous or hairy. Rachis usually clothed with bristles; outer glumes short, broad, 3-nerved, second and third about equal, the third enclosing a pale but no stamens. Fruiting glume minutely rugose, obtuse, but with the central nerve produced into a short awn-like point.

An excellent fodder grass for both horses and cattle. It is found chiefly on cultivated ground in the plains, and occurs on the Himalaya up to about 5,000 feet. The short awn-like point to the fruiting glume is its best distinguishing character.

P. humile, *Nees.* *Vern.*—Cent. Prov.: *Katki* and *uṛdiya* (Chánda).

A slender annual, about one foot in height. Leaves lanceolate acuminate, sparsely hairy. Panicle spreading; glumes acuminate prominently nerved.

I have seen specimens from the Punjab and Central Provinces, and have gathered it in Bundelkhand, where it is said to be a good fodder grass.

P. indicum, *Linn.* *Vern.*—*Lodi-gadi* (Chánda in Cent. Prov.).

Closely allied to *P. myosuroides* (*see* description), but not so plentiful in Northern India. It is a smaller plant, with much shorter and somewhat interrupted spikes. The spikelets are also much smaller, and more or less curved; the second glume is curved and gibbous at the base.

P. jumentorum, *Pers.* *Syn.*—*P. maximum,* Jacq.

Perennial. Stems tall, 3-5 feet, leaves broad, flat, acuminate; sheaths and nodes hairy. Panicle large and loose with numerous capillary much divided branches. Spikelets many, stalked. Lower outer glume one-fourth the length of the spikelet, ovate obtuse, the third glume encloses a male flower; fruiting glume acute, slightly rugose.

This is the "Guinea-grass," a native of Tropical Africa, and now extensively cultivated in most tropical countries. Although it seeds freely in this country, it is nevertheless found preferable to propagate it by root cuttings. In the United States it is usually planted in this way, as it rarely matures seed in that country. Manuring is beneficial where frosts prevail. Analysis shows it to be very rich in nutritive qualities; and, as it appears to thrive well in the plains of Northern India, its extended cultivation should be encouraged.

P. miliaceum, *Linn.** *Syn.*—*P. asperrimum,* Lagasc.; *P. Milium,* Pers. *Vern.*—General: *Chena, china, chinwa* and *chirwa;* Trans-Indus: *Tsedze,* (Ladak); Punjab: *Sálan* (Stewart), *anne* (Chenab basin), *zad* (Sutlej basin); Oudh: *Sáwan-chaitwa* and *sáwan-jethwa* (Bara Banki); Bundelkhand: *Bansi phikar* and *ráli;* Teling: *Worga* (Roxb.); South India: *Varágu.*

Annual, hairy. Stems erect, 2-4 feet high, leafy, simple or branched from the base. Leaves large, broad, acuminate, pilose or hispid; sheaths long, densely hairy. Panicle much branched; branches slender, elongate, spreading, ultimately bending over from the weight of the grain. Spikelets rather large, inflated, oblong, acute, smooth; lower glume one-third shorter than the spikelet, acute or cuspidate. Grain

* *See Plate* A., *Fig.* 2, of present Volume.

oval with longitudinal streaks. (For figures, *see* "Field and Garden Crops, N.-W. Provinces and Oudh," Part II., *Plate* XXIII., and Church's "Food Grains of India," *Fig.* 2).

A native of Egypt and Arabia. It is cultivated in various parts of N.-W. India on the plains as a hot weather crop; and on the Himalaya it is grown to some extent during the rainy season as a village crop at various elevations up to 11,000 feet. In this country it is cultivated almost entirely for the sake of its grain, a preparation of which constitutes a favourite kind of food at marriage ceremonies; it is therefore seldom used as fodder, although of excellent quality in the green state.

P. miliare, *Lamk.*,* (*Plate* XLVI.) *Syn.*—*P. psilopodium*, Trin.? *Vern.*—PUNJAB: *Kutki* (Stewart), *chin* (Hissar); N.-W. PROV.: *Mijhri*; BUNDELKHAND: *Kutki*; CENT. PROV.: *Kutki* (Chánda), *ban kutki* and *bagad* (Balaghát), *badi bhurbhuri* (Nagpur); BERAR: *Gomej ko kutki*; SANTAL: *Gundhi*; TELING: *Nella-shama* (Roxb.).

Annual, stems many, erect, 2-3 feet high. Leaves smooth, narrow and tapering to a fine point. Panicle slender, oblong, with many capillary hispid branches, ultimately bending over with the weight of the grain. Flowers in pairs, pedicels unequal, grain ovate, smooth, striated, becoming dark brown when ripe.

Not uncommon in the plains and up to moderate elevations on the Himalayas. It is cultivated locally for its grain by the poorer classes in Northern India and in the Central Provinces. Cattle are fond of the straw, and Mr. Coldstream states that it is good for grazing, and will stack. It is reckoned to be a good fodder grass in Bundelkhand.

P. myosuroides, *R. Br.* *Syn.*—*P. angustum*, Trin. *Vern.*—CENT. PROV.: *Dhidhina* (Chánda), *musapunchi* (Balaghát), *supedkar* (Seoni).

A smooth slender erect annual with long narrow leaves. Spikelets ovoid, obtuse, crowded into dense cylindrical spikes 1-4 inches long, often dark coloured.

Common in wet ground in the plains, and at low elevations on the hills. It is of little or no importance for fodder purposes. It extends to Queensland in Australia.

P. Myurus, *Lamk.*† *Syn.*—*P. interruptum*, Willd; *P. serrulatum*, Roxb.; *Hymenachne Myurus*, Beauv. *Vern.*—*Dhamsiria* (Rohilkhand).

A tall smooth grass growing in water. Stems 2-4 feet high, lower portions thick and rooting at the nodes. Leaves flat, broad. Spikelets crowded on the short branches of a dense cylindrical spike-like panicle which is sometimes lobed and interrupted at the base. Outer glume thin, transparent, 1-nerved, usually inserted at some distance below the others; second and third tapering to a fine point; flowering glume shorter, thin, transparent, stiff but not hardening round the grain.

It occurs in marshy ground and by water-courses in the plains of Northern India,

---

* I am unable to distinguish this species from *P. psilopodium*, Trin., under which name it is figured in Part II. of "Field and Garden Crops, N.-W. Provinces and Oudh," *Plate* XXVI. *See* also Church's "Food Grains of India," *Fig.* 2.

† *See Plate* A., *Fig.* 3, of present Volume.

but too local in its distribution to be reckoned as a useful fodder grass. In Australia, however, it is said to be very palatable and nutritious to stock.

P. paludosum, *(Roxb.). Syn.—P. decompositum*, R. Br. *Vern.*—BENGAL: *Boruti* and *kulus-nar* (Roxb.); TELING: *Soda* (Roxb.).

An aquatic grass with stout stems rooting at the lower nodes. Leaves long; ligule broad, ciliate. Panicle 6 inches to 1 foot long; branches filiform. Spikelets narrow, acute, pale coloured; lower outer glume short and truncate; fruiting glume smooth and without nerves.

Wet ground in Northern India, but not common. Baron von Müeller in his "Select Plants for extra-tropical Countries" says—"one of the most spacious of Australian nutritious grasses. The aborigines convert the small millet-like grains into cakes. This grass will thrive on poor soil."

P. Petiverii, *Trin. Vern.—Chápar* and *chaprur* (South-Eastern Punjab), *chaprura* (Falconer).

Annual. Stems decumbent, often bent and rooting at the lower nodes. Leaves rounded at the base, lanceolate acuminate, flat, smooth or hairy. Panicles erect, shortly pyramidal, simple or sub-compound; racemes linear, common rachis beset with rough bristles; spikelets shortly stalked, with rather long bristles at the base, in pairs or solitary, loose and rather large, light green, softly tomentose or smooth; lower glume one-third shorter than the spikelet, cordate-ovate, acute.

Plains of Northern India. Apparently a good fodder grass, but according to Symonds it is not suited for making into hay.

P. plicatum, *Lamk.* This is a tall grass, 3-4 feet, with very handsome foliage. It is usually found in damp shady places. I have not heard of its being used for fodder, though no doubt it may be sufficiently nutritious when young.

P. prostratum, *Lamk. (Plate* XLV.) *Syn.—P. procumbens*, Nees. *Vern.*—BUNDELKHAND: *Chaurila;* CENT. PROV.: *Choti semai* (Seoni), *sarpur* (Chánda).

Perennial. Stems cæspitose, ascending, or creeping and rooting at the nodes. Leaves glabrous or more or less hispid with bulbous-based hairs, broadly lanceolate acuminate from a cordate base, and undulate. Panicle short, ovate, one-sided; spikes shortly stalked or sessile, usually in pairs; spikelets in two ranks with bristles on their pedicels, ovate, acute, glabrous; outer glume cordate, amplexicaul, obtuse, five times shorter than the spikelet; hermaphrodite floret white, and minutely wrinkled.

Common in the plains. It is a good fodder grass, and the grain is used as food in famine times. Baron von Müeller states that it is recommendable for pastures in Australia.

P. repens, *Linn.*—Perennial glaucous. Stems extensively creeping. Leaves broad, cordate at the base and usually hairy; ligule short, ciliate. Panicle narrow, erect or spreading; spikes 4-10, short, sessile, equally inserted on the angular villous rachis; spikelets smooth, or minutely hairy on the nerves; outer glume less than one-half the spikelet; second and third acute or acuminate, prominently 3-5 nerved, the third enclosing a male flower.

Plains of Northern India. It occurs also in Australia, North Africa, South Europe, and on the coast of Brazil. Both Royle and Roxburgh state that cattle are fond of this grass.

P. sanguinale, *Linn.* (*Plate* VIII.)* *Syn.—Digitaria sanguinalis,* Scop.; *Dactylon sanguinale,* Vill.; *Paspalum sanguinale,* D.C. *Vern.*—GENERAL: *Takri* and *takriya;* TRANS-INDUS: *Khurásh* (Stewart); PUNJAB: *Bara takria* (Hissar), *dúbra* (North-Eastern Punjab), *mothi kabbal* (Stewart); RAJPUTANA: *Hen* (Mount Abu); N.-W. PROV.: *Kewai, charmara* (Bijnor); CENT. PROV.: *Korkol jodi* (Seoni); BERAR: *Chikhari.*

Stems decumbent, often rooting from the lower joints, 1-1½ feet high. Leaves flaccid, flat, glabrous or occasionally hairy on the sheaths. Spikes 4-8, sub-digitate, 2-4 inches long, on a long peduncle, secund; rachis angular, flexuose, scabrous. Spikelets in pairs, or three or four together on unequal pedicels, oblong, acute. Glumes 4, smooth, the lower outer one minute, second 3-nerved, third 5-nerved, fruiting glume shorter.

Common in the plains and at low elevations on the hills. It is much used as fodder. It occurs in Australia, South Europe, America, and in most warm countries. In the United States it is highly esteemed under the name of "Crab grass." The following quotations are from Prof. Vasey's "Agricultural Grasses of the United States":—

"It makes a sweet hay, and horses are exceedingly fond of it" (Prof. Killebrew).

"Crab grass is one of our best hay and pasture grasses. It will make two tons of first quality of hay per acre. All that is necessary is to plough and harrow the ground in April, May, or June, and you will be sure of a crop. It grows well in ordinary lands, but on sandy lands best (E. W. Jones of Buena Vista, Miss.)"

Var. **ciliare** (*Plate* IX.) *Syn.—P. ciliare,* Retz. *Vern.*—PUNJAB: *Dobra* (Simla Hills); N.-W. PROV.: *Kewai* (Aligarh), *siuri* (Allahabad); N.-W. PROV. and OUDH: *Kabdai* (Pilibhit), *sahri* and *sehri* (Bhira); BUNDELKHAND: *Kewai;* RAJPUTANA: *Chhinke* (Ajmere); CENT. PROV.: *Mandiya* (Chánda), *ráha* (Nagpur), *sikka* (Seoni and Balaghát); BENGAL: *Makur jalee* (Roxb.); TELING: *Shangali gaddi* (Roxb.).

Differs by having the lateral nerves and margin of the inner glumes clothed with long white hairs. It is found usually on dry sandy or rocky ground. From the reports I have received it evidently appears to be a good fodder grass, and is highly valued in Rájputána.

P. Teneriffæ, *R. Br. Syn.—Tricholæna Teneriffæ,* Parl.; *T. micrantha,* Schrad.; *Saccharum Teneriffæ,* Linn. f.

---

* *See* also *Plate* A., *Fig.* 4, of present Volume.

A perennial grass growing in tufts. Leaves glaucous and glabrous, narrowly linear, rigid. Spikelets solitary, irregularly panicled, clothed with long hairs; lower outer glume wanting.

It occurs in Sindh, and extends through Afghanistan to Arabia and Egypt. I have received no information as to its value for fodder purposes.

P. tenuiflorum, *R. Br.* *Syn.—Paspalum brevifolium,* Flügge. Stems from a much branched creeping base, one foot or more high. Leaves short, flat, and narrow; sheaths hairy, bearing a scarious jagged ligule. Panicle branches spike-like, digitate, filiform, 1-2 inches long; spikelets ovate, disposed along one side of the rachis; pedicels short, curved; outer empty glume wanting.

Probably common in North-West India, but no doubt often overlooked owing to its resemblance to a *Paspalum,* under which genus it is sometimes placed. I have specimens from the Siwalik range, and from Bundelkhand. It occurs in the warmer parts of Australia, where it is said to produce a fair amount of feed, and plenty of seed.

P. triflorum, *Edgew.* Found by Mr. Edgeworth among rocks at Banda, and in fields at Rudour in the Sikh States. It is distinguished (Mr. Edgeworth says) from other species of this genus by the number of the florets.

P. turgidum, *Forsk.* Perennial, glabrous, glaucous. Root fibres thick and velvety. Stems hard with proliferous fascicles at the swollen joints. Leaves often reduced to the spathe-like sheaths. Panicle terminal, short, narrow, with short erect branches. Spikelets shortly stalked, rather large, ovate, tumid, white.

A native of Sindh and Central India, extending to Arabia and Egypt. A coarse-looking hard grass, though probably nutritious when young. In Egypt a kind of bread is made from the grain.

P. vestitum, *Nees.* *Syn.—P. coccospermum,* Steud. Is recorded from Peshawar. Nutritive value unknown.

5. OPLISMENUS, *Beauv.* A small genus of about three or four species inhabiting tropical and sub-tropical countries. It resembles very closely some of the awned species of *Panicum,* but the awn in this genus is attached to the two lower glumes, of which the outer one in *Panicum* is never awned.

O. Burmanni, *Retz.,* (*Plate* XLVII.) *Syn.—Panicum Burmanni,* Linn. *Vern.*—N.-W. Prov.: *Chusa* (Pilíbhit); Cent. Prov.: *Chimakál gadi* and *utaniya* or *wataniya* (Chánda), *ghor-chubba* (Seoni), *yerwa* (Balaghát).

A small grass with the lower portion of the stems branching and procumbent. Leaves and sheaths hairy. Spikelets in a spike-like panicle. Glumes hairy, the two outer ones with long awns.

Common in the plains and at low elevations on the hills. Usually found under the shade of trees. Symonds says that cattle eat it, and that it makes good hay. In Oudh it is reported that cattle eat this grass with relish. At Balaghát it grows in the shade of bamboos, and cattle eat it when young.

Two other species, *O. acuminatus,* Nees. and *O. compositus,* R. & S., are not uncommon on the lower slopes of the Himalaya, extending to the dúns at the base of those mountains.

6. SETARIA, *Beauv.* A genus containing about 10 species, four of which occur within our area. *S. glauca* and *S. verticillata* are widely distributed throughout the tropics and the temperate regions of the world; and *S. italica* (*kangni*) is cultivated largely in India and in other warm countries. This genus may at once be recognized by its dense bristly spikes. These bristles, supposed to be abortive branches, are attached to the pedicels below each spikelet, and remain persistent after the spikelets have fallen off.

S. glauca, *Beauv.* (*Plate* X.) *Syn.*—*Panicum glaucum*, Linn.; *Pennisetum glaucum*, R. Br. *Vern.*—GENERAL: *Bandra* and *bandri*; PUNJAB: *Ban kangni* (Central and East Punjab), *dissi* (Salt Range), *kotu* (Kángra); N.-W. PROV.: *Bindra* (Dehra Dún); RAJPUTANA; *Kutta choti* (Ajmere), *soma* (Merwára), *billi* and *chhinchra* (Jeypur); BUNDELKHAND: *Dhusa, neori* (Banda); CENT. PROV.: *Pohwa* and *panhawa* (Chánda), *thontwa* (Balaghát); SANTAL: *Kukra*; BERAR: *Kuluku*; BENGAL: *Pingi-natchi* (Roxb.); TELING: *naka-kora* (Roxb.).

Annual. Stems erect, 1-3 feet high. Leaves broadly linear, acuminate, with scabrous edges, usually pale green. Panicle spike-like, densely cylindrical, 1-6 inches long. Spikelets solitary, ovoid, the awn-like barren branches beset with minute teeth directed upwards. Outer glume very small; the second shorter than the third. Fruiting glumes more or less gibbous, and transversely wrinkled. Dwarfed specimens with ovoid or sub-globose spikes are frequently to be found on barren and stony ground.

Very common all over the plains, and up to moderate elevations on the hills. It is generally considered to be a fairly good fodder grass. It thrives best in rich or cultivated ground. Symonds states that it affords a moderately good fodder, but is unsuited for making hay. In the Central Provinces it is used as fodder and the grain as food. In Australia it is highly relished by stock. In the United States, where it is called "Pigeon" or "Bottle grass," Dr. Vasey reports that it furnishes a considerable amount of fodder which is as nutritious as Hungarian grass (*S. italica*), but less productive.

S. intermedia, *R. & S. Vern.*—N.-W. PROV.: *Chiriya-chaina* (Aligarh); RAJPUTANA: *Chota sarsata* (Udaipur), *uñdar punchha* (Jeypur); CENT. PROV.: *Chota chikiya* (Chánda), *noktowa* (Seoni), *sawá* (Nagpur); BERAR: *Lundi.*

An annual species resembling small specimens of *S. verticillata*, but the spikes are narrower and more pointed, and interrupted towards the base. The bristles have the teeth pointing forwards.

Plains of Northern India, and at low elevations on the hills. In the Central Provinces it is found on both black and sandy soils. I have received no information regarding its nutritive value.

S. italica, *Beauv.* *Syn.*—*Panicum italicum,* Linn. *Vern.*—GENERAL: *Kangni* and *kákun;* TRANS-INDUS: *Gal;* PUNJAB: *Chiurr* (Jhelum basin); CHUTIA NAGPUR: *Kauni.*

Annual. Stems branching, round, smooth, erect, 3-5 feet high, or decumbent below and rooting from the lower nodes. Leaves broad, margins rough with forward bristles; mouth of sheath bearded. Panicles ovate forming dense cylindrical spikes which bend over as they become ripe. Spikelets 2-flowered, intermixed with setiform peduncles disposed in the form of involucres.

Both wild and cultivated in India, and largely grown in other warm countries. In Northern India it is usually sown as a subordinate crop accompanying juár or sáwan. It is cultivated on the Himalaya at low elevations. Its abundant and nutritious foliage yields an excellent forage if cut when in blossom.*

In Australia it is considered to be a good fattening pasture grass. In the United States, where it is known under the name of "Hungarian grass," it is much valued. Prof. Phares quoted by Dr. Vasey remarks:—"If cut at the right stage the whole plant is a safe and very valuable forage."

S. verticillata, *Beauv.* *Syn.*—*Panicum verticillatum,* Linn.; *Pennisetum verticillatum,* R. Br. *Vern.*—PUNJAB: *Chirchira* (Hissar), *barchitta* and *kutta* (East Punjab); N.-W. PROV.: *Barti* (Dehra Dún), *bardanni* (Royle); BUNDELKHAND: *Chirchitta;* RAJPUTANA: *Kutta bari* (Ajmere), *gádar puchha* (Jeypur); CENT. PROV.: *Bandri* (Seoni), *chakkarnitta-gadi* and *chikna bara* (Chánda), *lapti* (Balaghát), *chilaya* (Nagpur); BERAR: *Jaljatang-jhara;* SANTAL: *Bir kauni;* BENGAL: *Dora byara* (Roxb.); TELING: *Chicklenta* (Roxb.).

A coarse rank annual easily distinguished from the other species of *Setaria* by the downward direction of the teeth on the bristles. It is common in shady places, and in rich ground all over the plains of North-West India, and up to 6,000 feet on the Himalaya. Cattle eat it when young, that is, before the flowering spikes appear. The grain is eaten by poor people.

7. CENCHRUS, *Linn.* A genus of about 12 species found in tropical and subtropical regions of the world. The spikelets are surrounded by an involucre as in *Setaria,* but the bristles or scales of which it is composed are stiff and often connate at the base. The articulation of the pedicel occurs below this involucre, which therefore does not remain persistent as in *Setaria.*

C. catharticus, *Del.* (*Plate* XI.) *Syn.*—*C. echinatus,* Rich (non

* It is figured in Church's "Food Grains of India," *Figs.* 6 and 7, and in Part II. of "Field and Garden Crops, N.-W. Provinces and Oudh."

Linn.) *Vern.*—General: *Bhurt;* Punjab: *Basla* and *lapta* (Stewart); Rajputana: *Bharbhunt* (Jeypur); *bharont* (Ajmere); Bundelkhand: *Kukar* (Banda).

Annual. Stems erect or ascending, often bent below. Leaves rough, lanceolate acuminate, ciliate or glabrous. Involucres nearly sessile, arranged loosely in a cylindrical spike and furnished with numerous spines; spines stiff and sharp, connate into a cup at the base, outer row very short and spreading; inner thicker, erect, overtopping the flowers, sulcate on the back, downwardly hispid, often ciliate at the base. Glumes ovate, acute, membranous.

Plains of North-West India in sandy soil. It is much valued as a forage grass, on account of the early appearance of its foliage. Mr. Coldstream reporting from Hissar, says that it is much grazed when tender, but is not suitable for stacking; also that the seed mixed with bájra flour is much used by the poorer classes. The following anecdote is related in the Sirsa Settlement Report, p. 14:—"The Bágris tell that an emperor of Delhi was on his way with an army to attack Bikáner when a bhurt stuck on his arm; he picked it off and it stuck in his finger; he tried to bite it off and it stuck in his lip and gave him great pain. When told the country was full of these things, he did not venture further, and Bikáner was saved from invasion."

C. montanus, *Nees. (Plate* XLVIII.) *Syn.*—*C. Schimperi,* Steud. and Hochst.; *C. tripsacoides,* Fresen. *Vern.*—General: *Anjan* and *dháman;* Punjab: *Dhamman* (Central and North).

Annual. Stems several, ascending from a procumbent base. Leaves linear, acuminate, clothed with spreading hairs, or nearly smooth. Involucres shortly stalked, enclosing 1-2 spikelets, globose, arranged in a dense cylindrical spike; outer spines of involucre subulate, short, adpressed; inner spines 8-10, hardly exceeding the spikelets, lanceolate, pungent, connate into a cup one-third their length, erect, scabrid, sometimes with ciliate margins. Glumes nearly equal, membranous, ovate, acute, and somewhat keeled.

Common in sandy parts of the plains of N.-W. India. One of the most nutritious of Indian grasses, and by some considered to be the very best. It is a good grazing grass, and makes excellent hay. This species varies much in the size of the spikes, the compactness of the spikelets on the spikes, the length of the spines composing the involucre, also in the colour of the spikes, which are sometimes of a rich reddish brown or almost black.

8. PENNISETUM, *Pers.* This genus contains about 40 described species, the greater number being African. Of those occurring in India five are found in the plains, including the cultivated bájra (*P. typhoideum*). The flowers are arranged in cylindrical spikes as in *Setaria*, but the involucre usually falls off together with the pedicel as in *Cenchrus*. The bristles, however, are weak, not stiff and hard as in the latter named genus.

P. Alopecuros, *Steud.* *Syn.—Gymnothrix Alopecurus*, Nees ; *Cenchrus hordeiformis*, Rottl. *Vern.*—RAJPUTANA : *Moiyar* (Mount Abu) ; BUNDELKHAND : *Mo* (Lalitpur) ; CENT. PROV. : *Morthan* (Chánda), *mowa* (Seoni).

A coarse grass. Roots furnished with large fleshy fibres. Stems thick. Leaves very tough, narrow, hairy on both sides near the base ; sheaths inflated, polished. Bristles of involucre white or straw-coloured, not plumose. At Chánda in the Central Provinces it is said to grow on black soil near water. No information has been received regarding its nutritive value. This grass is abundant on Mount Abu along the sides of the water-courses ; it is used for making rope.

P. cenchroides, *Rich.* (*Plates* XII. and XIII.)* *Syn.—Cenchrus ciliaris*, Linn. *Vern.*—GENERAL : *Anjan, dháman;* TRANS-INDUS : *Taura;* PUNJAB: *Kurkán* (Stewart), *dhamman* (Central and South-West); N.-W. PROV. : *Charwa* (Aligarh), *bandri* (Allahabad) ; BUNDELKHAND : *Baiba* and *kusa* (Banda) ; RAJPUTANA : *Añdho* and *bharbhuñt* (Jeypur).

Perennial, tufted. Stems many, herbaceous, often decumbent and bent, or ascending, becoming much elongated and subscandent when growing amongst bushes. Leaves narrowly linear, acuminate ; sheaths smooth or hairy. Spikes cylindrical, dense ; rachis rough. Bristles of the sessile involucre numerous, unequal, reddish-violet rarely white ; inner widening towards the connate base, plumose, $1\frac{1}{2}$ times longer than the spikelet. Spikelets in pairs, rarely solitary.

Common all over the plains of N.-W. India, especially in sandy districts. It is an excellent fodder grass for both horses and cattle. In the Multan district it is considered to be the best kind of grass for increasing the milk of cows. It is the best grass in the Sirsa district, where it is called "dháman." In the Jhang Settlement Report it is stated :—" Dháman is the best of all grasses ....Zamindars believe that if in good condition this grass gives a semi-intoxicating effect to the milk of buffaloes who graze on it."

P. holcoides, *Schult.* (*Plate* XLIX.) *Syn.—Panicum holcoides*, Roxb. *Vern.*—BUNDELKHAND : *Laraiya* (Lalitpur) ; CENT. PROV. : *Jiral* (Seoni) ; BENGAL : *Sivati* (Roxb.).

Perennial. Stems erect, branching, 2-4 feet. Bristles of involucre of two sorts, the one twice the length of the flower and woolly from the middle downwards, the other shorter and without wool. The inner bristles appear to be connate, as in *Cenchrus*.

---

* *See also Plate* A, *Fig.* 5, in present Volume.

Abundant in Bundelkhand and in the Central Provinces, by roadsides and amongst bushes, where, like *P. cenchroides*, it assumes a climbing habit. It has all the appearance of being a good fodder grass, though no information has been received regarding it as such.

P. imberbe, *Edgew.* (*Plate* L.) *Vern.*—Rajputana : *Bajuria* (Udaipur); Cent. Prov. : *Chaj-já gadi* (Chánda).

Spikes slender, and much narrower than in *P. holcoides*. Bristles of involucre fewer, without wool, claret coloured. I have specimens from Rájputána and from the Central Provinces, where it flourishes in the black soil. I have received no special information as to its value for fodder.

P. typhoideum, *Rich.* *Syn.*—*Penicillaria spicata*, Willd., *Holcus spicatus*, Linn., *Panicum spicatum*, Roxb. *Vern.*—General : *Bájra, bajri* and *lahra;* N.-W. Prov.: *Bájra tangunanwa* (Azamgarh); Santal : *Lendha* (Campbell); Bengal : *Bujra* and *bujera* (Roxb.); Teling : *Pedda-gantee* (Roxb.); Madras : *Chambu.*

A tall erect grass, 5-6 feet high, with the spikelets crowded into a compact cylindrical spike 6-9 inches long and $\frac{3}{4}$ to 1 inch in diameter. Each spikelet is surrounded by an involucre of bristles, of which the inner ones are plumose hairy.

This is the bulrush or spiked millet. It is largely cultivated in Northern India, and the stalks and leaves are much used as fodder, though inferior to juar. In the United States, where it is known under many names, such as African cane, Egyptian millet, &c., it is extensively grown as a fodder plant, and many cuttings are obtained during the season. It is figured in Church's "Food Grains of India," also in Part I. of "Field and Garden Crops of N.-W. Provinces and Oudh."

TRIBE II. MAYDEÆ.

9. COIX, *Linn.* There are three or four described species, one of which is a common water grass in India. It is easily recognised by its numerous large roundish or pear-shaped pearly-white bead-like fruits. The flowers are monœcious, the fertile ones being situated at the base of the spikes. Male spikes drooping. The hard shell-like substance which covers the grain consists of a sheathing bract.

C. gigantea, *Koen.* *Vern.*—Berar : *Kesai ;* Bengal : *Danga gurgur* (Roxb.).

A tall erect water grass 8 to 15 feet high with large broad leaves. Florets of male spikes in threes, the central one stalked.

Plains of North-West India, in wet places.

C. Lachryma, *Linn.** *Vern.*—Punjab : *Sánklu* (Sabáthu Hills);

* *See Plate* A., *Fig.* 6, in present Volume, and *Fig.* 10 of Church's "Food Grains of India."

RAJPUTANA: *Dabhir* (Mount Abu); N.-W. PROV.: *Sankru* (Royle), *baru* (Sahâranpur); BUNDELKHAND: *Gandula* or *garun* (Lalitpur); CENT. PROV.: *Kasei* and *gulbi gadi* (Chánda), *gulu* (Seoni), *gurlu* (Balaghát); SANTALI: *Jargadi* (Campbell); BENGAL: *Gurgur* and *kunch* (Roxb.); MARATHI: *Rânjondhala* and *rânmaka* (Dymock).

Very similar to the preceding species, but not so tall. Leaves cordate at the base. Florets of male spikes in pairs.

Common in wet ground in the plains, and in warm valleys on the Himalaya. In Oudh it is largely eaten by cattle, and is said to be very fattening. The hard shell-like involucres, known as "Job's tears," are called "kassai-bij" in the Bombay Presidency, and are used there as a diuretic; and by the Chinese and Burmans the grain is used as an article of food. For further information *see* Church's Food Grains of India," p. 60, and Dymock's "Vegetable Materia Medica of Western India," p. 853.

10. CHIONACHNE, *R. Br.* There are three species, one of which is not uncommon on wet ground in Northern India. It resembles *Coix* in habit, and has also the curious polished stone-like fruit cases, which, however, in this genus are formed by the hardening of the outer empty glume.

C. barbata, *R. Br.* *Syn.—Coix barbata*, Roxb.; *C. Kœnigii*, Spreng. *Vern.*—CENT. PROV.: *Bhus* and *kirma-gilâram gadi* (Chánda), *kadpi* (Balaghát); MARATHI: *Varival* (Dymock); BENGAL: *Gurgur* (Roxb.); TELING: *Ghella gadee* (Roxb.).

Stems 3-6 feet high. Pedicels jointed, with a boat-shaped cuspidate spathe at the joint. Male spikes erect, florets in pairs.

Roxburgh says that owing to its coarse nature cattle do not eat this grass. At Balaghát in the Central Provinces, however, it is said to be used as fodder when young.

11. EUCHLÆNA, *Schrad.* There are two species, both natives of Mexico. The arrangement and structure of the flowers, which are monœcious, bear a close resemblance to that of maize (*Zea Mays*), so much so as to have suggested the probability of maize, which is not known in a wild state, having originated from a species of *Euchlæna*. Mr. Bentham remarks * that the affinity to *Zea* appears to be recognized in the country, for specimens have been received from Schaffner purporting to be known as "wild maize."

E. luxurians, *Ascheron.* An excellent fodder grass for a subtropical climate, attaining a height of 14 feet in rich ground. It has been grown successfully in this country under the name of *Reana luxurians;* but, as it requires a rich soil and plenty of irrigation, its extensive cultivation would prove too costly. It is highly valued in the warmer southern parts of the United States.

12. ZEA, *Linn.* Contains a single species, the well known Indian

---

* In Journ. Linn. Soc. (Botany), Vol. XIX., p. 53.

corn, or maize. The following remarks are taken from Mr. Bentham's valuable paper on the genera of grasses published in the Journal of the Linnean Society, and already referred to. "This most important, widely diffused, and most striking grass is only known in a cultivated state, or perhaps as an escape from cultivation. With most of the general characters of the tribe, to which it gives its name, it is exceptional not only in that tribe, but in the whole order by the manner in which its numerous female spikelets are densely packed in several vertical rows round a central spongy or corky axis. How far this arrangement may have gradually arisen after so many centuries of cultivation can only be a matter of conjecture."

Z. Mays, *Linn.* *Vern.*—General: *Makka;* Punjab: *Makki* and *kukri* (Stewart); N.-W. Prov.: *Bara juar* and *bari junri* (Eastern Districts); Bengal: *Makrai* and *jouar* (Chutia Nagpur), *mukka* (Roxb).; Santal: *Joudra* (Campbell); Teling: *Joona* and *moka* (Roxb.)

Extensively cultivated both in the plains and on the hills as a rainy season crop. The stalks and leaves when young contain a large amount of saccharine matter, and afford excellent fodder for cattle.

TRIBE III. ORYZEÆ.

13. HYGRORHIZA, *Nees.* Contains a single species confined to India. It is an aquatic grass, either floating on the surface of the water, or creeping on wet ground. Each spikelet contains only two glumes, of which the outer one is awned. The stamens are six, and there is no pale.

H. aristata, *Nees.* *Syn.*—*Leersia aristata,* Roxb. *Vern.*—Punjab: *Pastál* (Drummond); N.-W. Prov.: *Passai, passári* and *passáhi,* also *parsál* (Sahâranpur), and *tinni* (Partábgarh).

Stems long, lower portions usually submerged and emitting numerous roots from the joints. Leaves cordate, lanceolate, obtuse, scabrous. Spikelets narrow, 1-flowered.

Roxburgh says that cattle are fond of this grass. The grain, where the supply is plentiful, is eaten by certain of the poorer classes, who collect it by sweeping over the plants with baskets. The grain ripens in September.

14. ORYZA, *Linn.* Rice and its numerous varieties belong to this genus. It differs in floral structure from *Hygrorhiza* by having four glumes instead of only two; the two outer ones are minute or setiform, the inner upper ones (sometimes called pales) are rigid, and one of them is often awned. There are no pales, and the stamens are 6.

O. sativa, *Linn.** *Vern.*—Kashmir: *Dein* and *táni* (Stewart); Pun-

* *See* also *Plate* B., *Fig.* 7, of present Volume.

JAB: *Shálian* (Drummond), *tai* (Stewart); SINDH: *Dangara* (Watt.); RAJPUTANA: *Garri* (Lowrie), *sál* (Mount Abu); CENT. PROV.: *Deodhán* (Chanda); CHUTIA NAGPUR: *Uri dhán* (Campbell); SANTALI: *Horo* (Campbell); TELING: *Newaree* (Roxb.).

Cultivated on the plains of Northern India, and up to about 4,000 feet on the Himalaya. The straw is sometimes given to cattle, but is not considered a wholesome kind of fodder. Roxburgh says: "the rice of the wild sort is remarkably white, palatable, and reckoned very wholesome; so that it is carefully gathered and sells dear. The rich esteem it a dainty; and to make it still more delicate they boil it only in steam." An awned variety of wild rice grows abundantly in wet places on Mount Abu, and the grain is collected for food.

15. LEERSIA, *Swartz.* There are five species, all natives of America, including one which occurs also in Europe, and another in India. They are aquatic and similar in habit to *Oryza;* the spikelets, however, are smaller, the glumes, of which there are only two, are thinner, and there is no pale.

L. hexandra, *Swartz. Syn.—L. australis,* R. Br.

Found occasionally on wet ground in the plains of N.-W. India. Symond says that cattle are fond of it; and in Australia it is said to be much relished by stock.

TRIBE IV. TRISTEGINEÆ.

16. ARUNDINELLA, *Raddi.* A genus of 24 species spread over the tropical and subtropical regions of the world. The following are its chief distinguishing characters: glumes 4, the three lower of which are pointed but not awned; the fourth or fruiting glume is smaller than the others, and carries a slender twisted and bent awn. The inflorescence is variable. *A. nepalensis,* Nees, and *A. Wallichii,* Nees, extend into the plains from the Himalaya; and *A. pumila,* Steud. occurs in Sindh and in hilly parts of Rájputána. Nothing definite is known regarding their value as fodder.

17. RHYNCHELYTRUM, *Hochst.* A small genus of three or four species, one of which occurs locally in India, and the rest are tropical African. It is at once distinguished from the other genera of the tribe by the long hairs on the lower glumes.

R. Wightii, *Syn.—Tricholæna Wightii,* Nees; *Panicum megalanthum,* Steud. *Vern.*—RAJPUTANA: *Bard ghás* (Jeypore), *girri* (Ajmere).

Stems erect, 1–3 feet high. Spikelets large, in rather dense panicles; outer glumes thickly clothed with pink or lilac coloured pubescence.

This is a local grass, occurring in sandy soil. I have specimens from Jeypore, Ajmere and Udaipur. It is apparently of little value for fodder purposes.

18. THYSANOLÆNA, *Nees.* Contains a single species, *T. acarifera,* Nees, a native of tropical Asia. It is a tall handsome grass with large panicles of minute spikelets. It is not uncommon on the plains, and at low elevations on the hills, usually in the vicinity of water. This grass is called "karsar" in Chutia Nagpur. A decoction of the root is used as a rinse for the mouth in cases of fever (Rev. A. Campbell).

TRIBE V. ZOYSIEÆ.

19. TRAGUS, *Hall.* Contains a single species, which is widely distributed over tropical and temperate regions.

T. racemosa, *Hall.* (*Plate* XIV.)* *Syn.*—*Lappago racemosa,* Willd.; *L. biflora,* Roxb.; *Cenchrus racemosus,* Linn. *Vern.*—GENERAL: *Barchinte;* PUNJAB: *Barchinte choti* (Hissar); RAJPUTANA: *Dháman* (Merwára).

A small annual with procumbent stems and rooting from the lower nodes. Leaves short with ciliated margins. Spikelets in clusters of 3-5, arranged in compact spikes; upper outer glume stiff and covered on the back with hooked bristles.

Plains of Northern India on sandy soils. Mr. W. Coldstream says that it is common at Hissar both on bir and on cultivated land, that it is too small to stack, but being a very nutritious grass, it is much grazed in the rains. Mr. Symonds, however, says that cattle will not eat it, and Mr. Lowrie, writing from Ajmere, condemns it as a bad fodder grass. It is found in Australia, where it is regarded as good for winter feeding.

20. LATIPES, *Kunth.* Contains a single species, *L. senegalensis.* (*Syn.*—*Lappago Latipes,* Steud.), a native of tropical Africa, and extending eastward as far as Sindh. The spikelets are smaller than those of *Tragus,* and usually solitary, or rarely in pairs on the pedicel.

21. PEROTIS, *Ait.* Contains about three species, one of which *P. latifolia,* Ait.† (*Syn.*—*Anthoxanthum indicum,* Linn.; *Saccharum spicatum,* Linn.; *Agrostis spicæformis,* Linn. *f.*) is very common in the plains on barren and sandy soil. The plant is from 1 foot to 1½ feet high; leaves short and hairy; spikelets 1-flowered, arranged in a simple spike-like raceme. Of the three glumes the two outer ones are stiff and linear with slender terminal awns. The following are some of its vernacular names:—PUNJAB: *Chambar* (Sabáthu Hills); RAJPUTANA: *Puniya* (Ajmere), *undar puchha* (Jeypur); CENT. PROV.: *Banda puchhi* (Seoni). Roxburgh says that cattle are not fond of this grass; Mr. Lowrie, however, states that at Ajmere it is considered to be a good fodder grass.

TRIBE VI. ANDROPOGONEÆ.

22. IMPERATA, *Cyrill.* Of the three or four described species one is very common all over India, and is easily recognized by its pure white cylindrical spike-like panicles of silky spikelets. The thin transparent glumes are without awns, and there are only two stamens. This genus has one character in common with the following (*Miscanthus*), and

---

* See also *Plate* B., *Fig.* 8, of present Volume.

† *Plate* B., *Fig.* 9.

which is quite exceptional in the tribe, *viz.*, the branches of the panicle having no joints.

I. arundinacea, *Cyrill.* (*Plate* XV.)* *Syn.*—*I. cylindrica*, Beauv.; *I. Kœnigii*, Beauv.; *Saccharum cylindricum*, Lamk.; *Lagurus cylindricus*, Linn. *Vern.*—GENERAL: *Siru* and *ulu;* PUNJAB: *Dáb* (Simla Hills), *sil* and *sir* (Stewart), *kusa* (E. Punjab); N.-W. PROV.: *Usirh* (Aligarh); BENGAL: *Ooloo* (Roxb.).

A perennial grass with extensively creeping roots. Stems erect and stiff, 1-3 feet high; nodes usually with a tuft of long hairs. Leaves erect, narrow, the lower ones overtopping the stems, upper with very short blades. Panicle spike-like, cylindrical, 3-4 inches long, covered with silvery white hairs which completely conceal the glumes, but through which the stamens and stigmas protrude. There are only two stamens.

Widely dispersed over Northern India both in the plains and on the hills, more especially on clayey soils where water is near the surface. It forms a very large portion of the pasturage in Bengal, where, as Roxburgh observes, the fields are white with it when in flower after the first rains in April and May. Cattle relish it when young. The Telingas make use of it in their marriage ceremonies. In Australia it is called "blady grass," and the young succulent foliage which springs up after the occurrence of a fire is much relished by stock. I have observed the same effect resulting from periodical fires on certain parts of the Himalaya where this grass is plentiful.

23. MISCANTHUS, *Anders.* Contains 8 species, one of which, *M. fuscus*, Anders., (*Syn.*—*Saccharum fuscum*, Roxb.; *Eriochrysis fusca*, Trin.) occurs in the plains of Northern India. As in *Imperata* the panicle branches are not jointed, but it differs from that genus in having awns to the flowering glumes, and three stamens. It has also a very different looking inflorescence, the spikelets being arranged in a loose panicle. *M. fuscus* is a large rather handsome grass, and is usually found in damp spots. It is chiefly used as a thatching material, and pens are said to be made from its stems.

24. SACCHARUM, *Linn.* This genus contains about 12 species, including sugarcane. They are all tall grasses with large compound panicles, the branches are articulate and clothed with silky hairs. The spikelets are very small and the glumes are not awned. Belonging to this genus we have two other very familiar species, *viz.*, kañs, and munj grass.

S. ciliare, *Anders.* (*Plate* XVI.)† *Vern.*—GENERAL: *Sarr* and

---

* See also *Plate* B., *Fig.* 10, of present Volume.

† Professor Hackel informs me that Roxburgh's name, *S. Munja*, under which this well known grass has hitherto been identified in this country, is doubtful.

sarkanda; PUNJAB: *Kána* (Sirsa), *sarkara* (E. Punjab), *sarjbar* (Kángra); N.-W. PROV.: *Ikar* (Western districts), *patáwar* (Eastern districts); OUDH: *Palwar* (Bhira). Other names given to separate portions of the plant are—*munj* the sheath of the leaf and the fibre which it yields; *sar* the leaves (Punjab); *bind* the flowering stem (Doáb), *sarahri* (Eastern districts of N.-W. Provinces); *sentha* and *kána* the lower portion of the flowering stem; *sirki* and *til* the upper portion of flowering stem; *majori* the entire stem from the base (Punjab); *tilak* or *tilon* the blossom (Punjab), also called *ghua* (Eastern districts of N.-W. Provinces).

A tall handsome grass, 8-10 feet high, smooth. Leaves long and narrow, rough at the edges with minute forward prickles. Panicle large; branches in verticils, spreading. Spikelets densely clothed with long white silky hairs.

Plains of Punjab and N.-W. Provinces, becoming rare eastward of Allahabad. It is of too coarse a nature to be used for fodder except when quite young; it is used, however, for many other purposes; *e.g.*, in the manufacture of matting, rope, paper and for thatching; the stems are made into screens, sieves and baskets; the thicker portions of the stem are used for lining wells, and in the construction of chairs and couches. In the Jhang district of the Punjab it is stated that in the cold weather the leaves are often the only pasturage for the cattle. They are also chopped up and mixed with bhusa, with grain, oil cake, or green stuff. In the early spring the grass is fired, and the cattle graze on the green shoots that quickly sprout again. Only the inferior patches of sar are treated thus, as the plant seldom produces *munj kána* after being burnt (Jhang Settlement Report, p. 23).

S. officinarum, *Linn.* *Vern.*—PUNJAB: *Ganna* and *kamánd* (Stewart), *pona* (grown for chewing), *ikh* and *ikhári* (East of Sutlej), *kamád* (Central Punjab); RAJPUTANA: *Sántha* (Ajmere); N.-W. PROV.: *Ukh* and *ukhári* (Eastern districts), *paunda* (grown in Dehra Dún for chewing); BUNDELKHAND: *Baraii* (Lalitpur); BENGAL: *Katari* (Chutia Nagpur), *ak*, *kajooli*, *kooshiar*, *kullooa* and *poori* (Roxb.); TELING: *Cherukoo-bodi* and *cherukoo-duboo* (Roxb.). The inflorescence of this and other species of *Saccharum* is called *tilak*.

Sugarcane is cultivated largely in Northern India as a kharif crop, and sparingly in some of the warmer Himalayan valleys. It is propagated by cuttings, the plants very rarely yielding seed. There are several varieties, some of which are grown for the manufacture of sugar, and others for eating raw. The refuse cane yields a strong fibre, and is also used for torches, &c., in the central parts of the Punjab, where the strips are called pachchian. The leaves are used as fodder. Stewart mentions that sugarcane is sometimes grown without irrigation, the crop being used as *chari* for feeding elephants. For figures *see* "Field and Garden Crops, N.-W. Provinces and Oudh," Part I., and Church's "Food-Grains of India," *Fig.* 14.

S. Sara, *Roxb.* (*Plate* LI.) *Vern.*—PUNJAB : *Sarkara* and *kanda* (Watt); RAJPUTANA: *Panni;* BUNDELKHAND: *Sarpat* (Banda); OUDH: *Kanwar* (Bhira); BENGAL: *Shur* (Roxb.); SANTALI: *Sarghás* (Campbell).

A tall erect grass upwards of 12 feet high. Leaves flat, with cutting edges; sheaths 1–1½ feet long, with a tuft of hairs in the place of the ligule. Panicle dense, much branched, open when in flower, afterwards becoming condensed.

Common in Rájputána, Bundelkhand, and in the Punjab. Of too coarse a nature, except when quite young, to be used as fodder. Mr. Coldstream says that the young flowering tops are regarded as good fodder for milch cows. At Jeypur it is extensively used as a sand-binding plant; and the experiments which have been undertaken there for arresting the movement of sand prove it to be very suitable for the purpose. At Ajmere the flowering stems are called *sarkanda,* and the leaf sheaths are known as *munj.*

S. spontaneum, *Linn.* (*Plate* LII.) *Syn.*—*S. ægyptiacum,* Willd. *Vern.*—GENERAL: *Káns;* PUNJAB: *Kánh* (Jhang and Muzaffargarh), *káhi* (Stewart); SINDH: *Kahu* (Watt.); RAJPUTANA: *Kánh* (Mount Abu); N.-W. PROV. and OUDH: *Kansa* and *kansi* (Allahabad), *rara* (Lucknow), *khagar* (Kheri); CENT. PROV.: *Kore gadi* (Chánda), *padar* (Balaghát); HIND: *Kagara* (Roxb.), *kosa* (Watt.); TELING: *Relloo gaddy* (Roxb.).

Perennial. Roots extensively creeping. Stems varying in height from 5 to 15 feet according to the nature of the soil. Leaves long and narrow, with hispid margins; mouth of sheaths woolly. Panicle narrow, branches in verticels, simple. The quantity of wool-like pubescence which surrounds the base of the spikelets renders this plant a conspicuous object.

Common in the plains, and on the Himalaya up to 5 or 6,000 feet; usually in damp soils. Owing to its vigorous root-growth it is a most difficult plant to eradicate from cultivated land. It is a favourite fodder of buffaloes, and is also given to elephants when young. In the Jhang Settlement Report it is stated to be found in the moistest portions of lands adjoining the rivers, where it affords most valuable pastúrage for buffaloes. The zamindárs of those parts say that if there were no *káńh* there would be no buffaloes, and they consider it too valuable to be used for thatching. In other parts of the country where better fodder grasses are obtainable, this grass is very generally used as a thatching material.

Three other species of *Saccharum* are occasionally met with in Northern India, *viz.*:—

S. Narenga, *Benth.* *Syn.*—*Eriochrysis Narenga,* Nees.

S. procerum, *Roxb.* *Vern.*—BENGAL : *Teng* (Roxb.).

Roxburgh says that it is by far the most beautiful of the genus. It comes nearest in appearance to *S. officinarum,* but is a taller and much more elegant plant.

S. semidecumbens, *Roxb.* *Vern.*—BENGAL : *Khori* (Watt.), *khurree* (Roxb.). Lower portion of culms procumbent.

25. ERIANTHUS, *Mich.* Of the 12 described species only one is found in the plains of Northern India. Botanically it stands between *Saccharum* and *Pollinia,* having the inflorescence of the former, and the awned glumes of the latter.

E. Ravennæ, *Beauv.** *Syn.*—*Saccharum Ravennæ,* Linn.; *Andropogon Ravennæ,* Linn.; *Ripidium Ravennæ,* Trin. *Vern.*—N.-W. PROV.: *Dhaulsar* and *dholu.*

Plains of N.-W. India. A tall grass much resembling a *Saccharum* in general appearance.

26. SPODIOPOGON, *Trin.* Species 3, inhabiting temperate Asia and India. This genus differs from *Pollinia* as regards its inflorescence just as *Chrysopogon* does from *Andropogon.* The short branches of the panicle bear three spikelets, one sessile between two stalked ones, with occasionally a pair of spikelets below the three terminal ones ; but the branches never form the regular spikes of *Pollinia.*

S. albidus, *Benth.* *Syn.*—*Andropogon albidus,* Wall. *Vern.*—CENT. PROV.: *Kanka gadi* (Chánda).

Stems 1-3 feet, smooth, shining, and tinged with red. Leaves distinctly petioled, broad, flat, dark green, with a few long silky hairs ; midrib prominent, nearly white ; apex attenuated into a slender awn-like point ; sheaths inflated, edges membranous and with many bulbous-based hairs at the upper part. Panicles narrow ; clusters crowded, straw-coloured, and thickly clothed with silky pubescence.

I have specimens from the Central Provinces and from Bundelkhand, also some lately gathered by myself on Mount Abu, in Rájputána.

27. POLLINIA, *Trin.* About 25 species have been described. Those which occur in Northern India are mostly Himalayan. Of the three species found in the plains, the bhábar grass *(P. eriopoda)* is the most important, though of little value as fodder. Some of the species very much resemble *Andropogon* in habit, but the stalked spikelets are fertile, which is not the case in *Andropogon.*

P. argentea, *Trin.* (*Plate* LIII.) *Syn.*—*P. tristachya,* Thw.; *Erianthus tristachyius,* Trin.; *E. Roxburghii,* F. Muell. *Vern.*—RAJPUTANA :

---

* *See* also *Plate* B., *Fig.* 11, of present Volume.

Krer (Mount Abu); BUNDELKHAND: *Gándli* and *gonchi* (Lalitpur); CENT. PROV: *Chota kusal, liyun gadi,* and *tám* (Chánda), *chota kusal* (Seoni), *kaudi* (Balaghát); BERAR: *Sona-jhara.*

Stems 2–3 feet, erect, smooth at the nodes. Leaves narrow, hairy, the sheaths ciliate at the mouth. Spikes usually several, clustered at the summit of the peduncle, slender, 3-4 inches long. Rachis of spikes and the pedicels clothed with white silky hairs.

Plentiful in Rájputána, Bundelkhand and the Central Provinces, and extending to Queensland. It is said to afford excellent fodder for cattle when young, afterwards becoming coarse and more suitable for thatching purposes.

P. eriopoda, *Hance. Syn.—Spodiopogon angustifolius,* Trin.; *S. laniger,* Nees; *Andropogon involutus,* Steud.; *A. notopogon,* Nees. *Vern.*—GENERAL: *Bhábar;* PUNJAB: *Bhabar* (Salt Range and Himalaya), *munji* and *baggar* (Stewart), *babbar* (Sir W. Davies); N.-W. PROV. and OUDH: *Bankas* (Gorakhpur), *ban kush* and *baib* (Bhira); *bámoth* (Hamirpur); BENGAL: *Babui* (Chutia Nagpur), *bachkron* (Santál); CENT. PROV.: *Nulka gadi* (Chánda), *som* (Balaghát).

Stems 1½ feet or more, base bulb-like and covered with woolly pubescence. Leaves narrow, with involute edges, strong and firm. Spikeslets in pairs, imbricate, one sessile and the other stalked, both of them hermaphrodite.

This grass yields a well known and excellent material for cordage, and is now also largely used in the manufacture of paper. It is eaten by cattle when young.

P. nuda, *Trin. Syn.—P. imberbis,* Nees; *Leptatherum Royleanum,* Nees. Lower ranges of Himalaya, occasionally extending to the plains.

28. POGONATHERUM, *Beauv. P. saccharoideum,* Beauv., is plentiful on the Himalaya at low elevations; it occurs also on rocky hills in other parts of India. It is an ornamental grass with slender branches bearing simple spikes. The second glume is awned as well as the flowering glume. The Santáli name for this grass, in Chutia Nagpur, is *lukui.*

29. DIMERIA, *R. Br.* Species about 10, extending from tropical Asia to Australia. They are annual grasses with very slender spikes, narrow and rather rigid outer glumes, and only two stamens. *D. ornithopoda,* Trin. occurs in the Central Provinces, and is known, in the Chánda Division, under the name of "kore gadi."

30. ARTHRAXON, *Beauv.* Contains about 10 species, of which one occurs in hilly parts of N.-W. India. In general appearance they resemble *Pollinia,* but in this genus one spikelet of each pair is reduced to a rudimentary stalk.

A. ciliare, *Beauv. Syn.—Batratherum echinatum,* Nees; *Andropogon* *echinatum*, Heyne. *Vern.*—RAJPUTANA: *Undri* (Merwára), *undar gin* (Mount Abu).

Stems 1 foot or more, decumbent or creeping at the base. Outer glume with muricate nerves; flowering glume with a long dorsal awn from near the base.

Plains of N.-W. India and up to 7,000 feet on the Himalaya. Considered to be a good fodder grass in Rájputána.

31. ELIONURUS, *Munro.* Two of the 12 described species occur in Northern India; one is a characteristic desert grass, and the other is found on rocky ground in the neighbourhood of ravines. They resemble *Rottbœllia* in habit, but the spikes are clothed with long silky hairs.

E. hirsutus, *Munro.* (*Plate* XVII.) *Syn.*—*Rottbœllia hirsuta*, Vahl.; *Lasiurus hirsutus*, Boiss; *Saccharum hirsutum*, Forsk.; *Ischæmum hirsutum*, Nees. *Vern.*—PUNJAB: *Sin* (Hissar); RAJPUTANA: *Shinwan* and *siwan* (Bikanir), *gawán* (Jeypur).

A perennial grass with a hard cæspitose rhizome, from which strong cylindrical root-fibres are given off. Stems erect, 1-2 feet, hard and woody below. Leaves firm, acuminate, convolute. Spike terminal, densely clothed with long silvery pubescence; rachis brittle. Spikelets in threes at each node of the rachis.

A characteristic desert grass of N.-W. India. It is considered very nutritious, and affords excellent grazing when young. Tod mentions that in Bikanir, where this grass is abundant, the seed is collected, and mixed with bájra flour it is largely consumed by the people. This grass is also given to elephants as fodder. It becomes coarse and hard as it matures, and is then only fit for thatching purposes.

E. Royleanus, *Nees.* (*Plate* LIV.) *Syn.*—*Rottbœllia elegantissima*, Hochst. and Steud.; *Andropogon elegantissimus*, Steud.

Root slender. Stems cæspitose, branched, 6 inches to 1 foot long, pilose at the nodes. Leaves narrow; sheaths inflated, edges hyaline, mouth pilose; upper leaves reduced to spathe-like sheaths and almost concealing the spikes. Outer glume of the sessile hermaphrodite spikelet clothed with long silky hairs, margin beset with short conical hair-tipped crenations. A distinct and curious looking grass found on dry stony ground in the ravine country.

32. ROTTBŒLLIA, *Linn. f.* There are about 18 described species, of which one occurs in Northern India. Spikes terete. Spikelets in pairs at each excavation of the jointed rachis, one of them being sessile and fertile, the other stalked and sterile.

R. exaltata, *Linn. f.* *Vern.*—BERAR: *Barsali*; BENGAL: *Bura swooate* (Roxb.); TELING: *Konda panookoo* (Roxb.)

A tall grass with strong fibrous roots. Stems slightly compressed, 6–10 feet high. Leaves many, large, hairy on the inner side, margins hispid, sheaths very hairy, hairs stiff and swollen at the base. Spikes cylindrical, usually solitary.

Sub-Himalayan tract ascending to 4 or 5,000 feet. It is found also in North Australia.

33. OPHIURUS, *R. Br.* Species about 4, two of which are not uncommon in damp spots in Northern India. It resembles *Rottbœllia* in habit, but is technically distinguished by having the spikelets single at each excavation of the rachis, the second or sterile spikelet not being present, at any rate on the upper portion of the spike.

O. corymbosus, *Gœrtn.* *Syn.*—*Rottbœllia corymbosa,* Linn. *Vern.*—RAJPUTANA and BUNDELKHAND: *Sonthe;* BERAR: *Chotoe;* TELING: *Pedda panookoo* (Roxb.).

Glaucous. Stems many, erect, smooth, 3–5 feet high. Leaves few, sheaths short and smooth. Spikes fascicled, on filiform peduncles, terminal and from the upper axils; peduncles curved, jointed and bracteate near the base.

Common on the black soil in Bundelkhand and the Central Provinces. In Bundelkhand it is used chiefly for thatching, and as fodder when other grasses fail.

O. lævis, *Benth.* (*Plate* LV.) *Syn.*—*O. perforatus,* Trin.; *Rottbœllia perforata,* Roxb.; *Mnesithea lævis,* Kunth. *Vern.*—PUNJAB: *Satgatua* and *satgathia* (E. Punjab); N.-W. PROV. and OUDH: *Gandel* (Doáb), *sarwára* (Pilibhit); BENGAL: *Kurki* (Roxb.); TELING: *Panookoo* (Roxb.).

Stems erect, smooth, 3–5 feet. Spikes solitary; rachis perforated so that the backs of the glumes next to the rachis touch each other. Spikelets in lower part of the spike in pairs at each node as in *Rottbœllia,* but the two of each pair are separated by a kind of partition dividing the cavity of the rachis into two.

Not uncommon on low-lying pasture land in the plains, and also on the Himalaya, up to 5,000 feet. Cattle eat it when it is young and green.

34. MANISURIS, *Linn.* Is represented by a single species found in most tropical countries. It may be readily distinguished by the globular shape of the sessile fertile spikelet of each pair.

M. granularis, *Swartz.* (*Plate* LVI.)* *Syn.*—*Cenchrus granularis,* Linn. *Vern.*—RAJPUTANA: *Kangni* (Ajmere), *dhaturo ghás* (Udaipur); CENT. PROV.: *Agi-mali-gadi* (Chánda); BERAR: *Ratop.*

A hairy annual. Stems branching 1–2 feet. Spikes stalked, terminal and axillary, and sometimes in fascicles, ½–1 inch long. Spikelets in pairs, one sessile and fertile, the other male or neuter and stalked.

---

* *See* also *Plate* B., *Fig.* 12, of present Volume.

Glumes of fertile floret four, of which the outer one is hard, globular and rugose.

Plains of Northern India, and on the Himalayas up to 4 or 5,000 feet. It extends to North Australia. Mr. Coldstream says that it is both grazed and stacked (at Hissar, Punjab), but is not much relished by cattle. At Ajmere it is considered to be a good fodder grass.

35. HEMARTHRIA, *R. Br.* Species two or perhaps three. Two kinds occur in Northern India, inhabiting damp ground. In general appearance they closely resemble *Rottbœllia*, but the spikes are flattened, not terete, and the stalk of the sterile spikelet is adnate to the rachis.

H. compressa, *R. Br.** *Syn.*—*Rottbœllia compressa*, Linn.; *R. glabra*, Roxb. *Vern.*—Bengal: *Buksha* and *pansheroo* (Roxb.); Teling: *Shervoo* (Roxb.).

Perennial. Stems many, creeping or climbing, compressed, smooth. Leaves rather short, smooth and soft. Spikes 2–4 inches long, terminal and from the upper axils, 2–5 together, compressed.

Moist places in the plains, and at low elevations on the hills. Extends to Australia. Roxburgh says that cattle are fond of this grass. Baron Von Müeller says that it is highly esteemed by graziers in Gyppsland for moist pastures.

H. fasciculata, *Kunth.* (*Plate* LVII.) *Syn.*—*Rottbœllia fasciculata*, Desf. *Vern.*—N.-W. Prov.: *Biksa* (Rohilkhand).

This is probably only a form of *H. compressa*, differing by having shorter leaves and the spikes shorter and more crowded. It is found in similar localities.

36. ISCHÆMUM, *Linn.* Contains about 30 species, of which three are found in the plains. The spikes are solitary or 2–3 together at the summit of the common peduncle. The spikelets are attached in pairs alternately on the rachis of the simple spike, the one sessile and the other stalked. The sessile spikelet contains two florets, the upper one hermaphrodite and the lower male. The flowering glume usually has a bent and twisted awn as in *Andropogon.*

I. ciliare, *Retz.* *Syn.*—*Spodiopogon obliquivalvis*, Nees. *Vern.*—N.-W. Prov.: *Kála* (Doáb); Cent. Prov.: *Bara toriya-gadi* and *piyána-koru-gadi* and *paba* (Chánda); *guhera* (Balaghát).

Stems 1–2½ feet. Leaves tapering to a fine point, clothed with scattered bulbous-based hairs; sheaths inflated, the upper ones much longer

---

* *Plate* XVIII. probably represents *H. fasciculata*, and not *H. compressa*, which it closely resembles. *See* also *Plate* C., *Fig.* 13, of present Volume.

than the free blades, ligule prominent. Spikes over one inch long, two together at the summit of the peduncle, one of them attached a little lower down than the other; pedicels ciliate. Awn twisted and bent below the middle.

Plains of North-Western India on wet ground; common in the Central Provinces. Extends to Australia. It is occasionally used as a fodder grass.

Var. **villosum.** *Vern.*—Cent. Prov.: *Piyána-koru-gadi* (Chánda), *chotiáli* and *bhodore* (Seoni).

Rachis thickly clothed with silky hairs.

I. laxum, *R. Br.* (*Plate* LVIII.) *Syn.*—*I. nervosum*, Thw.; *Andropogon nervosum*, Rottb. *Vern.*—Rajputana: *Sairan* or *seran* and *hirn* (Ajmere), *sairan* (Udaipur). Cent. Prov.: *Sira* (Chánda), *sedwa* (Balaghát); Berar: *Sainad.*

Stems slender, 2–3 feet long. Leaves narrow tapering to a fine point. Spike single, 2–5 inches long, often slightly curved; rachis and pedicels clothed with white hairs. The second glume of the sessile spikelet has a long straight awn, and the flowering glume has a long bent and twisted awn.

This grass occurs in hilly parts of Rájputána, Bundelkhand and the Central Provinces. It is found also in Burma and Ceylon, and extends to Africa and Australia. Mr. Lowrie says that it is one of the best fodder grasses in the Ajmere district. In Australia it is said to yield a fair amount of feed, and is readily eaten.

I. pilosum, *Hack.* *Syn.*—*Andropogon pilosus*, Klein. *Vern.*—Cent. Prov.: *Khund* (Chánda).

Glaucous. Roots strong, and thick like those of the dáb. Leaves rather narrow. Spikes solitary or in pairs, 2-4 inches long, clothed with long white silky hairs.

Occurs in black soil in the Central Provinces.

I. rugosum, *Gærtn.* *Syn.*—*Mesochium rugosum*, Nees.; *Thelopogon elegans*, Roth. *Vern.*—Punjab: *Mehat* (Sabáthu Hills), *munmuna* (Karnál); Rajputana: *Jalgundya* (Ajmere), *toli* (Udaipur); N.-W. Prov. and Oudh: *Dhanua* (Pilibhit), *maror* (Kheri); Cent. Prov.: *Amarkarh* and *maggru gadi* (Chánda), *murdi* (Balaghát); Bengal: *Marudi* (Santál); Berar: *Tudi.*

Stems erect, branching. Leaves large and smooth; ligule bifid. Spikes in pairs, terminal and from the upper axils, 2–3 inches long, erect. Spikelets in pairs, one sessile, and the other on a thickened pedicel. Outer glumes hard and transversely rugose. Flowering glumes with a long twisted awn.

Common in wet ground in the plains and at low elevations on the hills. Cattle and horses eat it when it is young. In some parts of the Central Provinces the grain is used as food. Roxburgh remarks that it is generally found growing amongst rice, and is so much like it, that they are not, till in flower, to be distinguished.

Vossia speciosa, *Benth.* (*Syn.—Ischæmum speciosum,* Nees) is a Himalayan species occasionally extending to the base of the hills. It is a tall rather handsome grass.

37. HETEROPOGON, *Pers.* There are 5 or 6 species inhabiting warm countries, one of which, the well-known *Spear grass*, is common all over India. The spikes are always solitary, and the pairs of spikelets are closely packed so as to overlap each other. The spikelets are 1-flowered. The sessile spikelet of each pair is fertile and awned, and the stalked ones are male and without awns. The long twisted and bent awn of the fertile spikelet tapers at the base into a sharp point (the point of the spear).

H. contortus, *R. & S.* (*Plate* XIX.) *Syn.—H. hirtus,* Pers.; *H. Roylei,* Nees; *Andropogon contortus,* Linn. *Vern.*—TRANS-INDUS: *Barweza* and *sarmal* (Stewart); PUNJAB: *Sarári, surári, sariála* and *surwála, lamb* (Kángra and parts of Gujranwála), *suriála* (Salt Range), *sarála* (E. Punjab), *sarwála* (Hissar); RAJPUTANA: *hurwál* (Mount Abu); N.-W. PROV. and OUDH: *Kunura* (Kumaon), *sarwála* (Dehra Dún), *surwár* (Aligarh), *sarwár* (Muttra), *lap* (Agra), *pareba* (Etáwah), *paraura* (Cawnpore), *parba* and *musel* (Allahabad), *riskawa* (Kheri), *surwára* (Bhira); BUNDELKHAND: *Bandapuncha* (Banda), also *lamp, lampa, lampar, parba* and *parbi;* CENT. PROV.: *Hukara gadi* and *kusal* (Chánda), *kusáli* and *khar* (Nagpur), *kusal* (Balaghát); BERAR: *Pochati* and *saga;* BENGAL: *Kher* (Rev. A. Campbell); SANTALI: *Sauri ghás* (Rev. A. Campbell); TELING: *Yeddi* (Roxb.).

Stems ascending or erect, 1–2 feet high. Leaves narrow, upper surface with a few long scattered hairs; sheaths flattened, thin, mouths bearded. Spikes stalked, 1–2 inches long not including the awns. Male spikelets closely imbricate, in two rows along one side of the spike, awnless. Female spikelets mostly confined to the upper part of the spike, narrow, surrounded by silky brown hairs, and awned.

Abundant in the plains, and up to 7,000 feet on the Himalaya. Largely used as fodder both before and after it has flowered, but chiefly when it is young and tender. In Rájputána and Bundelkhand, where this grass abounds, it is cut and stacked after the rains are over. It is also cut for hay in the Hissar bir, and Mr. Coldstream states that it will keep good in stack for 12 years. On Mount Abu the people consider it the best fodder grass they have. In other districts it is said to be eaten only by buffaloes, or by cattle when they are hungry and cannot obtain other kinds of grass. It is much used for thatching. The spears which when the spikes are ripe adhere in masses are called *sali* at Ajmere. In Australia it is looked upon as a splendid grass for a cattle run, as it produces a great amount of feed.

38. ANDROPOGON, *Linn.* A large genus containing about 100 described species. They are perennial grasses, usually tall, and with strong wiry stems. The spikelets are 1-flowered, arranged in pairs on spikes which may be solitary, in pairs, or several together. The rachis of each spike is distinctly jointed where each pair of spikelets is given off, one of each pair of spikelets being sessile and fertile, and the other is stalked and sterile; the terminal joint has usually two stalked sterile spikelets on either side of a sessile and fertile one. This genus is represented in India by the *khas-khas* grass (*A. muricatus*), and two other sweet-scented kinds (*A. Schœnanthus* and *A. laniger*); also by two or three species known under the name of *palwal* or *palwán*, and which are more or less esteemed as useful fodder grasses.

A. annulatus, *Forsk.* (*Plate* XX.)* *Syn.—Lepeocercis annulatus,* Nees: *Vern.*—PUNJAB: *Palwán* (General), *miniyar* (Stewart), *palwánh* (Multán), *palwal* and *parwal* (S. E. Punjab); RAJPUTANA: *Báṅsi* (Jeypur), *karr* (Ajmere); N.-W. PROV.: *Palmaha* (Dehra Dún), *jarga* (Etáwah), *janewar* (Allahabad), *nalli* (Mainpuri), *nilon* (Aligarh); BUNDELKHAND: *Phulaira* (Lalitpur) and *donda* or *dunda* (Banda); the scandent form is called *khel* in the Lalitpur district; CENT. PROV.: *Máliyar* (Chánda).

Perennial. Stems branching, frequently subscandent; nodes hairy, the lower ones often bent. Spikes 5–6, terminal, sub-digitate, nearly sessile. Outer glume of the sessile hermaphrodite floret obtuse, and usually ending in three blunt teeth. Flowering glume reduced to a long bent and twisted awn four times as long as the spikelet.

Common all over the plains of Northern India by roadsides and in bushy places. It yields a considerable amount of fairly good fodder, which is largely made use of. It is very similar in habit to *A. Ischœmum* and *A. pertusus,* differing from the former by its blunt glumes, and from the latter by the absence of the pit on the back of the outer glumes. Specimens with the outer glumes 3-dentate at the apex have hitherto been referred to *A. Bladhii,* Retz., but Prof. Hackel informs me that the true *A. Bladhii* is a Chinese variety of *A. annulatus.*

---

* *Figs.* 1, 2 and 3 are copied from Roxburgh's original drawing of *A. Bladhii,* Retz.

A. brevifolius, *Swartz.* *Vern.*—CENT. PROV. : *Ware-gare* or *wanji-jári* (Chánda).

Stems slender, decumbent, much branched, ½–1½ feet long. Leaves narrow, short, 1–2 inches long, obtuse or with a short oblique point. Spikes solitary, very slender, seldom above one inch long.

A. caricosus, *Linn.* *Syn.*—*A. serratus*, Retz. ; *A. filiformis*, Pers. ; *Lipeocercis serrata*, Trin. *Vern.*—BUNDELKHAND : *Kheral* (Lalitpur) ; CENT. PROV. : *Palmanega gadi* (Chánda), *bilaria kandi* (Seoni) ; BERAR : *Killa machhar* ; BENGAL : *Detara*, and *detta* (Roxb.).

Perennial. Stems decumbent at the base ; upper nodes bearded. Spikes single or in pairs on filiform peduncles Lower outer glume of fertile floret obovate, obtuse, and ending in three teeth ; flowering glume reduced to a long golden coloured bent awn which soon becomes detached. From its general appearance one would be inclined to reckon its value for fodder about equal to that of *A. annulatus*.

A. fastigiatus, *Swartz.* *Vern.*—CENT. PROV.: *Liyur* (Chánda).

Apparently an annual with narrow finely pointed leaves. Spikes few, on very slender peduncles enclosed in narrow boat-shaped bracts. Rachis of spikes thickly clothed with white silky pubescence. Outer glumes with slender hair-like awns. Awns of flowering glumes much longer, bent and twisted.

A variety in which the whole plant assumes a reddish tinge, and the outer glumes are tinged with a darker colour, has been received from Chánda, in the Central Provinces, under the name of "lál kusal." Similar specimens from Parasnath in Behar bear the manuscript name of *A. Loharduggæ*, (C. B. Clarke.)

A. foveolatus, *Del.* (*Plate* XXI.) *Syn.*—*A. monostachys*, Spreng. *Vern.*—PUNJAB : *Girji munhák* and *sirwala* (Hissar), RAJPUTANA : *Boári* (Merwára), *junjhli* (Ajmere), *kard gandhel* (Jeypur) ; N.-W. PROV. : *Murjaini* (Etawah) ; BUNDELKHAND : *Girgua* (Jhánsi), *murjnah* or *mujna* (Lalitpur).

Perennial, glaucous, cæspitose. Stems erect or ascending, simple or branching ; nodes hairy. Leaves narrow, with bulbous-based hairs on lower surface and near the mouth of the sheath. Spikes solitary at the summit of the stem or of each branch, slender, linear. Spikelets distichously imbricate in pairs, the one sessile hermaphrodite or female and awned, the other stalked and male or neuter and without awns. Rachis of spike and pedicels of sterile spikelets clothed with white hairs. Glumes of fertile spikelet with a pit just below the summit. Flowering glumes of fertile spikelet reduced to a slender twisted and bent awn three or four times as long as the spikelet.

Abundant on sandy and rocky ground in the plains, and usually reckoned a good fodder grass.

A. gangeticus, *Hack.* *Vern.*—CENT. PROV. : *Kora gadi* (Chánda).

A tall slender (annual ?) grass with smooth and polished stems. Leaves narrow, scabrous ; midrib white, prominent beneath. Panicle narrow, rather lax. Spikelets small, pale green ; pedicels ciliate ; awns slender, bent, and twisted below.

A. glaber, *Roxb.* *Vern.*—MARATHI : *Támbat* (Dymock) ; BENGAL : *Gundhagoorana* (Roxb.).

Perennial. Stems suberect, branched, 3–4 feet high, smooth as also are the leaves. Panicles ovate; branches slender, verticillate. Outer glumes of perfect floret purplish, on one of which is a shallow pit.

It is found in localities similar to where *A. annulatus* grows, but is not in such abundance. Roxburgh says that it is found thinly scattered on rather elevated spots over Bengal.

A. intermedius, *R. Br.* *Syn.*—*A. fascicularis*, Thw. *Vern.*—Cent. Prov.: *Kasi gadi, kachi gadi*, and *mular* (Chánda); Berar: *Khar jhara*.

A tall rather coarse-looking grass with thick fibrous roots and long narrow leaves. It resembles *A. Ischæmum* and *A. pertusus* in general appearance, but the panicles are more elongated and much more loose.

Var. **punctatus.** *Vern.*—Cent. Prov.: *Koda johor* (Seoni).

Outer glumes indented with a dorsal pit as in *A. pertusus*. It occurs in the hilly parts of Northern India, and is abundant on the Himalaya up to moderate elevations. The Seoni specimens have three shallow pits on the outer glumes of the sterile florets, and one deep pit on the glumes of the hermaphrodite floret.

A. Ischæmum, *Linn.* (*Plate* XXII.)* *Vern.*—Trans-Indus: *Turmurgah* (Col. Strong); Punjab: *Palwan* (Rawal Pindi), *phalwán* (Bár), *palwán* (E. Punjab), *palwal* (S. E. corner of Punjab); Rajputana: *Bharo-bheru* (Jeypur); N.-W. Prov.: *Jarga* (Aligarh and Muttra), *janewa* (Allahabad).

Perennial. Root creeping. Stems erect, simple or with few branches; nodes smooth or clothed with very short hairs. Spikes 5–10, in fascicles, usually with a reddish tinge; rachis and pedicels of male spikelets clothed with white hairs. Outer glumes of hermaphrodite spikelets acute. Flowering glume reduced to a slender twisted and bent awn about three times as long as the spikelet. Very similar in general appearance to *A. pertusus* and *A. annulatus;* from the former it differs by the absence of the pit on the back of the outer glumes, and from the latter in having the outer glumes narrower and acute.

This species is common in the plains of Northern India, and is generally considered to be a good fodder grass.

A. lancifolius, *Trin.* *Syn.*—*Batratherum molle*, Nees.

A small species, often only of annual duration. Stems decumbent, 1–1½ feet, smooth except at the nodes. Leaves broadly ovate lanceolate with cordate amplexicaul base, acuminate, softly hairy; sheaths inflated. Spikes ½–¾ inch long, 2–5 together at the summit of slender capillary peduncles; nodes of rachis hairy. The flowering glume is furnished with a slender black awn bent below the middle, twice as long as the spikelets.

Hilly parts of Northern India. As this grass usually occurs on rocky ground, and often in more or less inaccessible positions, it is not well adapted for grazing purposes, though its nutritive properties may very possibly be of equal value to those of the more commonly utilized species of *Andropogon*.

A. laniger, *Desf.* (*Plate* XXIII.) *Syn.*—*A. Iwarancusa*, Roxb. (in part); *A. Oliverii*, Bois.; *Cymbopogon laniger*, Desf. *Vern.*—Trans-

* *See* also *Plate* C., *Fig.* 14, of present Volume.

Indus: *Sir ghurai* (Col. Strong); Punjab: *Solára, bur* (South Punjab), *khair* (Jhang), *gandhi* (J. R. D.), *khawi* (Central and N.-W. Punjab); Rajputana: *Gander* (Ajmere), *runa* (Merwára), *dabsulo* (Jeypur); N.-W. Prov.: *Babhori* (Etáwah); Marathi: *Jarámkush, azkhir,* and *khavi* (Dymock); Hindi: *Gandel* (Col. Strong).

Perennial, cæspitose. Stems erect, thick and woolly below. Leaves smooth, glaucous, stiff; blades narrow and convolute. Panicles erect, narrowly oblong, composed of distant fascicles of spikes surrounded at the base by blunt boat-shaped yellowish sheaths. Rachis and pedicels of the awnless male spikelets densely clothed with white hairs. Flowering glumes of hermaphrodite florets minute, transparent, bidentate, and with a very slender bent awn from between the teeth.

This is one of the sweet-scented grass, the roots of which are sometimes used like *khas-khas* in the manufacture of tatties. It is common on uncultivated land in Sindh, the Punjab, Rájputána and parts of the N. W. Provinces; it is also recorded from Tibet at an elevation of 11,000 feet. As a fodder grass it does not rank high in regard to its nutritive qualities. It is, however, largely made use of by cattle when it is young and tender. Its scent is said to affect the flavour of their milk. It is often stacked and forms a useful supply in times of scarcity. Mr. Coldstream says that it will keep good in stack for upwards of 10 or 12 years. For horses it is not to be recommended. Mr. J. B. Hallen tells me that the natives of Chattar in Beluchistan state that cattle eat it with impunity, but that horses suffer from colic after feeding on it. Col. Strong also mentions the same circumstance. In the Jhang Settlement Report it is stated that the *khair* grass grows in hollows where water collects, and seems to prefer *kallar*, that cows graze upon it if hard pressed, but not otherwise; also that the *bár* housewives use wisps of this grass to clean out vessels used for churning and holding milk. A perfume is manufactured from it, and the aromatic oil is sometimes used as a cooling medicine. For further information regarding the history and medicinal properties of this grass reference should be made to Dr. Dymock's "Vegetable Materia Medica of Western India," p. 850.

A. muricatus, *Retz.* (*Plate* XXIV.)* *Syn.*—*A. squarrosus*, Linn.; *Anatherum muricatum*, Retz.; *Rhaphis muricata*, Nees; *Vetiveria odorata*, Virey. *Vern.*—General: *Panni* and *khas-khas* (roots); Trans-Indus: *Mushkani* (Col. Strong); Punjab: *Biran* (stems) (Kángra), *pánni* (Bágri dialects and S. Punjab), *sink* (stems) (E. Punjab);

* See also *Plate* C., *Fig.* 15, of present Volume.

BUNDELKHAND: *Ganrar, onei, orai, durbachi* (Jhánsi); N.-W. PROV. and OUDH: *Sink-jháru* (Dehra Dún), *ganrar* (Muttra), *gánrár* (Allahabad), *garar* and *gandel* (Mainpuri), *gandar* (Bhira), *gânder* (Kheri); CENT. PROV.: *Urai* (Balaghát), *ursori* (Chánda); MARATHI: *Varelu* and *ushir* (Dymock); BENGAL: *Bena* (Roxb.), *Siron* (Santáli); TAMIL: *Woetiwear* (Roxb.); S. INDIA: *Vettiver*.

Perennial. Roots composed of long spongy brownish coloured fibres. Stems many, smooth, simple, erect, 4–6 feet high. Leaves near the base. bifarious, narrow, erect, smooth, 2–3 feet long. Panicle conical, 6 inches to 1 foot, composed of many simple linear spike-like racemes arranged in verticels. Flowers in pairs, without awns. Glumes of hermaphrodite florets nearly equal, muricated on the back.

Generally distributed throughout the plains of Northern India, especially on moist low-lying land. It affords good fodder when young, and is much relished by buffaloes. It is not stacked as fodder, and the cut grass is given to cattle only in seasons of excessive drought. This grass is used largely as a thatching material; and the fragrant roots, known under the name of *khas-khas*, are used all over Northern India in the manufacture of tatties. In the Sirsa Settlement Report it is stated that the roots are dug up by the villagers, who sometimes pay the owner of the ground a small fee of 4 annas per digger, and that they are sold at about a rupee a maund to banyas, who send them to Lahore and Ferozepur. In the Jhang Settlement Report mention is made of the tough roots being used for making rope, and also the brushes used by the weavers for arranging the threads of the web. The brushes of the Sahâranpur and Dehra Dún weavers are of the same material. Baskets are made of the stems (*sink*), which are sometimes dyed. At Bhira, in Oudh, a perfume called *itar* is extracted, and used medicinally under the name of *uraiya*. For further information regarding the medicinal properties of this grass, *see* Dr. Dymock's "Vegetable Materia Medica of Western India," p. 851.

A. pachyarthrus, *Hack.* (*Plate* LIX.) *Syn.*—*A. demissus,* Steud. *Vern.*—BUNDELKHAND: *Gangerua;* CENT. PROV.: *Málakaya* (Nagpur), *málka-phalka* (Chánda).

Stems erect, smooth, 6 inches to 1½ feet high. Leaves rather small, the upper ones reduced to sheaths. Panicles embraced by the leaf sheaths, of many terminal and axillary spikes on a slender jointed peduncle. Outer glume of hermaphrodite floret cuspidate; flowering glume reduced to a long slender bent awn.

Common on open usar soil in Rájputána and Bundelkhand, and on sandy soil in the Central Provinces. It is considered to be a good fodder grass for cattle, but not for horses.

A. pertusus, *Willd.* (*Plate* XXV.)* *Syn.*—*Lepeocercis pertusus*, Hassk.; *Holcus pertusus*, Linn. *Vern.*—General: *Palwa;* Punjab: *Palwal* and *parwal* (S.-E. Punjab), *palwán* (E. Punjab), *girji* (Hissar); Rajputana: *Chirrya* (Ajmere), *chapruro* (Jeypur); N.-W. Prov.: *Janewa* (Allahabad); Bundelkhand: *Rukah* (Banda) and *tikriya;* Cent. Prov.: *Chota piya* and *vida-gucha gadi* (Chánda), *gohhaya* (Nagpur), *malhar* (Balaghát); Berar: *Killa.*

Perennial. Stems creeping at the base, erect above, bearded at the nodes. Leaves narrow, tapering to a fine point, hairy at the mouth of the sheath. Spikes 5–9, fascicled. Rachis and pedicels of male spikelets clothed with white hairs. Outer glume of hermaphrodite spikelet hard, acute, clothed with long silky hairs below, and a little above the middle there is a round or ovate pit. Flowering glume reduced to a bent and twisted awn considerably longer than the spikelet.

This grass, which is met with all over the plains of Northern India, is universally esteemed as a good fodder grass, both for grazing and stacking. In Australia also it is highly valued, being regarded as one of the best grasses to stand long droughts, while it will bear any amount of feeding. It is useful also as a winter grass if the weather is not too severe.

A. Schœnanthus, *Linn.* (*Plate* XXVI.) *Syn.*—*A. Martini*, Roxb.; *A. pachnodes*, Trin.; *A. Calamus-aromaticus*, Royle. *Vern.*—Punjab: *Dang rhauṅs* and *mirchia gand* (Outer Simla Hills), *makora* (Kángra), *gandi* (N.-E. Punjab), *rosa* (Rawal Pindi,) *rauṅs* (Hissar), *panni* (S.-W. Punjab), *rhausa* (S.-E. Punjab); Rajputana: *Rhauṅsa* and *roiṅsa* (Ajmere), *rauṅs* (Mount Abu); Bundelkhand: *Mircha, mirchua, chipara, rauṅs, mirchia,* and *bhor* (Banda); Cent. Prov.: *Rosa* and *thikari* (Balaghát), *tikadi-moti* (Nagpur); Berar: *Tikhari;* Marathi: *Roshegavat* and *rohish* (Dymock); Bengal: *Gundha-bena, iwarankusha, ibharankusha* and *kurankusha* (Roxb.).

Perennial. Stems many, erect, 3–6 feet high, terete and finely striate; joints swollen; sheaths loose, smooth, shorter than the joints; ligule very short. Leaves broad, rounded and ½-amplexicaul at the base, smooth except the hispid margins. Panicle 1½ feet or more, contracted, composed of numerous fascicles of slender pedicelled spikes which are surrounded at the base and sometimes concealed within boat-shaped bracts. The bracts turn to a brilliant reddish colour when mature. Rachis and

---

* *See* also *Plate* C., *Fig.* 16, of present Volume.

pedicels clothed with white hairs. Flowering glume of fertile spikelet reduced to a slender bent awn.

Plentiful in certain parts of Northern India, and at low elevations on the Himalaya. It is largely used for fodder in Rájputána, Bundelkhand and in the Central Provinces, where it is abundant in company with *Heteropogon contortus*, *Andropogon muricatus*, and *Iseilema laxum* (*musel*), usually on low-lying swampy ground. It is not considered to be a very good fodder grass either for grazing or stacking. In Rájputána it usually forms the roof portion of the stacks composed of *musel* and *spear-grass*. It is much used for thatching and sometimes for tatties. A fragrant oil, known as *rusa ka tel*, is extracted, and is used as a remedy for rheumatism, and from the roots a drug is prepared and employed in cases of intermittent fever. For further information, *see* Dr. Dymock's "Vegetable Materia Medica of Western India," p. 847.

A. tropicus, *Spreng.* *Syn.*—*Holcus fulvus*, R. Br.; *Sorghum fulvum*, Beauv.; *S. muticum*, Nees. *Vern.*—OUDH : *Hutia* (Kheri).

A tall rather slender grass. Stems densely hairy at the nodes. Leaves narrow, scabrous. Panicle loose, 4–8 inches. Hairs of pedicels and spikelets of a rich brown colour. Sessile spikelets black and shining when ripe.

Hilly parts of Northern India. It is occasionally used as fodder.

39. CHRYSOPOGON, *Trin.* This genus, which consists of about 20 species distributed over tropical and temperate regions, is distinguished by having the spikelets in threes terminating the filiform jointed branchlets of the panicle, the central one being sessile and fertile, and the lateral stalked and sterile, with occasionally 1–3 additional pairs of spikelets below the terminal triplets.

C. aciculatus, *Trin.* *Syn.*—*Andropogon aciculatus*, Retz.; *A. acicularis*, Kunth; *Rhaphis trivialis*, Lour. *Vern.*—BENGAL : *Chora-kánta* (Roxb.).

Perennial, cæspitose. Stems prostrate, creeping, and much branched below. Leaves with long sheaths and shortish blades. Panicles narrow, compact; pedicels hairy.

Plains of Northern India, on wet barren soil. This grass is of little or no use as fodder.

C. cœruleus, *Nees.* (*Plate* LX.) *Syn.*—*Rhaphis cærulea*, Nees. *Vern.*—PUNJAB : *Dhaulian* (Himalaya), *khar* (Salt Range); N.-W. PROV. : *Dhaula* (Siwalik Range), *ghweia* (Kumaun); BUNDELKHAND : *Tigri*; CENT. PROV. : *Pálla paggar gadi* (Chánda); BERAR : *Jhingra-ka-jhara*, and *khidi*.

Perennial, cæspitose. Leaves glaucous, long and narrow, hispid. Panicle loose. Spikelets on long filiform peduncles, usually of a bluish tinge.

Common in hilly parts of Northern India, usually on stony or sandy soil. On the Siwalik range it is used extensively as fodder.

C. Gryllus, *Trin.** *Syn.—Andropogon Gryllus*, Linn.; *Holcus Gryllus*, R. Br. Perennial, cæspitose. Leaves long, narrow. Panicle loose, spreading, 3 to 6 inches long, branches numerous, simple, capillary, mostly verticellate, of unequal length. Second glume of fertile floret awned; awn of terminal one long and rigid.

Hilly parts of Northern India. It is said to be an excellent pasture grass in Australia.

C. montanus, *Trin.* *Syn.—C. parviflorus*, Benth.; *Andropogon montanus*, Roxb.; *A. monticola*, R. and S.; *Sorghum parviflorum*, Beauv. *Vern.*—RAJPUTANA: *Ballak* (Mount Abu).

Perennial. Stems 23 feet, more or less villous at the nodes. Leaves flat, tapering to a fine point; sheaths smooth or villous. Panicle 4-8 inches long, much branched; ultimate branches hair-like, supporting minute spikelets scarcely 1⅓ lines long. Central sessile spikelet with a tuft of white hairs at the base. Awn of flowering glume six or seven times its length.

Hilly parts of Northern India. On Mount Abu I found several patches of this very elegant grass growing in depressions of the hill overlooking the Civil station. It is said there to be an excellent fodder grass, and the grain is collected and used as food by the natives.

C. serrulatus, *Trin.* Is recorded from Jhelam (Aitchison), Moradabad (T. Thomson), and Banda (Edgeworth).

40. SORGHUM, *Pers.* There are two species, both of which occur in India; one is "juar," and the other a widely distributed grass known as "baru." The arrangement and structure of the spikelets is very similar to that of *Chrysopogon*, but the panicle branches are scarcely jointed, and the outer glume of the fertile spikelet is ovate and becomes hard.

S. halepense, *Pers.* (*Plate* XXVII.) † *Syn.—Holcus halepensis*, Linn.; *Andropogon halepensis*, Sibth.; *A. arundinaceus*, Scop. *Vern.*—GENERAL: *Baru*; KASHMIR: *Brahám* (Stewart); KUMAUN: *Bikhonda* (Watson); BUNDELKHAND: *Bájra, barru* and *bara* (Banda); CENT. PROV.: *Galla jári* and *padda jalla gadi* (Chánda); BERAR: *Kartál.*

A tall perennial with creeping rhizome which throws up many suckers. Stems many and branching. Leaves flat, smooth; midrib prominent beneath. Panicle pyramidal, with numerous spreading branches. Hermaphrodite spikelets ovate oblong. Male spikelets oblong lanceolate, all clothed with short hairs at the base; glumes pubescent, grain oblong.

---

* *See Plate* D., *Fig.* 17, of present Volume.

† *See* also *Plate* D., *Fig.* 18, of present Volume.

Common all over Northern India in cultivated and uncultivated ground. It is considered to be a good fodder grass both for grazing and as hay. Various reports however indicate its injurious effects on cattle if eaten when too young, or when the plants are stunted by drought. The same results have been observed to take place in the case of juár (*Sorghum vulgare*). Dr. Stewart was told in Hazára that cattle, after eating it, are often attacked by fatal head affections. In Gujranwála, Gujrát and Sháhpur districts it is said to be poisonous until the rains are over, when cattle eat it with impunity. Tod, in his "Rájasthán," Vol. ii., p. 170, mentions that the seed of this grass is collected, and mixed with *bájra* flour is eaten by the poorer classes in Bikanir. In Australia it is valued both for pasturage and hay, and is much sought after by cattle. Native pens are made from the stems of this plant. No allusion is made regarding the injurious properties of this grass when young, either in Australia or in the United States. In the latter country, where it is known as "Johnson grass," "Cuba grass," "Mean's grass," and "False Guinea grass," it is highly valued as the following extracts from Dr. Vasey's "Report on the Grasses of the South," pages 16 and 17 (1887) will show:—

"Mr. N. B. Moore has cultivated this grass for 40 years and prefers it to all others, is perennial, is as nutritious as any other, difficult to eradicate, will grow on ordinary soil, and yields abundantly.

"Horses and cattle are fond of it both in its dry and green condition. Probably no grass gives better promise for the dry arid lands of the West.

"This grass is best adapted to warm climates, and has proved most valuable on warm dry soils in the Southern States . . . . . . Its chief value is for hay, in regions where other grasses fail on account of drought. If cut early the hay is of good quality, and several cuttings may be made in the season.

"In California it is known as 'Evergreen' or 'Arabian Millet'. It roots deep in the subsoil, and where that is at all alkaline, it grows enormously, but at the same time absorbs so much of the unpalatable alkali that stock will not eat it. It is excellent for dry hills free from alkali."

S. vulgare, *Pers.* *Syn.*—*Holcus Sorghum*, Linn., *Andropogon Sorghum*, Brot. *Vern.*—General: *Juár*, *chari* (sown close for fodder); Punjab: *Joár* (Stewart), N.-W. Prov. and Oudh: *Junri* (Western Districts), *choti juár* and *choti junri* (Oudh and Benarés), *bájra-jhupanwa* (Azamgarh); Bengal: *Kasa-jonar* (Chutia Nagpur); Teling: *Janoo*, *konda* and *tella* (Roxb.); S. India: *Cholum*.

A tall handsome grass. Stems erect, thick, succulent, often tinged with red or yellowish blotches. Leaf blades broad, narrowing gradually to their tips, smooth except at their junction with the sheath; midrib prominent beneath, channelled above; sheaths very long. Flowers in dense ovate panicles; heads nodding before ripening. Spikelets in pairs, 1-flowered, one sessile and hermaphrodite, the other stalked and male. Glumes about equal, hard and firm, especially those of the fertile florets. Grain about ⅛-inch long, smooth, white or red. For figures, *see* "Field and Garden Crops, N.-W. Provinces and Oudh," Part I., *Plate* VI., and "Church's Food Grains of India," *Fig.* 15.

Largely cultivated all over India, chiefly for its grain. The stalks are extensively used as fodder, and when chopped up is known by the name of *karbi.* When specially grown for fodder purposes it is called *chari.* It is a valuable and favourite fodder for cattle, but is said to have injurious effects if eaten too young.

41. ANTHISTIRIA, *Linn. f.* Species about 8, mostly tropical. This genus is easily recognized by its inflorescence, the spikelets being arranged in short spikes or clusters. Each cluster is composed of seven or more spikelets, the two lower pairs being either empty, or with a male floret in each, and disposed in the form of an involucre surrounding the three inner ones. The central one of these three inner spikelets is sessile and fertile, the two lateral ones being stalked and sterile as in *Chrysopogon.* Occasionally there are one or more extra pairs of spikelets within those which form the involucre.

A. anathera, *Nees. Syn.—Androscepia anathera,* Anders. *Vern.*—PUNJAB: *Kohdi* (Gujrát).

Perennial, glaucous. Stems 2–4 feet, smooth, thickened at the nodes. Leaves long, narrow at the base, ciliate especially at the mouth of the sheaths. Clusters erect, stalked, arranged in an elongate loose panicle, and subtended by spathe-like reddish bracts. Spikelets about nine, without awns; the lower six male, their outer glumes clothed with long white hairs seated on tubercles; seventh spikelet hermaphrodite, glumes not ciliate; the two upper spikelets male, nearly smooth.

Hilly parts of Northern India, and up to 8,000 feet on the Himalaya, where it is largely used as fodder. Madden remarks that in Kumaun the roots are said to be frequently luminous, whence it is there called "jyotishmati."

A. arundinacea, *Roxb. Vern.—Bharua* (Stewart), *kangua* (Kumaun), *ula* (Oudh).

A tall perennial grass, 6–12 feet or more. Stems smooth, filled with spongy pith; joints large. Leaves 4–8 feet, with hispid margins; sheaths smooth, compressed. Clusters of many large slender stalked drooping spikelets, each subtended by a boat-shaped bract. Spikelets composed of four sessile awnless accessory male florets surrounding and inserted on a short club-shaped pedicel which supports an hermaphrodite awned floret and two stalked awnless ones. Outer glumes of male florets clothed with much golden coloured hair. Outer glumes of hermaphrodite floret villous, the flowering glume reduced to a long twisted and bent awn nearly four times the length of the spikelet.

This grass is found in large clumps in wet pasture land. It is eaten only when very young.

A. gigantea, *Cav.* Is another tall grass resembling the above, and occurring in similar localities. The spikelets are smaller, more crowded, and the hairs on the glumes are shorter and of a deep brown colour.

A. ciliata, *Linn. f.** *Syn.—A. australis,* R. Br.; *A. cæspitosa,* An-

* *See Plate* D., *Fig.* 19, of present Volume.

ders.; *Themeda ciliata*, Hack. *Vern.*—Cent. Prov.: *Chudur jahara* (Seoni); Berar: *Gondalli.*

Stems 1–3 feet high. Leaves narrow, ciliate at the base. Clusters of spikelets few, the lower ones on slender peduncles. Bracts subtending each spike sheathing at the base, and tapering into points longer than the cluster. Spikelets narrow, four male or barren ones sessile at the base of the bearded rachis, and two or one stalked at the top, glabrous or clothed with a few long hairs. Fertile terminal spikelet glabrous or shortly pubescent at the end; awn twice as long as the spikelet.

Hilly parts of Northern India, common on the Himalaya. It is abundant in Australia and Tasmania, and well known under the name of "Kangaroo grass." It is considered by Australian farmers an excellent grass for stock.

A. scandens, *Roxb.* (*Plate* LXI.) *Vern.*—N.-W. Prov.: *Bhoru* (Allahabad); Bundelkhand: *Guner*, *ganori*, *ganaiya* and *genehru*; Rajputana: *Gendar* (Mount Abu); Cent. Prov.: *Ghonyár* and *era-kolla-gadi* (Chánda), *ghonadi* and *ghonál* (Nagpur), *ghunhair* and *titar* (Balaghát).

Perennial. Stems scandent, branching and rooting from the lower joints. Panicles large, composed of verticelled fascicles of spikelets which turn to a bright reddish colour after flowering. Summit of glumes of outer spikelets of each fascicle beset with hairs seated on tubercles. Awn hairy, twisted, and slightly bent, much longer than the spikelet.

Common in Rájputána, Bundelkhand, and the Central Provinces. It is used for fodder and for thatching purposes. This species differs from *A. ciliata* in being a perennial, and usually scandent.

A. Themeda Forskalii, *Hack.* *Syn.*—*A. ciliata*, Auct. (non Linn.)

Vern.—Cent. Prov.: *Era-kolla-gadi* and *tatiyán* (Chánda). Stems thick, and swollen at the nodes. Resembles *A. scandens*, Roxb., in habit, but rachis of panicle more slender. Clusters in a more interrupted panicle, narrower and with shorter bracts. I have received specimens from Gwalior and from the Central Provinces.

Var. **major.** *Vern.*—Cent. Prov.: *Gudda-niko-gadi*, and *eraj-tukra-gadi* (Chánda).

Clusters larger and more compact; altogether a more robust plant than that of the type.

42. ISEILEMA, *Anders.* Species 3, of which two are Indian and one Australian. In habit they have a close resemblance to *Apluda*. The clusters of spikelets are small and glabrous. The spikelets are stalked, and each is enclosed within a sheathing bract.

I. laxum, *Hack.* (*Plate* XXVIII.) *Syn.*—*I. prostrata*, Anders. *Vern.*—General: *Gandhi* and *gándhi*; Punjab: *Champ* (Simla Hills), *luinji* (Kángra), *chhat* (Rawal Pindi), *gándi* (Hissar); Rajputana:

Karar-gandhel-dungarko (Jeypur); BUNDELKHAND: *Musel, musiál,* and *machauri* (Lalitpur); CENT. PROV.: *Masán, manchi-malwa* and *malwajari* (Chánda), *masán, tikha-lodan* and *gonda* (Nagpur), *ghorayal* (Seoni).

Annual. Stems numerous, suberect or prostrate, 1–2½ feet. Leaves rather short; blades of upper ones much reduced, ciliate at the mouth of the inflated sheaths. Panicles slender; clusters of spikelets terminal and axillary, rather distant. Bracts longer than the spikelets, membranous at the edges, and usually with the remnant of the blade which is ciliate at the base. Pedicels with tufts of hairs at the base. Hermaphrodite florets with long slender twisted and slightly bent awns.

Common in the plains of Northern India on low-lying land where the soil is good. In Bundelkhand this grass is abundant and largely used as fodder, and is prized above all other kinds. It is sweet scented when fresh. Mr. Coldstream says that it is very common in the Hissar bir swamps, in good land; and that where it will grow wheat will grow. It is both grazed and stacked, and is much eaten by buffaloes.

I. Wightii, *Anders. Syn.—Anthistiria Wightii,* Nees.; *A. Bladhii,* Wight; *A. prostrata,* Trin. *Vern.*—PUNJAB: *Ganni* (Gujranwála, Sháhpur and Lahore); N.-W. PROV.: *Gandel* (Aligarh); CENT. PROV.: *Ghor-masán, musán* and *pulsu-malwa-gadi* (Chánda), *musán* (Balaghát).

Very similar to the preceding species, but usually more diffuse and often quite prostrate. The clusters of spikelets are smaller, and usually more exserted from the bracts; and the keel and edges of the bracts are studded with papillose excrescences.

Plains of Northern India on low lying or swampy ground. In Bundelkhand and the Central Provinces it is frequently the prevailing grass on the black soil, its reddish coloured stems and spikelets rendering it a conspicuous object from a considerable distance. Its value as fodder is probably equal to that of *I. laxum.*

43. APLUDA, *Linn.** There are 2 species, both of them occurring in India. The arrangement of the spikelets is rather peculiar and somewhat puzzling. Each cluster contains a triple branch of spikelets enclosed in a sheathing bract; the central sessile branch is composed of a fertile floret with a male floret below it, and on either side are two flattened pedicels, each bearing a rudimentary or barren spikelet.

A. aristata, *Linn.* (*Plate* XXIX). *Syn.—A. rostrata,* Nees. *Vern.* —GENERAL: *Gandhi;* PUNJAB: *Ganni* (Lahore), *santhran* (Kángra),

---

* *See Plate* D., *Fig.* 20, of present Volume.

munmona (Patiála Hills), *murmuru* (E. Punjab); RAJPUTANA: *Gaván* (Jeypur), *bhankta* (Ajmere), *bonta* (Mount Abu); N.-W. PROV.: *Baru* (General), *bhajura* (Etáwah), *bhañjura* (Allahabad); BUNDELKHAND: *Bhangri* or *bhañjuri* and *send* (Banda); CENT. PROV.: *Gugar-gadi* and *kattingiya sufed* (Chánda), *bhus-jari* (Seoni); BENGAL: *Durhi ghás* (Santal), *goroma* (Roxb.); TELING: *Pootstrangali* (Roxb.).

Perennial. Stems creeping or scandent, often reddish coloured, lower parts naked. Flowering branches erect, one to several feet high. Leaves somewhat bifarious, backwardly hispid. Spikelets in a large leafy panicle; bracts boat-shaped, with an awn-like point, enclosing three sets of florets; the central branch contains a fertile awned floret with a male floret on one side of it; the lateral branches consist of sterile rudimentary florets supported by flattened pedicels.

Very common all over the plains of N.-W. India and at low elevations on the Himalaya. In hedges and bushy places it usually assumes a climbing habit. In forest land it often constitutes a large portion of the under-growth. It is considered to be a fairly good fodder grass, and is readily eaten by cattle when young.

SERIES B. POACEÆ.

TRIBE VII. PHALARIDEÆ.

44. PHALARIS, *Linn.* Two out of the nine or ten described species are found it Upper India, but neither of them possess any appreciable value as fodder plants. The spikelets are densely packed in an oval spikelike panicle. The two inferior glumes remain persistent under the joint; they are longer than the other glumes, and are furnished with a more or less broadly winged keel. *P. minor*, Retz., is a common weed on cultivated land in the plains, and up to about 4,000 feet on the Himalaya. *P. paradoxa*, Linn. f., has been recorded from Lahore by Stewart, but I have seen no specimens. *P. canariensis*, Linn., (Canary grass,) and *P. arundinacea*, Linn., are introductions.

45. CRYPSIS, *Ait.* Contains a single species inhabiting S. Europe, N. Africa, and N.-W. India. It is a small annual grass with prostrate stiff brittle branches. The spikelets are in dense heads, which are surrounded by 2–3 sheathing bracts. It has four glumes (none below the joint as in *Phalaris*), and two stamens.

C. aculeata, *Ait.* (*Plate* LXII.)* *Syn.*—*Schœnus aculeatus*, Linn.; *Anthoxanthum aculeatum*, Linn.; *Phleum schœnoides*, Jacq.; *Antitragus*

---

* *See* also *Plate* D., *Fig.* 21, of present Volume.

aculeatus, Gærtn.; *Heleochloa diandra*, Host. A prostrate glaucous annual with branching compressed brittle stems. Leaves spreading subulate; sheaths loose, shorter than its internode.

Not uncommon in N.-W. India on a sandy soil. This grass is nutritious looking, and not unlike dúb in texture and colouring; its value, however, is much lessened by being an annual.

46. ALOPECURUS, *Linn.* Species about 20, three of which occur in Northern India, including the well-known *Meadow Fox-tail grass* (*A. pratensis*). The flat spikelets are crowded into a cylindrical spike-like panicle. The two outer glumes are boat-shaped and have a prominent keel, and the flowering glumes are awned on the back. Pale and lodicules none.

A. agrestis, *Linn.** Annual, stems 1–2 feet. Panicle spikelike, narrow and acute. Empty glumes connate to about the middle.

Punjab plains in cultivated ground (Stewart). In Italy it is considered to be a good fodder grass fresh or dry.

A. geniculatus, *Linn.* Perennial. Stems procumbent and rooting at the lower nodes. Sheaths of upper leaves loose. Spikelike panicle slender, obtuse. Empty glumes connate at the base.

Plains of N.-W. India and up to 5,000 feet on the Himalaya. Mueller describes it as a good fodder grass for swampy land.

A. pratensis, *Linn.* Perennial. Stems erect, 1–3 feet. Sheaths of upper leaves inflated. Panicle cylindrical, 2–3 inches long, obtuse. Outer glumes nearly free at the base; keels hairy.

This species is well known in England as an excellent fodder grass. On the Himalaya it is abundant at moderate elevations, extending down to the plains in the Punjab. In Australia it is said to be one of the best of their perennial pasture grasses, and that sheep thrive well on it. In the United States, where it has been introduced, it is highly valued as being one of the earliest of the grasses to start in the spring. None of these species of *Alopecurus*, mentioned above, are sufficiently abundant in the plains to be considered of much account. They are all capable, however, of being cultivated as cold weather grasses, and as such might be advantageously utilized.

TRIBE VIII. AGROSTIDEÆ.

47. ARISTIDA, *Linn.* Species upwards of 100, chiefly characteristic of dry sandy tracts, and they are easily recognised by their thin feathery appearance. The flowering glume is terminated by a long slender

---

* *See Plate* D., *Fig.* 22.

awn divided into three branches. The cylindrical shaped grain is closely enveloped by the flowering glume. Of the North Indian species occurring in the plains the two following are the most important as fodder grasses owing to their greater abundance.

A. depressa, *Retz.* (*Plate* XXX.) *Syn.*—*A. cærulescens*, Desf. *Vern.* —PUNJAB: *Lamb* and *lamba* (General), *ghyán* and *ghyáni* (Kángra), *lam'e* (Cent. Punjab), *lam* (Jhang), *lámp* (Hissar); RAJPUTANA: *Rámpla* (Jeypur); BUNDELKHAND: *Choti parba* and *sinka* (Lalitpur); TELING: *Nalli-pootiki* (Roxb.).

A slender annual with hard wiry stems and narrow subulate leaves. Panicle spikelike 3–8 inches long, interrupted towards the base. Spikelets sessile narrow, crowded, often tinged with purple.

Common on sandy ground in North-West India. Opinions vary as to the value of this grass for fodder. Stewart described it as a favourite fodder for cattle in the Punjab. Symonds says that it is a troublesome grass which cattle will not eat. Coldstream states that it is grazed, but is too short and light to stack; that it covers the Hissar bir in vast sheets, is too fine to cut with a scythe, but is nutritious, and particularly relished by cattle. In the Jhang Settlement Report it is stated to be a grass of average quality, and is found growing in kallar. Neither at Ajmere nor at Jeypur is it considered to be a good fodder grass.

A. hystrix, *Linn. f.* (*Plate* XXXI.) *Vern.*—GENERAL: *Lámp*; RAJPUTANA: *Lápri dhauli* (Ajmere), *lál rámpla* (Jeypur); N.-W. PROV.: *Lappa* (Etáwah), *láppa* (Allahabad); TELING: *Shilpuroo-kalli* (Roxb.).

Stems 1–2 feet, branching, and rather straggling. Panicle large, oval, thin, branches spreading. A more rigid grass than the preceding, and with a broader and more open panicle.

Common on dry sandy or stony ground in Northern India. As a fodder grass it would be ranked as of equal value with the preceding.

Mr. Edgeworth in his "Florula Mallica" (Multan District) mentions the following additional species:—

(1). **A. articulata**, *Edgew.* Erect, glabrous. Leaves needle-like. Panicle contracted. Glumes about equal; awn jointed at the top of the stipe. Found in the Rechnab desert, Punjab. (2). **A. funiculata**, *Trin.* and *Rupr.* (3). **A. hirtiglume**, Steud. (4). **A. hystricula**, *Edgew.* Small, glabrous. Upper glume twice as long as the oval mucronate inferior one. Very unlike *A. hystrix*, Linn. f., in habit. Sindh and Multan. (5). **A. mallica**, *Edgew.* Leaves scabrous, pilose. Glumes nearly equal, the lower one a little the longer very acute terminating in a hispid bristle. This species is technically most like *A. Royleana*, Trin., but the habit is very different. It is of a reddish colour and very dwarf. (6). **A. plumosa**, *Linn.*, *Vern.*—*Lonak* or *ronak* (Stewart). Found by Edgeworth at Jhang and on the sand-hills to the south of the Multan district. (7). **A. pogonoptila**, *Jaub.* and

Spach. (8). **A. Royleana,** *Trin.* Mr. Edgeworth also records the following in his list of Banda plants—*A. capillacea*, Lamk., and *A. vulgaris.*

Allied to *Aristida* is the genus *Stipa* containing several Himalayan and Tibetan species, one of which, *S. siberica*, Lamk., is said to be poisonous to cattle in Kashmir and Afghanistan. Mr. A. E. Lowrie has sent specimens of a *Stipa* gathered near Ajmere, and which Professor Hackel tells me is undescribed. It is called *lápra dhaula* at Ajmere. It is of no use for fodder.

48. HELEOCHLOA, *Host.* Species 7 or 8, chiefly Mediterranean. Two of these occur in the drier parts of the Punjab and Sindh. The spikelets are crowded into dense ovoid or cylindrical spikes. The empty glumes are shorter than the flowering glumes and remain persistent below the joint. This last character distinguishes this genus from *Crypsis*, which superficially has a remarkable resemblance to some of the forms of *Heleochloa schœnoides.* Stamens two.

H. alopecuroides, *Boiss.* *Syn.—Crypsis phalaroides*, M. B.; *Phalaris geniculata*, Sm.

Annual, glaucous. Stems simple. Leaves narrowly linear, acuminate, margin and upper surface rough; sheaths not swollen. Spikes oblong, cylindrical, dense, often turning black.

H. schœnoides, *Host.** *Syn.—Phleum schœnoides*, Linn.; *Crypsis schœnoides*, Lamk. *Vern.*—Punjab: *Talaphetar* (Multan).

Annual, glaucous. Stems branched, compressed, spreading. Leaves linear, acuminate; upper sheaths swollen and open. Spikes ovate oblong dense. Bracts 1–2.

49. SPOROBOLUS, *R. Br.* Species upwards of 80, six or more of which are found in the plains of Northern India. The genus is distinguished by its minute awnless florets, which are arranged in a panicle either loose and spreading, or narrow and spikelike. The ripe grain becomes exposed, and readily detaches itself from the glume; the seed also is usually quite loose within the thin pericarp.

S. commutatus, *Boiss.* *Syn.—Vilfa commutata*, Trin.

A dwarf annual. Lower part of stems leafy, naked above. Leaves broadly linear, short, many nerved, and flat: margins cartilaginous and aculeate ciliate; sheaths subauriculate and pilose. Panicle branches in verticels, short, spreading. Florets very minute.

In sandy and stony localities. Not sufficiently abundant, however, to be considered of much importance for fodder.

S. coromandeliana, *Roxb.* *Syn.—Agrostis coromandeliana*, Linn. *Vern.*—Teling: *Yellika-tungoo-gadi* (Roxb.).

Stems 4–8 inches high. Panicle verticelled; branches simple, secund. Seeds naked, ovate, rugose.

This species is included in Edgeworth's list of Banda plants.

S. diander, *Beauv.* (*Plate* LXIII.) *Syn.—Agrostis diandra*, Linn. *Vern.*—Punjab: *Nonak* (Lahore); N.-W. Prov.: *Chiriya-ka-dána* (Allahabad); Bundelkhand: *Galphula*; Bengal: *Bena-joni* (Roxb.).

Smooth. Stems erect, 1–3 feet. Leaves very narrow, and tapering to a fine point; mouth of sheaths slightly bearded. Panicle narrow, often a foot long, usually bending over a little. Florets in pairs, diandrous.

---

* *See Plate E., Fig. 23.*

Common in the plains, and at moderate elevations on the Himalaya. It is said to be readily eaten by horses and cattle at Lahore; and is also favourably mentioned at Gujranwála and Sháhpur.

S. indicus, *R. Br.** *Syn.*—*S. tenacissimus*, Beauv.; *Vilfa tenacissima*, Trin. *Vern.*—Punjab: *Khir* (Gujranwála); Bundelkhand: *Ratua* (Banda); Cent. Prov.: *Ghorla* (Balaghát).

An erect grass growing in tufts, 1–2 feet high, glabrous except along the margin of the sheaths. Leaves mostly at the base of the stem, narrow, upper with long sheaths. Spikelike panicle long and narrow, continuous or interrupted. Spikelets numerous, crowded along the erect imbricate or distant branches.

Plains of North-West India, ascending to moderate elevations on the Himalaya, and generally spread over the tropical and subtropical parts of the world. In the Gujranwála district (Punjab) it is considered to be a good fodder grass, especially for horses. At Balaghát (Central Provinces) it is found on clay soils, and is used as fodder when young. In Australia it is valued as an excellent pasture grass for alluvial soils; it stands drought well, and is greedily eaten by stock.

In the United States, this grass, which is known there under the name of "Smut grass," is of considerable value, for grazing purposes if frequently cut or grazed down, but if allowed to remain untouched long, cattle and horses will not eat it unless very hungry, as it becomes tough and unpalatable. Mr. J. N. Brashear of Port Gibson, Miss., quoted by Dr. Vasey, remarks in reference to this species—"It is common all over our pasture lands, and is very hardy, standing any sort of weather. It grows well on almost any kind of land, but does best on rich moist bottoms. It is not used to any considerable extent for hay, but it makes splendid feed if cut while young. It will yield about 1½ tons per acre...............It makes a splendid pasture plant, and that is what we generally use it for. Stock are generally fond of it until it goes to seed, and they sometimes use it when dry in winter."

S. orientalis, *Kunth.* (*Plate* XXXII.)† *Syn.*—*Vilfa orientalis*, Nees. *Vern.*—Punjab: *Tandua* (Kángra), *kheo* (Cent. and S. Punjab); N.-W. Prov.: *Usar-ki-ghás* (General), *kar-usara-ghás* and *kálusra* (Awa).

Perennial. Stems extensively creeping and rooting at the nodes after the manner of *dúb*, but very different both in foliage and inflorescence. Leaves crowded at the base of the stems, rather narrow, and convolute, tapering to a fine point. Flowering stems long, wiry, and naked above. Panicle loose pyramidal; branches verticillate. Spikelets many, minute. Outer glume hyaline, rounded at the apex, much smaller than the inner and darker coloured glumes.

This grass is strictly confined to saline soils, and is found on all the

---

* *See Plate* F., *Fig.* 24, of present Volume.

† *Fig.* 1 of *Plate* XXXII. is from Roxburgh's drawing of *Agrostis tenacissima*, Linn. = *Spor. tenacissimus*, Beauv. and *Spor. indicus*, R. Br.

usar tracts in Northern India, often constituting the entire vegetation. As such it is not only useful as an unmistakeable indicator of reh-infected soils, but also by affording an abundant supply of fodder over large areas of land where other plants are unable to exist. The experiments now being undertaken at Aligarh and Cawnpore for the reclamation of reh-infected land are of great interest in regard to the changes affecting the growth of this grass. The immediate effect of excluding all cattle from usar land is the production of a more luxuriant growth of the usar grass, and its rapid extension over what were formerly bare efflorescent patches. At the same time other kinds of grasses quickly take advantage of the improved condition of the soil consequent on the more vigorous growth of the usar grass; for the thicker coating of usar grass helps to moderate the scorching rays of the sun, and in this way diminishes the upward capillary movement of the reh salts. On all usar tracts there are usually to be seen patches of various sizes scattered here and there, usually in the form of ridges or mounds. These raised portions are nearly always found to support an assortment of plants indicating a distinctly different condition of soil compared to that of their surroundings. *Dúb* and other valuable grasses form a large proportion of the vegetation of these raised patches, and are ever ready to encroach wherever the ground in their immediate neighbourhood becomes fitted for their existence. The usar grass does not appear to be able to hold its own on ground which is capable of supporting these other grasses; it will, therefore, gradually disappear as the reclamation of the reh-infected tracts proceeds.

S. pallidus, *Nees.* *Syn.*—*Vilfa pallida,* Nees. *Vern.*—PUNJAB: *Budhan* and *budhar* (E. Punjab), *palinji* (Hissar); N.-W. PROV.: *Karno* (Royle).

Similar in height and habit to *S. orientalis,* but the stoloniferous rhizomes are much shorter; the panicles are narrower, their branches shorter and more erect.

Common in the Punjab and Rájputána on sandy ground, growing gregariously, and affording a considerable amount of forage.

50. POLYPOGON, *Desf.* Species about 10, inhabiting temperate regions of the world. Panicle densely spikelike. The long weak awns which give it a soft and brush-like appearance arise from the outer empty glumes, the flowering glumes have very short awns.

P. monspeliensis, *Desf.** *Syn.*—*Alopecurus monspeliensis,* Linn.; *A. paniceus,* Linn.; *Phleum crinitum,* Schreb.; *Agrostis panicea,* Willd. *Vern.*—PUNJAB: *Malhar* (Salt Range), *mandusi* (Karnál). RAJPUTANA: *Chitra* (Ajmere).

Stems about one foot high. Awn of empty glumes three or four times as long as the glume.

---

* *See Plate E., Fig.* 25, of present Volume.

A common weed in cultivated ground. It is an ornamental grass, but of little value for fodder.

P. fugax, *Nees.*

The spike-like panicles are larger and more distinctly branched than those of *P. monspeliensis*. The much shorter awns and larger spikelets give it also a very different aspect.

Plains and hills of Northern India, usually on wet ground. It occurs also in Australia. It is of little value for fodder.

TRIBE IX. AVENEÆ.

51. **AVENA**, *Linn.* Species about 40, chiefly confined to the temperate regions of the old world. The spikelets are 3–5 flowered and arranged in a loose panicle. The flowering glume is rounded on the back, 2–cleft at the summit, and many-nerved; from its back arises a long twisted and bent awn. The ripe grain which is usually adherent to the pale is furrowed in front. There are no indigenous species to be found in the plains of Northern India. The two which will be presently mentioned are the cultivated *oat*, and the other is an introduced weed, which occasionally makes its appearance in wheat and barley fields, and has been supposed by some to be a degenerate form of oats.

A. fatua, *Linn.* *Vern.*—PUNJAB: *Gandal*, *ganer*, and *jei* (Stewart), *ganhel* (Cent. Punjab), *gozang* (Chenáb), *jandel* (Cent. and S.-W. Punjab).

Flowering glumes of a firm texture at the base, and covered outside with long brown hairs.

I have received no particular information as to its value for fodder in this country. Dr. Vasey in his "Report on the Agricultural Grasses of the United States" mentions—

"that some people have thought this species to be the original of the cultivated oats, but that the alleged facts are not sufficiently established. It differs from it in having more florets in the spikelets, in the long brown hairs which cover the flowering glumes, in the constant presence of the long twisted awn, and in the smaller size and lighter weight of the grain. It is a great injury to any grain field, in which it may be introduced, but for the purpose of fodder, of which it makes a good quality, it has been much employed in California."

A. sativa, *Linn.*,* (Oats). *Vern.*—*Jai* or *jawi.*

Cultivated in N.-W. India principally as green fodder for horses. It is largely grown for this purpose at the Sahåranpur and Hapur Stud depôts, and at the Hissar Cattle Farm, and is also stacked. For description and figure, *see* "Field and Garden Crops, N.-W. Provinces and Oudh," Part I.

52. **TRISTACHYA**, *Nees* There are 8 species, American and tropical African, and one (*T. Stocksii*) mentioned by Boissier as occurring in Sindh and Beluchistan. Spikelets in threes at the ends of the panicle branches, 2–flowered.

* *See Plate* E., *Fig.* 26, of present Volume.

Lower floret male, upper hermaphrodite or female. Awn of the flowering glume terminal between the two lobes. Nothing appears to be known regarding its value for fodder.

TRIBE X. CHLORIDEÆ.

53. SCHŒNEFELDIA, *Kunth.* Contains a single species confined to tropical Africa and the drier portions of N.-W. India.

S. gracilis, *Kunth.*,* (*Plate* LXIV.) *Syn.*—*S. pallida,* Edgew.; *S. ramosa,* Trin.

Annual. Stems many. Leaves narrow. Spikes long, solitary or 2–4 together at the top of the stem. Awns of the flowering glumes long and slender, often becoming curved. Whole plant of a pale straw colour.

Grows in dry sandy ground in N.-W. India, also in the ravines bordering the Jumna and Chambal rivers.

54. CYNODON, *Pers.* This genus contains four species including the widely spread and well known *dúb.* They all occur in Australia, two of them being confined to that country. The genus is distinguished by the following characters :—Spikes 2–6, slender, proceeding from the summit of the peduncle. Spikelets small, 1-flowered, without awns, sessile along one side of the simple spike-like branches of the panicle. Rachilla produced beyond the floret into a small point or bristle. The *Cynodons* have a superficial resemblance to some of the digitate-spiked species of *Panicum,* but differ from them by the spikelets being arranged singly and not in pairs on the rachis.

C. Dactylon, *Pers.*, (*Plate* XXXIII.)† *Syn.*—*C. stellatus,* Willd.; *Panicum Dactylon,* Linn.; *Digitaria Dactylon,* Scop.; *Paspalum Dactylon,* D.C. *Vern.*—General: *Dúb;* Trans-Indus: *Baráwa* (Stewart); Punjab: *Khabbar* (Stewart), *khabbal* (Central and Western Punjab), *talla* and *tilla* (S.-W. and W. Punjab), *dubra* (Karnál); Rajputana: *Dob* (Ajmere), *nili dub* (Merwára); Bundelkhand: *Duba;* N.-W. Prov. and Oudh: *Káli ghás* (Doáb), *rám ghás* (Bhira); Cent. Prov.: *Dhupsa* (Seoni), *hariáli* (Chánda); Marathi: *Durva, harala, haryeli* (Dymock); Chutia Nagpur: *Dhobi-ghás* (Santal); Bengal: *Doorba* (Roxb.); Teling: *Ghericha* (Roxb.); Tamil: *Arugam-pilla* (Roxb.); Madras: *Hariáli.*

Perennial, glaucous. Stems prostrate, creeping and rooting from many nodes. Leaves short. Flowering stems ascending. Panicle of 3–5 slender spikes, each 1-1½ inches long. Spikelets less than a line long; outer glumes nearly equal, open, narrow and pointed; flowering glumes rather larger and much broader, becoming hardened when in fruit, smooth on the sides, rather rough on the keel and edges.

---

* *See Plate* E., *Fig.* 26, of present Volume.

† *See also Plate* E., *Fig.* 27.

Abundant in the plains of North-West India, and up to 7 or 8,000 feet on the Himalaya. It is rarely found in the very sandy parts of Western Punjab, and in the black soils of Central India it is also scarce. *Dúb* is by far the most useful of all fodder grasses, especially for horses. It is perennial, and flowers nearly all the year round. The foliage becomes scanty during the cold weather months, at which time it may be said to be at rest. It varies considerably in habit as well as in its nutritive qualities, according to the nature of the soil or climate. It makes excellent hay, and will keep good for many years in stack. It is considered to be a first class fodder grass in Australia, where it is widely distributed, though in all probability introduced with cultivation. This grass is highly valued in the United States, where it is generally known under the name of "Bermuda grass." The following extracts are from Dr. Vasey's "Report on the Grasses of the South," pages 26–28 (1887):—

"In Louisiana, Texas, and the south generally, it is and has been the chief reliance for pasture for a long time, and immense herds of cattle on the southern prairies subsist principally on this food . . . . It has the capacity to withstand any amount of heat and drought, and months that are so dry as to check the growth of *blue grass* (*Poa arachnifera*) will only make the *Bermuda grass* green and more thrifty" (Professor Killebrew).

"*Bermuda grass* grows on any kind of soil in Texas, but will not stand the trampling of stock on loose sandy soil. It is hard to beat for a grazing grass, though long continued droughts cause it to dry up" (Mr. M. M. Martin, Central Texas).

"While this is the most northern limit of *Bermuda grass*, it is also the most southern limit of *Blue grass*. The two growing together on the same land produce a most perfect pasture, as the *Blue grass* is green all the fall, winter, and spring months, while during the heat of summer, which prevents the growth of the *Blue grass*, the *Bermuda* flourishes. The two together in good strong soil make a perfect pasture, good all the year round" (Mr. J. B. Wade, N. Georgia).

"The time is not far distant when all the rough feed consumed on plantations will be made of this grass, and when the planter will consider his hay crop of more importance than his sugar and cotton. No other grass will yield such an amount of valuable hay, surpass it in nutritious qualities, or support on an acre of pasture such an amount of stock" (Mr. Affleck in Professor Killebrew's Grasses of Tennessee).

55. CHLORIS, *Swartz.* There are about 40 species, all of them occurring in warm latitudes. The spikes are either crowded at the summit of the peduncle, or are arranged in verticels. Spikelets 1-flowered, placed in two rows on one side of the simple spikes. Flowering glumes awned.

C. barbata, *Swartz. (Plate* XXXIV.*)* *Syn.—Andropogon barbatus*, Linn.; *C. decora*, Nees. *Vern.*—PUNJAB: *Ganni* (Kángra), *jharna* (S. and E. Punjab); RAJPUTANA: *Phundi* (Ajmere), *punji* (Merwára), *chhinkri* (Jeypur); N.-W. PROV.: *Gandi gavung* and *paluah* (Royle), *jargi* (Allahabad) ; CENT. PROV. : *Bárdiya* (Chánda), *phulkia* (Balaghát) ; BERAR : *Botya jhara*.

Stems creeping below and branching, joints smooth. Leaves bifarious at the base of the stems, their margins and mouths of sheaths ciliate. Spikes 6–12, digitate, secund, 1–2 inches long ; rachis striated, not hairy. Spikelets 2-flowered ; upper floret composed of one or more empty glumes ; the lower one fertile and sessile. Flowering glume and pale with hairs at the base.

Common in N.-W. India especially on sandy soils. It is considered a good fodder grass up to the time of flowering, after which time cattle will not touch it.

C. Roxburghiana, *Edgew.* (*Plate* LXV.) *Syn.—C. digitata,* Steud ; *Melica digitata,* Roxb. *Vern.*—RAJPUTANA : *Bámna* (Ajmere) ; BUNDELKHAND : *Mathaniya* (Lalitpur) ; CENT. PROV. : *Hika gadi* and *salakodam gadi* (Chánda).

Stems procumbent, or erect when growing amongst bushes. Both surfaces and sheaths of leaves hairy. Spikes terminal, 4–5, secund, filiform, 6–9 inches long hairy at the base. Spikelets in two rows, sessile. Outer glumes unequal, inner 3–4 times longer, and shortly awned. Flowering glume with a long awn issuing just below its apex from outside. This grass has a superficial resemblance to *Panicum sanguinale.*

Not uncommon in Northern India, and ofter growing amongst bushes, where its stems attain a considerable height. Mr. Lowrie tells me that it is considered to be a good fodder grass at Ajmere.

C. tenella, *Roxb.* (*Plate* LXVI.) *Vern.*—RAJPUTANA : *Kágya* (Ajmere), *morbhaga ghás* (Udaipur).

Stems erect from a decumbent base, about one foot high, smooth. Leaves rather large in proportion to the plant, smooth and soft. Spikes solitary or in pairs, secund, about 2 inches long. Spikelets 3-5-flowered, the fifth one being rudimentary.

Rájputána, Bundelkhand, and Central Provinces. At Ajmere it is said to be a good fodder grass.

56. MELANOCENCHRIS, *Nees.* Species 3, one of which is found in Northern India. The spikelets are arranged in many short scattered clusters, which fall away at the joints. The two lower empty glumes are clothed with long feathery hairs ; the flowering glumes are 3-fid, their lobes almost aristate.

M. Royleana, *Nees.* (*Plate* LXVII.) *Syn.—Eutriana abyssinica,* R. Br. ; *M. Jacquemontiana,* Jaub. and Spach.

Annual. Stems many, 6–10 inches. Leaves narrow, upper sheaths long, edges of leaves and their sheaths ciliate. Spikelets in separate clusters, directed to one side of the curved common peduncle. Empty glumes densely hairy below, and awned.

A diminutive and very elegant grass, not uncommon in sandy or stony ground in Northern India. It is said to be a good grazing grass when young, though rather too small to be of much account.

57. TETRAPOGON, *Desf.* There are 4 species, one of which is plentiful in certain parts of Northern India. In general appearance it resembles a *Chloris*, but the spikelets are 3–4-flowered; whilst in *Chloris* they are only 1–flowered. The spikes are erect, 1–3, and covered with long silky hairs. Flowering glumes awned.

T. villosus, *Desf.* (*Plate* LXVIII.) *Syn.*—*Chloris villosa*, Pers. *Vern.*—PUNJAB : *Khera-madhána* and *sager* (Salt Range); RAJPUTANA : *Kalia* (Ajmere); N.-W. PROV.: *Phulni* (Etah), *kokuna* (Cawnpore); CENT. PROV.: *Phundra jadi* (Seoni).

Perennial, cæspitose. Stems erect, upper parts rather free of foliage. Leaves glabrous, narrowly linear. Spikes in pairs, often coalescing so as to appear single. Spikelets 4–5-flowered. Lower glume acute, upper mucronate from a rounded apex; flowering glume obovate, obtuse, with long silky hairs from the back, with an awn twice as long as itself springing from just below the obtuse or retuse apex.

Common on sterile land in the plains of Northern India, and considered to be a good fodder grass at Ajmere. It is very abundant on some of the saline usar tracts in the Doáb, frequently constituting the sole vegetation, but usually selecting less infected patches than those occupied by the true usar grass, *Sporobolus orientalis*.

58. DINEBRA, *Jacq.* This genus contains a single species, which is confined to tropical Africa and Northern India. Spikes several, scattered along the peduncle. Spikelets 2–3-flowered. Flowering glumes bluntish, much shorter than the somewhat awned lower empty ones.

D. arabica, *Beauv.** *Syn.*—*D. retroflexa*, Panz.; *D. ægyptiaca*, Jacq.; *Leptochloa arabica*, Kunth; *Cynosurus retroflexus*, Vahl; *Dactylis paspaloides*, Willd.; *Eleusine calycina*, Roxb. *Vern.*—CENT. PROV.: *Bara sarpot* (Chánda), *maljhanji* (Seoni); TELING: *Wadata-toka gaddee* (Roxb.).

Annual. Stems erect or prostrate, 1–3 feet, leafy at the base. Panicle narrow; spikes numerous, alternate, often reflexed, reddish when young. Spikelets 3–flowered; outer glumes equal, longer than the flowering glumes.

---

* *See Plate F., Fig.* 28, of present Volume.

Punjab, Rájputána, and in the Central Provinces; also in Bundelkhand, where I have usually found it in arhar fields on the black soil. A very ornamental grass, and probably nutritious, but being only an annual, and not very plentiful, it does not take a high place as a fodder grass.

59. ELEUSINE, *Gærtn.* Contains about 7 species according to Bentham, nearly all of which are to be met with in Northern India. One of them is largely cultivated under the name of *mandua,* and the other species are more or less valuable for fodder. The spikes are digitate at the top of the peduncle, or verticellate. Spikelets many-flowered, sessile, crowded, and flattened. The flowering glumes have no awns, and they are longer than the two inferior empty ones. The seed is transversely wrinkled, and often, especially in *mandua,* loose within the thin shell-like pericarp.

E. ægyptiaca, *Pers.* (*Plate* XXXV.)* *Syn.—E. cruenta,* Lamk; *Dactyloctenium ægyptiacum,* Willd.; *Cynosurus ægyptiacus,* Linn. *Vern.* —General: *Makra;* Trans-Indus: *Chubrei* (Stewart); Punjab: *Madhána* (Punj. Plains and Salt Range), *Kark-madhána* (Gujranwála and Sháhpur Districts), *Kar-madhána* (Lahore); Rajputana: *Malicha* (Ajmere), *mansa* (Mount Abu); N.-W. Prov.: *Khermakra* (Allahabad); Bundelkhand: *Maka makna* and *tipakia* (Banda); Cent. Prov.: *Mathna* (Balaghát), *chikára* (Nagpur), *chikára, chota mandya,* and *ute-sirkum jári* or *ute-sirla gadi* (Chánda); Santal: *Suntu bukrui* (Campbell); Hind.: *Makur jali* (Roxb.).

Stems tufted, erect or creeping and rooting at the nodes after the manner of *dúb.* Leaves flat, tapering to a fine point, ciliate. Spikes 3–5, digitate, varying from ½ to 2 inches in length. Spikelets regularly and closely packed on the underside of, and at right angles to, a prominent angular rachis. Outer glume acute; the second broader, its keel produced into a dorsal awn; rachis of spikelets produced beyond the outer glumes. Flowering glumes broad, tapering into short spreading points. Seed oval, 3–sided, transversely rugose, enclosed in a loose pericarp.

Common all over Northern India, especially on cultivated ground. On dry sterile soils it assumes a more creeping habit, and produces very small spikes. It is generally considered to be a very nutritious grass both as forage and fodder. The seeds are eaten by the poorer classes. In the Lahore district it is said to be eaten by cattle, but not by horses. It occurs also in Australia, where it is much valued as a pasture grass.

---

* *See* also *Plate* F., *Fig.* 29, of present Volume.

E. Coracana, *Gærtn.* *Syn.—Cynosurus coracanus*, Linn. *Vern.*—GENERAL: *Mandua, makra* and *marua;* PUNJAB: *Kodoṅ, koda, kutra* and *mandwa* (Himalaya), *kodra* (Biás and Chenab basins), *mandal* (Rávi basin); BUNDELKHAND: *Rotka* (Jalaun); BENGAL: *Murha* (Campbell); SANTAL: *Kode* (Campbell); TELING: *Pedda* and *sodee* (Roxb.); S. INDIA: *Rági.*

Stems erect, 2–4 feet high, compressed. Spikes digitate, usually incurved. Spikelets 3–6-flowered. Glumes all obtuse. Pericarp loosely investing the small globular seed. Roxburgh's *E. stricta* is a luxuriant variety with straight spikes.

Cultivated as a kharif crop in Northern India, but chiefly on the lower slopes of the Northern Himalaya, where it sometimes provides the principal food of the people. The stalks are given to cattle as fodder. It is figured in "Field and Garden Crops, N.-W. Provinces and Oudh," Part II., *Plate* XXVIII., and in "Church's Food Grains of India," *Figs.* 17 and 18.

E. flagellifera, *Nees.* (*Plate* XXXVII.) *Syn.—E. arabica*, Hochst.; *E. stolonifera*, R. Br. *Vern.*—GENERAL: *Chhimbar;* TRANS-INDUS: *Chubrei* and *bháru* (Stewart); PUNJAB: *Chemri* (Stewart), *chembri* (Multán), *chhembar* (West of Sutlej), *gathil* (S. Punjab), *ganthil* and *kharimbar* (Sirsa), *dubra* (E. Punjab); RAJPUTANA; *Ganthia* (Ajmere), *gáṅth dob* (Jeypur); DOAB: *Ghurdub* (Royle).

Perennial, glaucous. Stems many from the bulb-like rooting nodes of a prostrate extensively creeping rhizome. Leaves narrowly linear, acuminate, stiff, distant, upper very short. Spikes 3–5, digitate, 5–8-flowered. Glumes lanceolate, smooth, the upper one very acute.

Plains of Northern India, preferring a sandy soil. It is generally considered to be a very good fodder grass, both for horses and cattle, though in the Gujránwála and Sháhpur districts it is supposed to diminish the milk of cattle if eaten dry. In the Jhang Settlement Report it is mentioned as being the most common grass in the *bar*, and also one of the best.

E. indica, *Gærtn.* (*Plate* LXIX.) *Syn.—Cynosurus indicus*, Linn. *Vern.*—RAJPUTANA: *Mandwa* (Ajmere); N.-W. PROV. and OUDH: *Jhingri* (Royle), *makraila* (Allahabad), *gadha-charwa, gadha-mandwi* and *lijhas* (Bhira); BUNDELKHAND: *Gurcháwa;* CENT. PROV.: *Ghod-chabba* (Balaghát), *gurra gadi* and *kakariya* (Chánda), *madanya* (Nagpur), *mandiál jori* (Seoni); HIND.: *Mal-ankuri* (Roxb.); TELING: *Kuror* (Roxb.).

Annual. Stems erect, 1–2 feet, compressed, smooth, branching below. Leaves glabrous, flat; ligule pilose. Spikes long, erect, 5–7, digitate, and often with one or two spikes added below. Spikelets 3–5–flowered. Glumes obtuse or shortly mucronate. Seeds oblong, 3–sided, rugose; pericarp loose.

Common in the plains of Northern India, and up to moderate elevations on the Himalaya. It is a somewhat coarser grass than the preceding. It is eaten by horses and cattle, and in some districts is considered to be a good fodder grass, though Roxburgh says that cattle are not fond of it; this remark may, however, apply chiefly to the Bengal form, which the nature of the climate would render more rank and unpalatable. It is considered to be a good pasture grass in Australia. It is also much valued in United States, where it is known under the following names :— *Yard grass*, *Crow's foot*, *Crab grass*, and *Wire grass*. Prof. Phares, quoted by Dr. Vasey in his "Report on the Agricultural Grasses of the United States," writes—

"It grows in rich cultivated ground and produces an immense quantity of seeds. It is a very nutritious grass, and good for grazing, soiling and hay. The succulent lower part of the stems, covered with the sheaths of the leaves, renders it difficult to cure well, for which several days are required. It may be cut two or three times, and yields a large quantity of hay."

E. scindica, *Duthie* (*Plate* XXXVI.) *Syn.—Dactyloctenium scindicum,* Boiss. *Vern.*—SINDH: *Mandjiro;* PUNJAB: *Bhobra* (Hissar), *bobriya* (S. Punjab); RAJPUTANA: *Ganthya, ganti ghás* and *jangli malicha* (Ajmere), *kharo makro* (Jeypur).

Perennial. Stems branching from a short bent and prostrate rhizome. Flowering stems elongate, erect, slender, almost naked. Leaves short, linear acuminate, flat, their edges near the base clothed with a few bulbous-based hairs; ligule truncate, ciliate. Spikes 3–5, very short, ovate and slightly curved; rachis mucronate. Lower glume oblong, acute; upper larger, ovate, and ending abruptly and obliquely in a short awn. Flowering glume oblong, lanceolate, obtuse, its keel scabrid and ending in a short point, lateral nerves prominent.

Sandy ground in the plains of N.-W. India extending west to Aden. It is considered to be a good fodder grass. It bears a slight resemblance to *makra*, but is altogether a much more slender grass.

E. verticillata, *Roxb.* (*Plate* LXX.) *Syn.—Cynosurus verticillatus,* Wight; *Leptochloa verticillata,* Kunth; *Acrachne eleusinoides,* Nees. *Vern.*—PUNJAB: *Jharna* (Hissar); RAJPUTANA: *Chhinke* or *kuri chinke* (Ajmere), *kangsi* (Merwára).

Erect, smooth, 1–4 feet. Leaves bifarious. Panicle erect, oblong, composed of many verticels of sessile spreading linear spikes like those of *E. indica*. Spikelets numerous, panicled, 8–12–flowered. Glumes jagged. Seeds oblong, rugose.

It is considered to be a good fodder grass for cattle both in the Punjab and in Rájputána.

60. LEPTOCHLOA, *Beauv.* Contains about 12 species, one of which occurs in Northern India. The flattish spikelets are sessile, or nearly so, and are attached to one side of the slender branches of a long panicle. Glumes without awns; inferior ones empty.

L. chinensis, *Nees.* (*Plate* LXXI.) *Syn.*—*L. tenerrima,* R. and S.; *Poa chinensis,* Kœn.; *P. decipiens,* R. Br.; *Eragrostis decipiens,* Steud. *Vern.*—N.-W. Prov.: *Chánhel* (Allahabad); Cent. Prov.: *Chipa-chima gadi* (Chánda), *jhira* and *phulkia* (Seoni).

Stems creeping below and rooting from the lower nodes, ascending, 2–3 feet, slender, glabrous. Leaves narrow, flat, tapering to a fine point. Panicle upwards of one foot long; branches many, simple, scattered or in clusters along the rachis. Spikelets sessile or nearly so, narrow, 4–6–flowered. Outer empty glumes rather unequal, acute; flowering glumes broader, acute.

Common in the plains of Northern India and used more or less for fodder, though nothing definite appears to be known regarding its real value.

TRIBE XI. FESTUCEÆ.

61. PAPPOPHORUM, *Schreb.* Out of 20 described species the four following are recorded as occurring in the Punjab: *P. Aucheri,* Jaub. and Spach; *P. brachystachyum,* Jaub. and Spach (*Syn.*—*P. arabicum,* Hochst); *P. elegans,* Nees. (*Syn.*—*Calotheria elegans,* Wight); and *P. nanum,* Steud. They are perennial grasses with dense spike-like panicles, and the flowering glumes are furnished with numerous and usually plumose awns. I have received no information as to their value for fodder.

62. DIPLACHNE, *Beauv.* Species upwards of 14, distributed over the hotter parts of the world. Panicle branches long and slender. Spikelets sessile or nearly so, linear, scattered along the rachis, in two rows, but not sufficiently regular and unilateral for the genus to be placed amongst the *Chlorideæ,* to which it is sometimes referred.

D. fusca, *Beauv.* *Syn.*—*Festuca fusca,* Linn.; *Leptochloa fusca,* Kunth. *Vern.*—N.-W. Prov.: *Choti gandar* and *narri* (Aligarh).

Perennial. Stems prostrate below, and rooting from the lower nodes. Leaves long, linear, rough. Panicle narrow, with long erect spike-like branches. Sipkelets many, short; pedicels compressed, 5–9–flowered. Outer glumes linear lanceolate, unequal, acute. Flowering glumes with two teeth a little below the mucronate apex, keeled.

Plains of Northern India, on low-lying land where water is liable to lodge. I have observed it growing in great abundance in the more depressed portions of the saline usar tracts in the Aligarh district. Buffaloes are said to be very fond of this grass.

63. ARUNDO, *Linn.* Contains 6 or 7 species, of which three occur in Northern India. They are tall handsome perennial grasses, with large branching panicles clothed with silky hairs. Flowering glumes pilose on the back. They are of little or no value as fodder for cattle.

A. Donax, *Linn.* *Syn.—Donax arundinaceus,* Beauv. *Vern.*—PUNJAB : *Bánsi* (E. Punjab), *sukna* (Hoshiarpur). This species is commonly met with throughout the Mediterranean region, and is possibly an introduction in Northern India.

A. madagascariensis, *Kunth.* *Syn.—Donax Thouarii,* Beauv. Hilly parts of Northern India.

A. mauritanica, *Desf.* *Syn.—A. Pliniana,* Turr. This species occurs at the base of the Himalaya in the Punjab, extending from the Mediterranean region. It has narower leaves than *A. Donax,* and the spikelets are much smaller.

64. PHRAGMITES, *Trin.* There are 2 species, both of which occur in Northern India. This genus is closely allied to *Arundo,* the chief difference being that in *Phragmites* the lowest floret of the spikelet is male. They are tall handsome reeds with large branching panicles clothed with silky hairs on the axis.

P. Roxburghii, *Kunth.* *Syn.—Arundo Karka,* Roxb. *Vern.*—TRANS-INDUS : *Drumbi, dwarena,* and *gwarga* (Stewart) ; KASHMIR : *Nai* (Stewart) ; PUNJAB : *Nal* and *naria* (Stewart), *nar* (Chenab basin), *nalu* (Rávi basin), *bag-narri* (Jhelum basin), *narsal* (E. Punj.) ; SINDH : *Sar ;* N.-W. PROV. : *Bansi* (Dehra Dún) ; OUDH : *Narkul, narkat,* and *narsal ;* CENT. PROV. : *Paika gadi* (Chánda) ; MARATHI : *Deonal* or *deonál* (Dymock) ; BENGAL : *Nal* (Roxb.), *karka* (Watt) ; TELING : *Naga-sara maitantos* and *patoo-ederoo* (Roxb.) ; HIND. : *Nuda-nar* (Watt).

Stems erect, 8–12 feet, stout, covered with the leaf sheaths. Leaves flat, broad. Panicle erect or slightly drooping, 1½ feet or more. Spikelets numerous, crowded, each with 3–5 distant florets. Flowering glume of lowest floret, which is usually male, tapering but not awned, the others smaller and more pointed.

Var. **angustifolia.** *Vern.—Nalli.* Leaves narrower. This may possibly be the plant described by Retzius under the name of *Arundo bifaria* (*Syn.—P. nepalensis,* Nees).

Common in the plains of Northern India near water. The stems are used for making chairs, baskets and the pipes of hukahs ; and in Bengal mats are made of the split stems. Watson mentions that this grass has proved poisonous to cattle in Kumaun. In any case it is much too coarse a grass for fodder purposes.

P. communis, *Trin.** *Syn.—Arundo Phragmites,* Linn. *Vern.*—PUNJAB : *Dila* (Jhelum basin).

Of smaller stature than the preceding, with long creeping root-stock. Panicle somewhat one-sided, often of a purplish tinge. Spikelets at first very narrow, flat and spreading when in seed. The long silky hairs proceeding from the rachis give the panicle a beautiful silvery aspect.

Plains of North-West India and up to 14,000 feet on the Punjab Himalaya. Eaten by cattle in Ladak, where also sandals are made from the stems. It can only be used as fodder when quite young.

65. ELYTROPHORUS, *Beauv.* Contains a single species easily recognized by its inflorescence, which is composed of minute many-flowered spikelets crowded together into subglobose fascicles and forming an interrupted spike. Stamen 1.

---

* *See Plate* F., *Fig.* 30, of present Volume.

E. articulatus, *Beauv.* (*Plate* LXXII.)* *Syn.—Echinalysium strictum*, Trin.; *Dactylis spicata*, Willd. *Vern.*—N.-W. PROV.: *Balha* (Doáb); CENT. PROV.: *Kolhati* (Seoni), *suria* (Balaghát); SANTAL: *Khet kapuri* (Campbell).

An erect glabrous annual 6 inches to 1 foot high. Leaves flat, often longer than the stem; sheaths loose. Spikelets small, numerous, disposed in globular sessile clusters, and forming a cylindrical spike, which is often interrupted, and sometimes shortly branched from the base. Pale with two dorsal wings.

Plains of Northern India, on damp clay soils, not common.

66. LAMARCKIA, *Mœnch.* Contains a single species, which is abundant in the Mediterranean region, and has been recorded from Peshâwar by Stewart.

L. aurea, *Mœnch.* *Syn.—Cynosurus aureus*, Linn.; *Chrysurus cynosuroides*, Pers.; *C. aureus*, Spreng.

A small annual with handsome golden-coloured inflorescence. Spikelets in a dense unilateral panicle.

67. KŒLERIA, *Pers.* This genus contains about 12 species, the most of which are European. The spikelets are arranged in a dense cylindrical spike-like panicle. The flowering glumes are scarious and transparent.

K. phleoides, *Pers.* *Syn.—Festuca phleoides*, Vill.

Annual. Panicle densely cylindrical. Flowering glumes ending in two teeth, and with a short awn between the teeth. A common Mediterranean grass, extending through Afghanistan to the Punjab. Dr. Aitchison in his "Flora of the Jhelum District" recommends this grass for cultivation as likely to be of great use during the cold weather for fodder.

Another species, *K. cristata*, Pers., is abundant at moderate elevations on the Himalaya, and is a good fodder grass. It is a perennial species. The panicle is spikelike, often interrupted at the base. The flowering glumes are neither toothed nor awned.

68. ERAGROSTIS, *Beauv.* This genus contains about 100 described species, which are distributed over all parts of the world. In the plains of Upper India there are upwards of 15 species. The spikelets are numerous, somewhat compressed, many-flowered, and arranged in a panicle which is either spreading or compact. The outer glumes are shorter than the distichously imbricate flowering ones. The flowering glumes are awnless, 3-nerved, and prominently keeled.

E. bifaria, *W. and A.* (*Plate* LXXIII.) *Syn.—Poa bifaria*, Kunth. *Vern.*—RAJPUTANA: *Punya-safed* and *chota bhánkta* (Ajmere), *moi* (Mount Abu); TELING: *Wooda-tallum* (Roxb.).

Stems straight, wiry, 1–2 feet high. Spikes narrow, compact, 4–8 inches long. Spikelets sessile, in two rows from one side of the rachis; upper many-flowered, lower ones 4–6-flowered.

---

* *See* also *Plate* F., *Fig.* 31, of present Volume.

Sandy and rocky ground in North-West India, common in Rájputána. At Ajmere it is considered to be a good fodder grass, and is eaten by cattle on Mount Abu.

E. Brownei, *Nees. Syn.—Poa Brownei,* Kunth.; *P. polymorpha,* R. Br.; *Megastachya polymorpha,* Beauv. *Vern.*—N.-W. PROV.: *Jenkua* (Rohilkhand); BUNDELKHAND: *Khari* (Lalitpur); CENT. PROV.: *Asata* and *chir* (Seoni); BERAR: *Choti khidi.*

Stems usually 1 foot or more in height. Leaves narrow, flat or convolute. Panicle variable, sometimes quite simple and dense, or with long distant and spreading branches. Spikelets shortly stalked, flattened, tapering almost to a point. Flowering glumes closely distichous, their lateral nerves prominent, nearly central on each side. Easily recognized by its closely packed florets arranged in dark coloured and flattened spikelets.

Plains of North-West India, and at low elevations on the Himalaya, usually near water. It extends to Australia, where it is looked upon as a good pasture grass, yielding an abundance of feed both winter and summer.

E. ciliaris, *Link. Syn.—P. ciliaris,* Linn.; *P. ciliata,* Roxb. *Vern.*—RAJPUTANA: *Uṅdar-puṅchho* (Jeypur); SANTAL: *Tor chandbol* (Campbell).

Annual. Stems procumbent below. Leaves narrowly linear acuminate; mouth of sheaths pilose. Panicle narrow, spike-like, cylindrical, or occasionally with the lower portions branched. Spikelets 5–8–flowered; glumes acute; pales thickly clothed with long white stiff hairs.

Plains of Northern India on sandy ground. It affords good grazing wherever it occurs in sufficient quantity.

Var. **brachystachya,** (*Plate* XXXIX.) *Vern.*—RAJPUTANA: *Chaen* (Merwára). *Syn.—E. arabica,* Jaub. and Spach. A smaller plant with short dense cylindrical panicles. It is found on dry, sandy or stony ground in North-West India.

E. cynosuroides, *R. and S.* (*Plate* XL.) *Syn.—Poa cynosuroides,* Retz.; *Briza bipinnata,* Linn.; *Uniola bipinnata,* Linn. *Vern.*—GENERAL: *Dáb* or *kusa;* PUNJAB: *Dab* or *dib* (Cent. and W. Punjab), *dhab* (Multan), *dráb* (Kángra), *drábh* (Jhang); N.-W. PROV. and OUDH: *Kush* (Pilibhit), *dhab* and *kus* (Bhira); BUNDELKHAND: *Dabvi* (Banda); CENT. PROV.: *Chir, dabhat* and *kusha* (Balaghát); MARATHI: *Darbha* (Dymock); HINDI: *Davolia* (Stewart); BENGAL: *Koosha* (Roxb.); TELING: *Dubha, durbha,* and *durpa* (Roxb.).

A perennial with a thick creeping rhizome. Stems 1–3 feet, thick, terete, leafy. Leaves many, long, chiefly from the base of the stem, convolute above, hispid. Panicle spike-like or conical; branches horizontal, short and stiff. Spikelets in two rows from the under side of each branch, 6–12–flowered.

Abundant in the plains of Northern India in all kinds of soil. In saline usar soils it is usually found in the lower-lying portions where water collects. Cattle do not eat it as a rule, though it is liked by buffaloes when young. Its vigorous extensively creeping roots help to keep it fresh in dry weather. When other grasses fail it is often used as fodder mixed with gram and wheat. It produces a fairly strong fibre which is much used for making ropes. In the Karnál Settlement Report it is stated that the fibre is used for the ropes of the Persian wheel where they will last three months or more. This species is considered sacred amongst the Brahmins. It is often spread beneath the dead bodies of Hindus, the chief mourner wearing a ring of it on his finger. The rhizome is used as a diuretic.

E. elegantula, *Nees.* (*Plate* LXXIV.) *Syn.—Poa elegantula,* Kunth; *P. elegans,* Roxb. *Vern.*—N.-W. Prov.: *Kaluargi* (Doáb), *bhulwa* (Cawnpore); Cent. Prov.: *Asara* (Balaghát), *chota asara* (Seoni).

Annual, smooth. Stems 1–3 feet. Leaves few, small, quite smooth except the pilose mouths of the sheaths. Panicle oblong, nodding; branches rather distant, linear, appressed. Spikelets stalked, 8–12–flowered, purplish.

Not uncommon in the plains of North-West India, usually occurring on low-lying swampy ground. It is eaten by cattle either fresh or dry. At Balaghát in the Central Provinces it is used for brooms.

E. megastachya, *Link.* (*Plate* LXXV.) *Syn.—E. major,* Host; *Poa Eragrostis,* Sibth.; *Megastachya Eragrostis,* Beauv.; *Briza Eragrostis,* Linn. *Vern.*—N.-W. Prov.: *Chiriya ke chaolai* (Royle).

Annual. Stems ascending. Leaves linear; mouth of sheaths pilose. Panicle ovate oblong; pedicels shorter than the spikelets. Spikelets large, solitary or in clusters, linear oblong, 15–20–flowered. Flowering glumes mucronate; lateral nerves prominent.

Common all over the plains, and up to 5,000 feet on the Himalaya. It is used more or less as fodder.

E. nutans, *Nees.* (*Plate* LXXVI.) *Syn.—E. interrupta,* Beauv.; *Poa interrupta,* Kön.; *P. nutans,* Retz. *Vern.*—Punjab: *Kutti-pushli* and *sur* (Multán), *lumra* (Lahore); N.-W. Prov.: *Lamcha* (Etáwah), *rasaurah* (Allahabad), *ghui* (Pilibhit); Bundelkhand: *Lál báli* and *asaunra* (Banda), *mumkára* (Lalitpur); Cent. Prov.: *Ghodila* (Nagpur), *ghorila* (Chánda), *khajuria* (Seoni); Teling: *Nakurmaral* and *urenke* (Roxb.).

Annual, glabrous. Stems erect, 1–3 feet high, smooth and polished. Leaves long and flat. Panicle erect, 6–12 inches, contracted; lower branches often distant, two or more proceeding from the same level and giving the panicle a verticellate appearance. Spikelets small, quite smooth, often deeply tinged with red.

Plains of Northern India in heavy retentive soils. It is not considered a first class fodder grass, but cattle eat it readily when other better kinds have failed.

E. pilosa, *Beauv.* *Syn.—E. verticellata*, R. & S.; *Poa pilosa*, Linn.; *P. verticellata*, Cav. *Vern.*—Punjab: *Nika sáṅwak* (Multán), *gádar ppunch* (Hissar); N.-W. Prov.: *Chiriya ka dána* (Allahabad); Rajputana: *Palichhi* (Ajmere); Cent. Prov.: *Kutaki.*

Annual. Stems slender. Leaves flat, linear acuminate; mouth of sheaths pilose. Panicle much branched; branches at first appressed, afterwards spreading, the lower ones in verticels. Pedicels usually longer than the spikelets. Spikelets minute, narrow, linear, loose, 5–11-flowered, often tinged with purple.

Common in the plains of Northern India, usually in damp or swampy ground where it is relished by buffaloes. Mr. Symonds says that cattle eat it readily, and that it would make good hay. Mr. Lowrie tells me that at Ajmere it is considered to be a good fodder grass, and that the seeds are eaten. In Australia it is said to be very productive as a pasture grass.

E. plumosa, *Link.* (*Plates* XXXVIII. and LXXVII.) *Syn.—Poa plumosa*, Retz. *Vern.*—Punjab: *Budhan* and *palinji* (E. Punjab); Rajputana: *Chiri ka khet* (Ajmere), *chiri ko bajro* (Jeypur); N.-W. Prov. and Oudh: *Bara bhurbhura* and *bharbhuri* (Doáb), *bholoni* and *jhusa* (Allahabad), *galgala* (Lucknow); Bundelkhand: *Phularwa* (Banda); Cent. Prov.: *Bharbhuri bara* and *sipar gadi* (Chánda), *bharbusi* (Balaghát), *pithi* (Nagpur), *safed bhurki* (Seoni).

Annual. Stems erect or ascending. Leaves linear acuminate. Panicle oblong or somewhat pyramidal; branches slender, spreading, ciliate at the axils. Pedicels longer than the spikelets. Spikelets very numerous, small, lax, 5–7-flowered; axis articulate. Flowering glume obliquely truncate at the apex. Pales ciliate with stiff spreading hairs. This species varies very much both as to stature and in the form of the panicle. Some specimens have their panicles so narrow and contracted as to be hardly distinguishable from *E. ciliaris*, Link.

Common in the plains of Northern India especially on sandy soils. It is also abundant on saline usar soil in company with the usar grass (*Sporobolus orientalis*). Capt. Wingate tells me that at Allahabad it grows extremely well along with *dub*, and makes a useful light hay for mixing with coarser hay, and that both horses and cattle like it. At Ajmere it is also considered to be a good fodder grass.

E. poæoides, *Beauv.* *Syn.—E. poæfermis*, Link; *Poa Eragrostis*, Linn.

Annual. Stems erect, or bent at the base. Leaves linear, flat; mouth of sheaths bearded. Panicle branches spreading; pedicels slender, shorter than the spikelets. Spikelets linear lanceolate, 8–20-flowered. Flowering glumes with prominent lateral nerves. Cosson and Durieu in their flora of Algeria have described this and *E. megastachya* as varieties of *E. vulgaris*, Coss. and Germ.

Plains of Northern India and up to 8,000 feet on the Himalaya.

E. tenella, *Beauv.* (*Plate* LXXVIII.) *Syn.—E. tenuissima*, Schrad.; *Poa tenella*, Linn. *Vern.*—N.-W. Prov.: *Bharbhuri* (Muttra); Cent. Prov.: *Mondia jori* (Seoni); Santal: *Ichkoi* (Campbell).

Annual. Stems erect, 1–2 feet. Leaves smooth, narrow and finely pointed. Panicle usually very long and narrow; branches ascending or spreading, verticellate. Spikelets small, numerous, ovate, 5–7–flowered, often tinged bright red; axis articulate. Pales glabrous, not ciliate.

Common in the plains of Northern India, especially in cultivated ground, along with *sugar-cane*, *juár* and *arhar*. It is eaten by cattle both fresh and dry, and the seeds are said to be nutritious. It is highly relished in Australia.

E. tremula, *Hochst.* (*Plate* LXXIX.) *Syn.—Poa multiflora*, Roxb. *Vern.*—Punjab: *Chankan buti* (Multán), *lukki* (Lahore); Rajputana: *Chiri ka khet* (Ajmere), *chiri ka chanwaliá* (Jeypur); N.-W. Prov.: *Kalunji* (Royle), *bhamiri* (Aligarh), *bánsa* (Rohilkhand).

Annual. Stems slender, 1-1½ feet, bent below. Leaves few, mostly from the base, narrow and tapering to a fine point; mouth of sheaths bearded. Panicle pyramidal, bowing, much branched, lax; branches very slender, pilose at the axils. Pedicels equalling or longer than the spikelets. Spikelets many-flowered, somewhat flattened, long and narrow, nodding. The very slender pedicels which support the long many-flowered spikelets give rise to the constant tremulous motion exhibited by this species when in flower.

Common in light sandy soils in the plains, especially on poorly cultivated ground. It is said to be a good fodder grass at Ajmere, but its foliage is too scanty to be of much value. Its grain is said to have been extensively utilized by the starving population in certain parts of the Punjab during a famine which took place about 60 years ago, and which is even now remembered as the "lukkiwala sál."

E. uniloides, *Nees.* *Syn.—E. amabilis*, W. and A.; *Poa uniloides*, Retz. *Vern.*—Cent. Prov.: *Chanda mama gadi*, *chota loniya*, and *loniya* (Chánda), lahoria, (Seoni); Santal: *Ichkoch* (Campbell); Bengal: *Konee* (Roxb.).

Annual. Stems 1–2 feet, branching from the base. Leaves small, broad at the base, and tapering to a fine point; mouth of sheaths bearded. Panicle erect, oblong; branches filiform. Spikelets 16–20–flowered, ovate, closely imbricate, usually tinged with purple; axis not articulate.

Plains of Northern India, and up to 5,000 feet on the Himalaya, usually on wet ground. I have received no information regarding its value for fodder.

E. viscosa, *Trin.* (*Plate* LXXX.) *Syn.*—*Poa viscosa,* Willd. *Vern.*—N.-W. Prov.: *Bhurbhur* (Doáb), *bhulni* (Cawnpore); Cent. Prov.: *Bhurbhusi* (Nagpur), *chikti* (Balaghát), *chippal* (Seoni).

Annual. Stems numerous, 9–18 inches long. Leaves rather short, broad below and tapering to a fine point; mouths of sheaths clothed with long white hairs. Panicle linear oblong, 2–4 inches long; branches spreading, verticellate; main rachis rather thick and stiff. Whole plant, especially the inflorescence, covered with a sticky glutinous substance.

Plains of Northern India on sandy soils, often accompanying *E. plumosa,* and probably of equal value for fodder purposes.

E. abyssinica is a species which has lately been introduced into this country for experimental cultivation. It is a native of Abyssinia, where it is cultivated to a large extent at high elevations, and yields a small grain, of which the bread of the country is generally made. Its native name is *Teff, Thaff* or *Thief.* There are two kinds, one called "Thaf-Hagaiz," and the other "Thaf-Tseddia." The former is sown in the cold season, and the latter at the commencement of the rainy season, *i.e.,* in June or July. "Thaf-Hagaiz" yields a white grain, and is considered greatly superior to the other variety, of which the grain is of a reddish colour. Full particulars of this plant, and the mode of cultivating it in Abyssinia, are given in the "Bulletin of Miscellaneous Information," No. 1 (Royal Gardens, Kew, 1887).

Experimental sowings were last year made at Sahāranpur from a supply of seed received from the Director of the Royal Gardens, Kew. Both kinds were sown in ordinary garden soil in the month of March, and they yielded grain in May. After the fruiting stems were cut the plants renewed their growth and produced an excellent crop of fodder in the rainy season. Another sowing was made during the rains, which yielded an abundant crop of fodder, and this was made into hay which proved to be of superior quality, and was greedily eaten by the garden bullocks in preference to *chari.* The grain, useful as it appears to be in Abyssinia, is never likely to be much in request in this country, except possibly in those districts where *mijhri* or *kutki* (*Panicum miliare*) is grown. As a fodder plant, however, it promises to be of great value, and the results of further experiments, now in course of being undertaken, will indicate to what extent it can be profitably grown.

69. ÆLUROPUS, *Trin.* Contains 3 species, which extend from the Mediterranean region to Arabia and Central Asia, and one of them to the Punjab. They have creeping prostrate stems, and short rigid often prickly leaves. The spikelets, which are many-flowered, are arranged in dense spike-like heads. The flowering glumes are broad at the apex and mucronate. The Punjab representative, *Æ. littoralis,* Parl., var. *repens,* is characteristic of saline tracts in the Western parts of the Province, where it appears to take the place of *dub,* which it somewhat resembles in habit.

70. POA, *Linn.* Species about 80, distributed over the cooler regions of the world. On the Himalaya there are several species, including some which are well-known in Europe and America as valuable fodder plants. The spikelets are few-flowered and arranged in panicles, which are usually lax. The flowering glumes are 5- or more-nerved, membranous, keeled, and without awns.

P. annua, *Linn. Vern.*—BUNDELKHAND : *Chirua* (Banda).

A tufted annual, rarely exceeding one foot in height. Leaves flat and flaccid. Panicle loose and spreading. Spikelets shortly stalked, 3–6-flowered ; rachis glabrous.

Plains of N.-W. India, and up to 8 or 9,000 feet on the Himalaya. It is a very nutritious grass, but the yield of foliage is too small to be of much account.

71. BROMUS, *Linn.* There are about 40 species, nearly all being restricted to temperate parts of the world. Several kinds are found on the Himalaya. The only species with which we are now concerned is a fodder grass introduced from Australia under the name of "Prairie grass," *Bromus uniloides,* H. B. & K. (*Syn.—Ceratochloa uniloides,* Beauv.).

Müeller describes it as one of the richest of all grasses, growing extensively and spreading readily from seed, particularly in fertile and somewhat humid soils. It is not indigenous to Australia, having been introduced into that country from America, where, especially in the Southern States, it is much valued as a good winter grass, "affording in the earlier months of spring a much-relished nutritious food as well as a good hay.......It withstands drought fairly well, but escapes the worst period of summer drought by ripening early in the season" (Dr. G. Vasey, "Report on the Grasses of the South," U. S. A.) Other names for this grass are—"Australian Oats," "Rescue grass," and "Schader's Brome grass."

The results of some trials made with this grass at Sahárapur showed it to be less productive than oats, and not capable of replacing the latter at any other season of the year.

TRIBE XII. HORDEÆ.

72. LOLIUM, *Linn.* Reducible to 2 or 3 species according to Bentham, and confined to temperate parts of the world. The position of the spikelets on the rachis distinguishes this genus from all others belonging to this tribe, the spikelets being so placed as to have their margins facing the rachis.

L. temulentum, *Linn.* (Darnel).

Annual. Outer glume of the lateral spikelets usually as long as or longer than the whole spikelet. Flowering glumes oblong, usually obtuse, with an awn as long or longer than the glume itself.

Plains and hills of the Punjab and N.-W. Provinces. The seeds of this grass have for a long time been supposed to possess poisonous properties, and numerous instances have been given of the ill-effects after eating flour or bread into which the grains of this grass have been purposely or accidentally introduced. Recent experiments however indicate that healthy *darnel* grain is perfectly innocuous, and that only grains which are ergotized or otherwise diseased are injurious. For further information *see* Bentley and Trimen's "Medicinal Plants," p. 295.

L. perenne, *Linn.* (Perennial Rye-grass).

A well-known and most important fodder grass. It grows wild on the Himalayan ranges up to 11,000 feet. It is said to stand the dry heat of the Australian summer very well, and would probably be found to thrive as a cold weather fodder crop in N.-W. India. In Europe it is largely grown along with clover.

73. TRITICUM, *Linn.* There are about 10 species, which are confined to Western Asia and the Mediterranean region. The spikelets are few-flowered, somewhat compressed, and are placed on the rachis so as to have the margins of the glumes facing the rachis. The flowering glumes are oblong or ventricose, rounded on the back or keeled above, 5–9–nerved, the lateral ones short and not joining towards the apex, or produced into a distinct awn, as in bearded wheat.

T. sativum, *Lamk.* (Wheat). *Vern.*—GENERAL: *Gehun* or *gohun*; LADAK: *Tokar* (white), *tomar* (red), and *tro* (Stewart); N. TIBET: *Dro* (Stewart); PUNJAB HIMALAYA: *Nis* (Stewart), *sud* (Kunáwar and Bassahir); PUNJAB PLAINS: *Kanak* (Stewart), *khasil* and *khawid* (cut as fodder). BENGAL: *Gom* (Roxb.), *gau* (Watt).

The cultivation of this important plant is of pre-historic antiquity, and wheat is now nowhere known to occur in a wild state. DeCandolle believes that it originated somewhere in the Euphrates region, whilst other authors give reasons in favour of its developement from a species of

Ægylops, which is now classed as a section of *Triticum*. Many varieties are in cultivation both in the plains and on the Himalaya. The most obvious variations are those which affect the consistency of the grain (hard or soft), or its colour (white or red); also the presence or absence of awns on the flowering glumes (bearded or beardless). On the Himalaya wheat is grown at various elevations, and in Tibet it has been observed as high as 16,000 feet above the sea. A variety called "oi" is cultivated in Byans (N. E. Kumaun), from which a strong spirit is manufactured. For fodder purposes wheat is used both green and dry; the latter composed of the chaff and chopped-up straw, and commonly known as *bhusa*, is a valuable and largely used form of fodder in all wheat-growing districts. For further information *see* Church's "Food Grains of India"; "Field and Garden Crops, N.-W. Provinces and Oudh," Part I.; Bentley and Trimen's "Medicinal Plants"; Royle's "Illustrations of Himalayan Plants"; DeCandolle's "Origin of Cultivated Plants."

74. OROPETIUM, *Trin.* Contains a single diminutive species confined to India. The spikes are solitary, cylindrical, and with the spikelets completely immersed in the axis as in *Rottbœllia* and *Ophiurus*, but the outer persistent glumes compel its retention amongst the *Hordeæ*.

O. Thomæum, *Trin. Syn.—Rottbœllia Thomæa*, Linn.

Open ground in the plains of the Punjab, also in Rájputána and in the ravine country about Agra and Etáwah. It is too small to be considered of much account for fodder purposes.

75. HORDEUM, *Linn.* Species about 12, confined to temperate regions. The spikelets are in threes at each node, and 1-flowered. The empty glumes are subulate and rigid, often resembling an involucre.

H. vulgare, *Linn.** (Barley). *Vern.*—General: *Jau*; Ladak: *Jhotak, spiroka, shruk, soa, yangma,* and *tro* (Stewart); Kashmir: *Jawa, nai,* and *thazatt* (Stewart); Punjab: *Ne* (Stewart), *chák* (Upper Sutlej basin), *chung* (Upper Chenab basin); Marathi: *Jav* and *yava* (Dymock); Bengal: *Jab* (Watt), *juba* (Roxb.).

Annual. Stems many, 2–3 feet, smooth. Leaves few, the upper one close to the spike; sheaths smooth, striate; ligule very short; blade rounded at the base, and tapering gradually to the apex, glaucous green. Spikes oblong, compressed, 2–2½ inches long (without the awns.) Spikelets sessile, arranged in threes on either side of a flattened rachis, the lateral ones occasionally barren or rudimentary (in 2-rowed barley). Outer glumes small, setiform. Flowering glumes firm, 5-ribbed, rounded on the back, and ending in a long stiff awn rough with forward prickles. Grain usually adhering to the pale.

Barley is supposed by DeCandolle to have originated in Western

* *See Plate V, Fig.* 32, of present Volume.

temperate Asia. It is extensively cultivated in Northern India, either alone, or mixed with wheat, or with gram, mustard and linseed. There are two important varieties, *viz.*, the 2-rowed (*H. distichon*), and the 6-rowed (*H. hexastichon*), the latter being the one more usually grown in this country. Barley succeeds better as a hill crop than wheat, and is cultivated at higher elevations. A curious beardless variety (*H. ægiceras*, Royle) is found in Tibet; another, called *rasuli* barley (*H. gymno-distichon*) differs from the ordinary in having the grains free of the pales; and Siberian barley (*H. cœleste*). *Vern.*—*Uyan* or *ua jau* has been recorded from Pángi (Stewart), Lahoul (Moorcroft), and Kumaun (Watson). For further information see works referred to under wheat.

TRIBE XIII. BAMBUSEÆ.

76. BAMBUSA, *Schreb.* Species about 24, distributed over tropical and subtropical Asia, one occurring in America.

B. arundinacea, *Retz.* *Syn.*—*B. orientalis*, Nees; *Arundo Bambos*, Linn.; *Bambos arundinacea*, Pers. *Vern.*—PUNJAB: *Magar báns* and *nál báns;* N.-W. and CENT. INDIA: *Báns*, and *kattang báns;* MARATHI: *Mándgái* (Dymock); TELING: *Vedroo* and *mulkas* (Roxb.).

Perennial. Stems woody, 30–50 feet high, forming compact clumps, green; branches spreading, alternate, bifarious, spinescent; cavity of joints small; spines strong, curved, in pairs at the base of the branches, or in threes, the central one being the longest. Leaves small, shortly stalked, bifarious, lanceolate, thin; sheaths persistent, coriaceous, downy, 1–2 inches long. Spikelets mostly sessile, in dense ½-whorled clusters, glabrous and shining. Empty glumes 2–4. Flowering glumes 4–10, the upper ones sterile. Edges of pale fimbriate. Lodicules 3. Stamens 6. Pericarp thin, adnate to the seed.

Common in Central and Southern India, and extensively cultivated in parts of North-West India and Bengal. The leaves and twigs are a favourite fodder of elephants. The various purposes to which this plant is put, too numerous to be here mentioned, are given in Dr. Watt's "Dictionary of the Economic Products of India," Vol. I., p. 390. *See* also Brandis' "Forest Flora," Roxburgh's "Flora Indica," II., 191, and Dymock's "Vegetable Materia Medica of Western India," p. 856.

Roxburgh, in describing the inflorescence of this species, says—"When in flower the tree is generally destitute of leaves, and as the extremity of every ramification is covered with flowers, the whole tree seems one entire, immense panicle, composed of innumerable, somewhat verticelled spikes, each verticel is composed of several, distichous, oblong, pointed, sessile, rigid spikelets, such as those of *Eleusine*, &c." The flowering of this species takes place periodically about every 30 years, when almost every individual specimen blossoms and dies. The grain produced on these occasions is abundant, and of great value as an article of food. It is supposed on more than one occasion during the present century to have prevented a famine. The food value of the grain, according to Prof. Church, is high, though deficient in oil and mineral matter.

77. DENDROCALAMUS, *Nees.* There are 9 species, inhabiting India, the Malay Archipelago, and China. In habit they resemble *Bambusa,* but there are no lodicules, and the pericarp of the fruit (caryopsis) is free from the seed.

D. strictus, *Nees.* (Male bamboo). *Syn.—Bambusa stricta,* Roxb. *Vern.*—General : *Báñs, báñsi* and *kussub* (Royle), *báñs kabban* (Watt); Santal : *Buru mat* (Campbell) ; Bengal : *Kopar* (Watt.) ; Teling : *Sadanapa-vedroo* (Roxb.).

Usually of smaller stature than that of *Bambusa arundinacea,* stems nearly or quite solid, lower part often variously bent, spreading above and frequently curved downwards. Leaves deciduous, arising from fasciculate branches enclosed in shining cartilaginous persistent sheaths, distichous, rough, and hairy on the lower or on both sides. Flowers produced annually on certain portions of the tree, the other stems remaining leafy. Spikelets spinescent, hairy, collected into dense globose heads on long interrupted spikes.

Common in Northern India, and often gregarious. The leaves become yellow and fall during winter, except in moist places where the tree remains evergreen. The young foliage appears again in the hot weather. The stems die away after flowering. This bamboo is much valued on account of its strong elastic stems, which are used for a variety of purposes. The foliage affords abundant fodder for elephants.

NOTE ON SELECT FODDER GRASSES.

As a guide to those who may wish to know which are the best kinds of fodder grasses to cultivate, or to encourage the growth of, in particular soils and localities, I have selected from the foregoing list a certain number of the more desirable kinds, and have arranged them into groups under the following headings—(1), Those grasses which are generally considered to be of first class excellence for fodder. (2), Fodder grasses which thrive in or near water. (3), Grasses which thrive on black soil; (4), Grasses which are more or less characteristic of saline soils.

1. **First class Fodder Grasses**:—Panicum colonum, *Linn.* (rich ground). P. flavidum, *Retz.* (rich ground). P. frumentaceum, *Roxb.* (cult. ground). P. helopus, *Trin.* (rich ground). P. jumentorum, *Pers.* (cult. ground). P. miliaceum, *Linn.* (cult. ground). P. miliare, *Lamk.* (light culturable ground). P. prostratum, *Lamk.* (rich ground). P. sanguinale, *Linn.* (rich ground). Cenchrus catharticus, *Del.* (sandy soil). C. montanus, *Nees.* (sandy soil). Pennisetum cenchroides, *Rich.* (light culturable soil). Euchlæna luxurians, *Ascheron* (rich moist soil). Zea Mays, *Linn.* (cult. ground). Elionurus hirsutus, *Munro* (sandy soil). Ischæmum laxum, *R. Br.* (sandy soil). Heteropogon contortus, *R. and S.* (hardly to be recommended for cultivation, but wherever it exists in abundance it will be found to be a very serviceable fodder grass). Andropogon annulatus, *Forsk.* (almost any kind of soil). A. foveolatus, *Del.* (stony and sandy ground). A. Ischæmum, *Linn.* (light soil). A. laniger, *Desf.* (sandy soil). A. pertusus, *Willd.* (light soil). Sorghum vulgare, *Pers.* (cult. ground). Iseilema laxum, *Hack.* (heavy clay soil). I. Wightii, *Anders.* (clay soil). Alopecurus pratensis, *Linn.* (rich ground). Sporobolus indicus, *R. Br.* (light soil). Avena sativa, *Linn.* (cult. ground). Cynodon Dactylon, *Pers.* (light soil). Eleusine ægyptiaca, *Pers.* (rich ground). E. flagellifera, *Nees.* (sandy soil). Eragrostis plumosa, *Link.* (sandy soil). Triticum sativum, *Lamk.* (cult. ground). Hordeum vulgare, *Linn.* (cult. ground).

2. **Those kinds which thrive in or near water**:—Paspalum Kora, *Willd.* Eriochloa polystachya, *H. B. and K.* Isachne australis, *R. Br.* Panicum Crus-Galli, *Linn.* P. fluitans, *Retz.* P. Myurus, *Lamk.* P. paludosum, *Roxb.* Coix Lachryma, *Linn.* Hygrorhiza aris-

tata, *Nees.* Leersia hexandra, *Swartz.* Imperata arundinacea, *Cyrill.* Saccharum-spontaneum, *Linn.* Hemarthria compressa, *R. Br.* H. fasciculata, *Kunth.* Ischæmum rugosum, *Gærtn.* Andropogon caricosus, *Linn.* A. muricatus, *Retz.* A. Schœnanthus, *Linn.* Diplachne fusca, *Beauv.* Eragrostis Brownei, *Nees.* E. cynosuroides, *R. and S.* E. elegantula, *Nees.* E. nutans, *Nees.* E. uniloides, *Retz.*

3. **Grasses characteristic of black soil**:—Panicum erucæforme, *Sibth.* and *Sm.* (usually on cultivated ground). P. miliare, *Lamk.* (usually on cultivated ground). Pennisetum holcoides, *Schult.* P. imberbe, *Edgew.* Pollinia argentea, *Trin.* Ophiurus corymbosus, *Gærtn.* Ischæmum ciliare, *Retz.* I. pilosum, *Hack.* Andropogon caricosus, *Linn.* A. pachyarthrus, *Hack.* Anthisteria scandens, *Roxb.* Iseilema laxum, *Hack.* I. Wightii, *Anders.* Dinebra arabica, *Beauv.* Elytrophorus articulatus, *Beauv.* Eragrostis nutans, *Link.*

4. **Grasses which more or less characterize saline soils**:—Andropogon muricatus, *Retz.* (damper parts). Iseilema Wightii, *Anders.* (damper parts). Aristida depressa, *Retz.* (more sandy parts). Sporobolus orientalis, *Kunth.* (usar grass). Cynodon Dactylon, *Pers.* (on the less infected parts). Chloris barbata, *Swartz.* (more sandy parts). Tetropogon villosus, *Desf.* Diplachne fusca, *Beauv.* (damper parts). Eragrostis cynosuroides *R.* and *S.* (damper parts). E. elegantula, *Nees.* (damper parts). E. pilosa, *Beauv.* E. plumosa, *Link.* E. viscosa, *Trin.* Æluropus littoralis, *Parl., var* repens (Punjab).

LIST OF VERNACULAR NAMES.

These names have been collected from various sources; partly from books, such as Roxburgh's "Flora Indica," and Stewart's "Punjab Plants;" a large number were contributed, together with specimens of the grasses to which they refer, by correspondents in various parts of Northern India; the remainder were obtained personally during my tours in Northern and Central India.

With the exception of Roxburgh's names the orthography has, as far as possible, been made to conform to the present recognized rules. There doubtless still remain for correction many errors both of omission and commission, and which I hope to be able by degrees to rectify. The list, however, such as it is, will serve, it is hoped, as a means of identifying the majority of the more important kinds of fodder grasses.

Several of the names given in this list are obviously vague and unsatisfactory, especially as regards nearly allied species, as for instance those belonging to large genera such as *Panicum*, *Andropogon*, and *Eragrostis*.

Special care has been taken in regard to the local names of such kinds as are most useful, whether for fodder or other purposes; and, although the names applied to these are more numerous than in the case of inferior fodder grasses, they are, nevertheless, as a rule, more dependable by reason of the recognized value of such grasses.

Vernacular name.	Botanical name.
A.	
Agi mali gadi, ..	Manisuris granularis, Swartz.
Ak, ..	Saccharum officinarum, Linn.
Amarkarh, ..	Ischæmum rugosum, Gærtn.
Añdho, ..	Pennisetum cenchroides, Rich.
Anjan, ..	Pennisetum cenchroides, Rich.
Anjan, ..	Cenchrus montanus, Nees.
Anne, ..	Panicum miliaceum, Linn.
Aruga, ..	Paspalum Kora, Linn.
Aruga, ..	Paspalum scrobiculatum, Linn.
Arugam-pilla, ..	Cynodon Dactylon, Pers.
Asara, ..	Eragrostis elegantula, Nees.
Asata, ..	Eragrostis Brownei, Nees.
Asauñra, ..	Eragrostis nutans, Nees.
Azkhir, ..	Andropogon laniger, Desf.
B.	
Babbar, ..	Pollinia eriopoda, Hance.
Babhori, ..	Andropogon laniger, Desf.
Babui, ..	Pollinia eriopoda, Hance.
Bachkron, ..	Pollinia eriopoda, Hance.
Badi bhurbhuri, .	Panicum miliare, Lamk.
Bagad, ..	Panicum miliare, Lamk.
Baggar, ..	Pollinia eriopoda, Hance.
Bagnarri, ..	Phargmites Roxburghii, Kunth.
Baib, ..	Pollinia eriopoda, Hance.
Baiba, ..	Pennisetum cenchroides, Rich.
Bájra, ..	Pennisetum typhoideum, Rich.
Bájra, ..	Sorghum halepense, Pers.
Bájra jhupanwa,	Sorghum vulgare, Pers.
Bájra tangunanwa,	Pennisetum typhoideum, Rich.
Bájri, ..	Pennisetum typhoideum, Rich.
Bajuria, ..	Pennisetum imberbe, Edgew.
Balha, ..	Elytrophorus articulatus, Beauv.
Ballak, ..	Chrysopogon montanus, Trin.
Bámna, ..	Chloris Roxburghiana, Edgew.
Bandar puchhi, ..	Perotis latifolia, Ait.
Bandarpuncha, ..	Heteropogon contortus, R. & S.
Bandra, ..	Setaria glauca, Beauv.
Bandri, ..	Setaria glauca, Beauv.
Bandri, ..	Setaria verticillata, Beauv.
Bandri, ..	Pennisetum cenchroides, Rich.
Ban kangni, ..	Setaria glauca, Beauv.
Bankas, ..	Pollinia eriopoda, Hance.
Ban kodo, ..	Paspalum scrobiculatum, Linn.
Ban-kush, ..	Pollinia eriopoda, Hance.
Ban-kutki, ..	Panicum miliare, Lamk.
Báns, ..	Bambusa arundinacea, Retz.
Báns, ..	Dendrocalamus strictus, Nees.
Báñsá, ..	Bambusa arundinacea, Retz.
Báñsa, ..	Eragrostis tremula, Hochst.
Báñsi, ..	Andropogon annulatus, Forsk.
Bañsi, ..	Panicum miliaceum, Linn.
Báñsi, ..	Arundo Donax, Linn.
Báns kabban, ..	Dendrocalamus strictus, Nees.
Bara, ..	Sorghum halepense, Pers.
Bara bhurbhura,	Eragrostis plumosa, Link.
Baraii, ..	Saccharum officinarum, Linn.
Bara juár, ..	Zea Mays, Linn.
Bara sáñwak, ..	Panicum Crus-Galli, Linn.
Bara sarpot, ..	Dinebra arabica, Beauv.
Bara takria, ..	Panicum sanguinale, Linn.
Bara toriya gadi,	Ischæmum ciliare, Retz.
Baráwa, ..	Cynodon Dactylon, Pers.
Barchinte, ..	Tragus racemosus, Hall.
Barchinte choti, ..	Tragus racemosus, Hall.
Barchitta, ..	Setaria verticillata, Beauv.
Bardanni, ..	Setaria verticillata, Beauv.
Bard ghás, ..	Rhynchelytrum Wightii.
Bárdíya, ..	Chloris barbata, Swartz.
Bari gagli, ..	Panicum antidotale, Retz.
Bari junri, ..	Zea Mays, Linn.
Bari bhodore, ..	Panicum Crus-Galli, Linn.
Baro bheru, ..	Andropogon Ischæmum, Linn.

Vernacular name.	Botanical name.
Barru, ..	Sorghum halepense, Pers.
Barsali, ..	Rottbœllia exaltata, Linn. f.
Barti, ..	Setaria verticillata, Beauv.
Baru, ..	Panicum antidotale, Retz.
Baru, ..	Apluda aristata, Linn.
Baru, ..	Sorghum halepense, Pers.
Baru, ..	Coix Lachryma, Linn.
Barwári, ..	Panicum antidotale, Retz.
Barweza, ..	Heteropogon contortus, R. & S.
Basaunta, ..	Panicum helopus, Trin.
Basla, ..	Cenchrus catharticus, Del.
Baunri, ..	Panicum flavidum, Retz.
Behor báns, ..	Bambusa spinosa, Roxb.
Bena, ..	Andropogon muricatus, Retz.
Bena-joni, ..	Sporobolus diander, Beauv.
Bhábar, ..	Pollinia eriopoda, Hance.
Bhabar, ..	Pollinia eriopoda, Hance.
Bhajura, ..	Apluda aristata, Linn.
Bhamiri, ..	Eragrostis tremula, Hochst.
Bhaṅgri, ..	Apluda aristata, Linn
Bhañjura, ..	Apluda aristata, Linn.
Bhañjuri, ..	Apluda aristata, Linn.
Bhankta, ..	Apluda aristata, Linn.
Bhar bhunt, ..	Cenchrus catharticus, Del.
Bharbhuri, ..	Eragrostis tenella, Beauv.
Bharbhuri, ..	Eragrostis plumosa, Link.
Bharbhusi bara, ..	Eragrostis plumosa, Link.
Bhar-haria, ..	Eragrostis ciliaris, Link., *var.* brachystachya.
Bharo-bheru, ..	Andropogon Ischæmum, Linn.
Bharont, ..	Cenchrus catharticus, Del.
Bharta, ..	Panicum Crus-Galli, Linn.
Bharti, ..	Panicum flavidum, Retz.
Bharti, ..	Panicum Crus-Galli, Linn.
Bharu, ..	Eleusine flagellifera, Nees.
Bharua, ..	Anthistiria arundinacea, Roxb.
Bhobra, ..	Eleusine scindica, Duthie.
Bhodore, ..	Ischæmum ciliare, Retz., *var.* villosum.
Bholoni, ..	Eragrostis plumosa, Link.
Bhor, ..	Andropogon Schœnanthus, Linn.
Bhoru, ..	Anthistiria scandens, Roxb.
Bhulni, ..	Eragrostis viscosa, Trin.
Bhulwa, ..	Eragrostis elegantula, Nees.
Bhurbhur, ..	Eragrostis viscosa, Trin.
Bhurbhusi, ..	Eragrostis viscosa, Trin.
Bhurbusi, ..	Eragrostis plumosa, Link.
Bhurt, ..	Cenchrus catharticus, Del.
Bhus, ..	Chionachne barbata, R. Br.
Bhus jari, ..	Apluda aristata, Linn.
Bikhonda, ..	Sorghum halepense, Pers.
Biksa, ..	Hemarthria fasciculata, Kunth.
Bilaria kandi, ..	Andropogon caricosus, Linn.
Billi, ..	Setaria glauca, Beauv.
Bind, ..	Saccharum ciliare, Anders.
Bir, ..	Bambusa spinosa, Roxb..
Biran, ..	Andropogon muricatus, Retz.
Bir-kanni, ..	Setaria verticillata, Beauv.
Boári, ..	Andropogon foveolatus, Del.
Bobriya, ..	Eleusine scindica, Duthie.
Bonta, ..	Apluda aristata, Linn.
Bonta-shama, ..	Panicum frumentaceum, Roxb.
Boruti, ..	Panicum paludosum, Roxb.
Botya-jhara, ..	Chloris barbata, Swartz.
Braham, ..	Sorghum halepense, Pers.
Budhan, ..	Sporobolus pallidus, Nees.
Budhan, ..	Eragrostis plumosa, Retz.
Budhar, ..	Sporobolus pallidus, Nees.
Bujera, ..	Pennisetum typhoideum, Rich.
Bujra, ..	Pennisetum typhoideum, Rich.
Buksha, ..	Hemarthria compressa, R. Br.
Bur, ..	Andropogon laniger, Desf.
Bura-jál-ganti, ..	Panicum helopus, Trin.
Bura-shama, ..	Panicum Crus-Galli, Linn.
Bura-swooate, ..	Rottbœllia exaltata, Linn. f.
Buru lukui ghás, ..	Arundinella, sp.
Buru mat, ..	Dendrocalamus strictus, Nees.
Buttam gadí, ..	Panicum colonum, Linn.
C.	
Chaen, ..	Eragrostis ciliaris, Link. *var.* brachystachya.
Chaj-já-gadi, ..	Pennisetum imberbe, Edgew.
Chák, ..	Hordeum vulgare, Linn.
Chakkarnittagadi,	Setaria verticillata, Beauv.
Chambar, ..	Perotis latifolia, Ait.
Chambu, ..	Pennisetum typhoideum, Rich.
Champ, ..	Iseilema laxum, Hack.
Chanda mama gadi	Eragrostis uniloides, Nees.
Chánhel, ..	Leptochloa chinensis, Nees.
Chankan buti, ..	Eragrostis tremula, Hochst.
Chápar, ..	Panicum Petiverii, Trin.
Chapraila, ..	Panicum helopus, Trin.
Chaprur, ..	Panicum Petiverii, Trin.
Chaprura, ..	Panicum Petiverii, Trin.
Chapruro, ..	Andropogon pertusus, Willd.
Chari, ..	Sorghum vulgare, Pers.
Charmara, ..	Panicum sanguinale, Linn.
Charwa, ..	Pennisetum cenchroides, Rich.
Chatta, ..	Panicum colonum, Linn.
Chatta, ..	Panicum helopus, Trin.
Chaurila, ..	Panicum prostratum, Lamk.
Chemri, ..	Eleusine flagellifera, Nees.
Chena, ..	Panicum miliaceum, Linn.
Cherukoo-bodi, ..	Saccharum officinarum, Linn.
Cherukoo-duboo,	Saccharum officinarum, Linn.
Chhat, ..	Iseilema laxum, Hack.
Chhembhar, ..	Eleusine flagellifera, Nees.
Chhenbri, ..	Eleusine flagellifera, Nees.
Chhimbar, ..	Eleusine flagellifera, Nees.
Chhiñchra, ..	Setaria glauca, Beauv.
Chhinke, ..	Panicum ciliare, Retz.
Chhinki, ..	Eleusine verticillata, Beauv.
Chhinkri, ..	Chloris barbata, Swartz.
Chichohi, ..	Panicum colonum, Linn.
Chichwi, ..	Panicum flavidum, Retz.
Chicklenta, ..	Setaria verticillata, Beauv.
Chikára, ..	Eleusine ægyptiaca, Pers.
Chikhari, ..	Panicum sanguinale, Linn.
Chikna bara, ..	Setaria verticillata, Beauv.
Chikti, ..	Eragrostis viscosa, Trin.
Chilaya, ..	Setaria verticillata, Beauv.
Chima kál gadi, ..	Oplismenus Burmanni, Linn.
Chin, ..	Panicum miliare, Lamk.
China, ..	Panicum miliaceum, Linn.

Vernacular name.	Botanical name.
Chinda mámá gadi	Eragrostis uniloides, Nees.
Chini,	Paspalum Royleanum, Nees.
Chinke,	Paspalum Kora, Linn.
Chinwa,	Panicum miliaceum, Linn.
Chinwári,	Panicum erucæforme, Sibth. & Sm.
Chipa chima gadi,	Leptochloa filiformis, R. & S.
Chipara,	Andropogon Schœnanthus, Linn.
Chippal,	Eragrostis viscosa, Trin.
Chir,	Eragrostis Brownei, Nees.
Chir,	Eragrostis cynosuroides, R. & S.
Chirchira,	Setaria verticillata, Beauv.
Chirchitta,	Setaria verticillata, Beauv.
Chiri-chira,	Paspalum pedicellatum, Nees.
Chiri ka chanwalia,	Eragrostis tremula, Hochst.
Chiri ka khet,	Eragrostis tremula, Hochst.
Chiri ka khet,	Eragrostis plumosa, Link.
Chiri ko bajro,	Eragrostis plumosa, Link.
Chiriya chaina,	Setaria intermedia, R. & S.
Chiriya ke chaolai,	Eragrostis megastachya, Link.
Chiriya ka dána,	Eragrostis pilosa, Beauv.
Chiriya ka dána,	Sporobolus diander, Beauv.
Chirrya,	Andropogon pertusus, Willd.
Chirua,	Poa annua, Linn.
Chirwa,	Panicum miliaceum, Linn.
Chitra,	Polypogon monspeliensis, Desf.
Chiurr,	Setaria italica, Kunth.
Cholum,	Sorghum vulgare, Pers.
Chora-kánta,	Chrysopogon aciculatus, Trin.
Chota asara,	Eragrostis elegantula, Nees.
Chota bhánkta,	Eragrostis bifaria, W. & A.
Chota chikiya,	Setaria intermedia, R. & S.
Chota kusal,	Pollinia argentea, Trin.
Chota loniya,	Eragrostis uniloides, Nees.
Chota mandiya,	Eleusine ægyptiaca, Pers.
Chota piya.	Andropogon pertusus, Willd.
Chota sarsata,	Setaria intermedia, R. & S.
Chotiáli,	Ischæmum ciliare, Retz., *var.* villosum.
Choti juár,	Sorghum vulgare, Pers.
Choti junri,	Sorghum vulgare, Pers.
Choti khidi,	Eragrostis Brownei, Nees.
Choti parba,	Aristida depressa, Retz.
Choti semai,	Panicum prostratum, Lamk.
Chotæ,	Ophiurus corymbosus, Gærtn.
Chubrei,	Eleusine flagellifera, Nees.
Chubrei,	Eleusine ægyptiaca, Pers.
Chudur jabara,	Anthistiria ciliata, Linn. f.
Chung,	Hordeum vulgare, Linn.
Chusa,	Oplismenus Burmanni, Linn.

D.

Vernacular name.	Botanical name.
Dáb,	Imperata arundinacea.
Dáb,	Eragrostis cynosuroides, R. & S.
Dab,	Eragrostis cynosuroides, R. & S.
Dabhat,	Eragrostis cynosuroides, R. & S.
Dabhir,	Coix Lachryma, Linn.
Dabsulo,	Andropogon laniger, Desf.
Dabvi,	Eragrostis cynosuroides, R. & S.
Dang rhauns,	Andropogon Schœnanthus, Linn.
Danga gurgur,	Coix gigantea, Kœn.
Dangara,	Oryza sativa, Linn.
Darbha,	Eragrostis cynosuroides, R. & S.
Datia,	Panicum Crus-Galli, Linn. *var.*
Datunya,	Chloris sp.
Davolia,	Eragrostis cynosuroides, Retz.
Dein,	Oryza sativa, Linn.
Deodhán,	Oryza sativa, Linn.
Deonal,	Phragmites Roxburghii, Kunth.
Deonál,	Phragmites Roxburghii, Kunth.
Detara,	Andropogon caricosus, Linn.
Detta,	Andropogon caricosus, Linn.
Dhab,	Eragrostis cynosuroides, R. & S.
Dháman,	Pennisetum cenchroides, Rich.
Dháman,	Tragus racemosus, Hall.
Dháman,	Cenchrus montanus, Nees.
Dhamman,	Pennisetum cenchroides, Rich.
Dhamman,	Cenchrus montanus, Nees.
Dhamsiria,	Panicum Myurus, Lamk.
Dhand,	Panicum Crus-Galli, Linn.
Dhanera,	Panicum flavidum, Retz.
Dhanna,	Ischæmum rugosum, Gærtn.
Dhaturo ghás,	Manisuris granularis, Swartz.
Dhaula,	Chrysopogon cœruleus, Nees.
Dhaulian,	Chrysopogon cœruleus, Nees.
Dhidhina,	Panicum myosuroides, R. Br.
Dhobi ghás,	Cynodon Dactylon, Pers.
Dholu,	Erianthus Ravennæ, Beauv.
Dhupsa,	Cynodon Dactylon, Pers.
Dhusa,	Setaria glauca, Beauv.
Dib,	Eragrostis cynosuroides, R. & S.
Dila,	Phragmites communis, Trin.
Dissi,	Setaria glauca, Beauv.
Dob,	Cynodon Dactylon, Pers.
Dobra,	Panicum ciliare, Retz.
Donda,	Andropogon annulatus, Forsk.
Doorba,	Cynodon Dactylon, Pers.
Doosa,	Panicum fluitans, Retz.
Dora byara,	Setaria verticillata, Beauv.
Dráb,	Eragrostis cynosuroides, R. & S.
Drábh,	Eragrostis cynosuroides, R. & S.
Dro,	Triticum sativum, Lamk.
Drumbi,	Phragmites Roxburghii, Kunth.
Dub,	Cynodon Dactylon, Pers.
Dúba,	Cynodon Dactylon, Pers.
Dúbha,	Eragrostis cynosuroides, R. & S.
Dúbra,	Panicum sanguinale, Linn.
Dúbra,	Eleusine flagellifera, Nees.
Dubra,	Cynodon Dactylon, Pers.
Dul,	Panicum Crus-Galli, Linn.
Dúnda,	Andropogon annulatus, Forsk.
Durbachi,	Andropogon muricatus, Retz.

Vernacular name.	Botanical name.
Durbha, ..	Eragrostis cynosuroides, R. & S.
Durhi ghás, ..	Apluda aristata, Linn.
Durpa, ..	Eragrostis cynosuroides, R. & S.
Durva, ..	Cynodon Dactylon, Pers.
Dwárena, ..	Phragmites Roxburghii, Kunth.
E.	
Eraj tukra jari, ..	Themeda Forskalii, Hack., *var.* major.
Era-kolla gadi, ..	Anthistiria scandens, Roxb.
Era kore gadi, ..	Dimeria ornithopoda, Trin.
Erba, ..	Setaria italica, Kunth.
G.	
Gádar puchha, ..	Setaria verticillata, Beauv.
Gádar punch, ..	Eragrostis pilosa, Beauv.
Gadha charwa, ..	Eleusine indica, Gærtn.
Gadha mandwi, ..	Eleusine indica, Gærtn.
Gal, ..	Setaria italica, Kunth.
Galgala, ..	Eragrostis plumosa, Link.
Galla jári, ..	Sorghum halepense, Pers.
Galphula, ..	Panicum helopus, Trin.
Galphula, ..	Sporobolus diander, Beauv
Ganaiya, ..	Anthistiria scandens, Roxb.
Gandal, ..	Avena fatua, Linn.
Gandar, ..	Andropogon muricatus, Retz.
Gandel,	Andropogon laniger, Desf. / Iseilema Wightii, Anders.
Gandel, ..	Andropogon muricatus, Retz.
Gandel, ..	Ophiurus lævis, Benth.
Gánder, ..	Andropogon muricatus, Retz.
Gander, ..	Andropogon laniger, Desf.
Gándhi, ..	Iseilema laxum, Hack.
Gandhi, ..	Apluda aristata, Linn.
Gandhi, ..	Iseilema laxum, Hack.
Gandhi, ..	Andropogon laniger, Desf.
Gandi, ..	Andropogon Schœnanthus, Linn.
Gandi, ..	Chloris barbata, Swartz.
Gándi, ..	Iseilema laxum, Hack.
Gándli, ..	Pollinia argentea, Trin.
Ganer, ..	Avena fatua, Linn.
Gangerua, ..	Andropogon pachyarthrus, Hack.
Ganhel, ..	Avena fatua, Linn.
Ganna, ..	Saccharum officinarum, Linn.
Ganni, ..	Iseilema Wightii, Anders.
Ganni, ..	Apluda aristata, Linn.
Ganni, ..	Chloris barbata, Swartz.
Ganori, ..	Anthistiria scandens, Roxb.
Gánrár, ..	Andropogon muricatus, Retz.
Ganrar, ..	Andropogon muricatus, Retz.
Gánth dob, ..	Eleusine flagellifera, Nees.
Ganthia, ..	Eleusine flagellifera, Nees.
Ganthil, ..	Eleusine flagellifera, Nees.
Garar, ..	Andropogon muricatus, Retz.
Garri, ..	Oryza sativa, Linn.
Gathil, ..	Eleusine flagellifera, Nees.
Gau, ..	Triticum sativum, Lamk.
Gavung, ..	Chloris barbata, Swartz.
Gáwa, ..	Panicum colonum, Linn.
Gawán, ..	Apluda aristata, Linn.
Gawán, ..	Elionurus hirsutus, Munro.
Gehun, ..	Triticum sativum, Lamk.
Gendar, ..	Anthistiria scandens, Roxb.
Genehru, ..	Anthistiria scandens, Roxb.
Ghamur, ..	Panicum antidotale, Retz.
Ghamrur, ..	Panicum antidotale, Retz.
Gharam, ..	Panicum antidotale, Retz.
Ghella-gadee, ..	Chionachne barbata, R. Br.
Ghericha, ..	Cynodon Dactylon, Pers.
Ghirri, ..	Panicum antidotale, Retz.
Ghodchabba, ..	Eleusine indica, Gærtn.
Ghodila, ..	Eragrostis nutans, Nees.
Ghonadi, ..	Anthistiria scandens, Roxb.
Ghonál, ..	Anthistiria scandens, Roxb.
Ghonyár, ..	Anthistiria scandens, Roxb.
Ghorayal, ..	Iseilema laxum, Hack.
Ghorchubba, ..	Oplismenus Burmanni, Linn.
Ghorila, ..	Eragrostis nutans, Nees.
Ghorla, ..	Sporobolus indicus, R. Br.
Ghor masán, ..	Iseilema Wightii, Anders.
Ghua, ..	Saccharum ciliare, Anders.,
Ghui, ..	Eragrostis nutans, Nees.
Ghunhair, ..	Anthistiria scandens, Roxb.
Ghurdub, ..	Eleusine flagillifera, Nees.
Ghwarga, ..	Phragmites Roxburghii, Kunth.
Ghweia, ..	Chrysopogon cœruleus, Nees.
Ghyán, ..	Aristida depressa, Retz.
Ghyáni, ..	Aristida depressa, Retz.
Girgua, ..	Andropogon foveolatus, Del.
Girji, ..	Andropogon foveolatus, Del.
Girji, ..	Andropogon pertusus, Willd.
Girri, ..	Rhynchelytrum Wightii.
Girui, ..	Panicum antidotale, Retz.
Gohhaya, ..	Andropogon pertusus, Willd.
Gohun, ..	Triticum sativum, Lamk.
Gom, ..	Triticum sativum, Lamk.
Gomej-ko-kutki,	Panicum miliare, Lamk.
Gonchi, ..	Pollinia argentea, Trin.
Gonda, ..	Iseilema laxum, Hack.
Gondalli, ..	Anthistiria ciliata, Linn. f.
Goroma, ..	Apluda aristata, Linn.
Gozang, ..	Avena fatua, Linn.
Gudda-niko-gadi,	Themeda Forskalii, Hack., *var.* major.
Gugar gadi, ..	Apluda aristata, Linn.
Guhera, ..	Ischæmum ciliare, Retz.
Guhria, ..	Panicum erucæforme, Sibth.
Gulbi gadi, ..	Coix Lachryma, Linn.
Gulu, ..	Coix Lachryma, Linn.
Gundha-bena, ..	Andropogon Schœnanthus, Linn.
Gundha goorana,	Andropogon glaber, Roxb.
Gundhi, ..	Panicum miliare, Lamk.
Guner, ..	Anthistiria scandens, Roxb.
Gunthya, ..	Eleusine scindica, Duthie.
Gurcháwa, ..	Eleusine indica, Gærtn.
Gurgi, ..	Coix Lachryma, Linn.
Gurgur, ..	Coix Lachryma, Linn.
Gurgur, ..	Chionachne barbata, R. Br.
Gurlu, ..	Coix Lachryma, Linn.
Gurra gadi, ..	Eleusine indica, Gærtn.

Vernacular name.	Botanical name.
H.	
Hál,	Oryza sativa, Linn.
Harala,	Cynodon Dactylon, Pers.
Hariáli,	Cynodon Dactylon, Pers.
Haryeli,	Cynodon Dactylon, Pers.
Hen,	Panicum sanguinale, Linn.
Hika gadi,	Chloris Roxburghiana, Edgew.
Hirn,	Ischæmum laxum, R. Br.
Homa,	Panicum flavidum, Retz.
Horo,	Oryza sativa, Linn.
Hukara gadi,	Heteropogon contortus, R. & S.
Hurwal,	Heteropogon contortus, R. & S.
Hutia,	Andropogon tropicus, Spreng.
I.	
Ibharankusha,	Andropogon Schœnanthus, Linn.
Ichkoch,	Eragrostis uniloides, Nees.
Ichkoi,	Eragrostis tenella, Beauv.
Ikh,	Saccharum officinarum, Linn.
Ikhári,	Saccharum officinarum, Linn.
Iwarankusha,	Andropogon Schœnanthus, Linn.
J.	
Jab,	Hordeum vulgare, Linn.
Jai,	Avena sativa, Linn.
Jal-ganti,	Panicum helopus, Trin.
Jalgundya,	Ischæmum rugosum, Gærtn.
Jaljatang jhara,	Setaria verticillata, Beauv.
Jandel,	Avena fatua, Linn.
Janewa,	Andropogon pertusus, Willd.
Janewa,	Andropogon Ischæmum, Linn.
Janewar,	Andropogon annulatus, Forsk.
Jangli malicha,	Eleusine scindica, Duthie.
Jangli sámak,	Panicum colonum, Linn.
Jangli sáṅwak,	Panicum colonum, Linn.
Janhe,	Paspalum scrobiculatum, Linn.
Janoo,	Sorghum vulgare, Pers.
Jarámkush,	Andropogon laniger, Desf.
Jarga,	Andropogon annulatus, Forsk.
Jarga,	Andropogon Ischæmum, Linn.
Jargadi,	Coix Lachryma, Linn.
Jargi,	Chloris barbata, Swartz.
Jarota,	Panicum Crus-Galli, Linn.
Jau,	Hordeum vulgare, Linn.
Jaudal,	Avena fatua, Linn.
Jav,	Hordeum vulgare, Linn.
Jawa,	Hordeum vulgare, Linn.
Jawi,	Avena sativa, Linn.
Jei,	Avena fatua, Linn.
Jenkua,	Eragrostis cilaris, Link., *var.*
Jhangora,	Panicum frumentaceum, Roxb.
Jharai,	Panicum colonum, Linn.
Jharna,	Eleusine verticillata, Roxb.
Jharna,	Chloris barbata, Swartz.
Jhingri,	Eleusine indica, Gærtn.
Jhingri ka jhara,	Chrysopogon cœruleus, Nees.
Jhira,	Leptochloa filiformis, R. & S.
Jhotak,	Hordeum vulgare, Linn.
Jhungara,	Panicum frumentaceum, Roxb.
Jhusa,	Eragrostis plumosa, Link.
Jiral,	Pennisetum holcoides, Schult.
Joár,	Sorghum vulgare, Pers.
Joona,	Zea Mays, Linn.
Jouar,	Zea Mays, Linn.
Joudra,	Zea Mays, Linn.
Juár,	Sorghum vulgare, Pers.
Juba,	Hordeum vulgare, Linn.
Jud-jhara	Apluda aristata, Linn.
Junglee dal,	Hygrorhiza aristata, Nees.
Junjhli,	Andropogon foveolatus, Del.
Junri,	Sorghum vulgare, Pers.
Jyotishmati,	Anthistiria anathera, Nees.
K.	
Kabdai,	Panicum ciliare, Retz.
Kachi gadi,	Andropogon intermedius, Br., *var.* genuina.
Kadpi,	Chionachne barbata, R. Br.
Kagara,	Saccharum spontaneum, Linn.
Kágya,	Chloris tenella, Roxb.
Káhi,	Saccharum spontaneum, Linn.
Kahu,	Saccharum spontaneum, Linn.
Kajooli,	Saccharum officinarum, Linn.
Kakariya,	Eleusine indica, Gærtn.
Kákni,	Setaria italica, Kunth.
Kákun,	Setaria italica, Kunth.
Kála,	Ischæmum ciliare, Retz.
Kalgehun,	Avena fatua, Linn.
Kalia,	Tetrapogon villosus, Desf.
Káli ghás,	Cynodon Dactylon, Pers.
Kalla báṅs,	Bambusa arundinacea, Retz.
Kaluargi,	Eragrostis elegantula, Nees.
Kalunji,	Eragrostis tremula, Hochst.
Kálusra,	Sporobolus orientalis, Kunth.
Kamád,	Saccharum officinarum, Linn.
Kamánd,	Saccharum officinarum, Linn.
Kámrori,	Heteropogon contortus, R. & S.
Kán,	Saccharum spontaneum, Linn.
Kána,	Saccharum ciliare, Anders.
Kanak,	Triticum sativum, Lamk.
Kanda,	Saccharum Sara, Roxb.
Kangna,	Panicum flavidum, Retz.
Kangni,	Manisurus granularis, Swartz.
Kangni,	Setaria italica, Kunth.
Kangsi,	Eleusine verticillata, Roxb.
Kangua,	Anthistiria arundinacea, Roxb.
Káṅh,	Saccharum spontaneum, Linn.
Kanka gadi,	Spodiopogon albidus, Benth.
Káṅs,	Saccharum spontaneum, Linn.
Kaṅsa,	Saccharum spontaneum, Linn.
Káṅsi,	Saccharum spontaneum, Linn.
Kanwar,	Saccharum Sara, Roxb.
Karar gaṅdhel dungarko,	Iseilema laxum, Hack.
Kard gaṅdhel,	Andropogon, foveolatus, Del.
Karela,	Paspalum Royleana, Nees.
Karka,	Phragmites Roxburghii, Kunth.
Kark-madhána,	Eleusine ægyptiaca, Pers.
Kar madhána,	Eleusine ægyptiaca, Pers.
Karno,	Sporobolus pallidus, Nees.
Karr,	Andropogon annulatus, Forsk.
Karsar,	Thysanolæna acarifera, Nees.
Kartál,	Sorghum halepense, Pers.

Vernacular name.	Botanical name.	Vernacular name.	Botanical name.
Kar usara ghás,..	Sporobolus orientalis, Kunth.	Kodela, ..	Paspalum scrobiculatum, Linn.
Kasa-jonar, ..	Sorghum vulgare, Pers.	Kodeli, ..	Paspalum scrobiculatum, Linn.
Kásamm, ..	Avena fatua, Linn.	Kodo, ..	Paspalum scrobiculatum, Linn.
Kasei, ..	Coix Lachryma, Linn.	Kodoṅ, ..	Paspalum scrobiculatum, Linn.
Kasi gadi, ..	Andropogon intermedius, Br. *var*. genuinus.	Kodoṅ, ..	Eleusine coracana, Gærtn.
Katari, ..	Saccharum officinarum, Linn.	Kodra, ..	Paspalum scrobiculatum, Linn.
Katki, ..	Panicum humile, Nees.	Kodra, ..	Eleusine coracana, Gærtn.
Kattang báṅs, ..	Bambusa arundinacea, Retz.	Kodrám, ..	Paspalum scrobiculatum, Linn.
Kattingiya sufed,	Apluda aristata, Linn.		
Kaudi, ..	Pollinia argentea, Trin.	Kodu, ..	Paspalum Kora, Linn.
Kauni, ..	Setaria italica, Kunth.	Kohdi, ..	Anthistiria anathera, Nees.
Kesai, ..	Coix gigantea, Kœn.	Kokuna, ..	Tetrapogon villosus, Desf.
Kewai, ..	Panicum sanguinale, Linn.	Kolhati, ..	Elytrophorus articulatus, Beauv.
Kewai, ..	Panicum ciliare, Retz.		
Khabbal, ..	Cynodon Dactylon, Pers.	Konda, ..	Sorghum vulgare, Pers.
Khabbar, ..	Cynodon Dactylon, Pers.	Konda panookoo,	Rottbœllia exaltata, Linn. f.
Khajuria, ..	Eragrostis nutans, Nees.	Konee, ..	Eragrostis uniloides, Nees.
Khagar, ..	Saccharum spontaneum, Linn.	Koori chinke, ..	Eleusine verticillata, Roxb.
Khair, ..	Andropogon laniger, Desf.	Koosha, ..	Eragrostis cynosuroides, R. & S.
Khar, ..	Chrysopogon cœruleus, Nees.		
Khar, ..	Heteropogon contortus, R. & S.	Kooshiar, ..	Saccharum officinarum, Linn.
Kharang, ..	Aristida, sp.	Kopar, ..	Dendrocalamus strictus, Nees.
Khari, ..	Eragrostis Brownei, Nees.	Kora, ..	Paspalum Kora, Linn.
Kharimbar, ..	Eleusine flagellifera, Nees.	Kora, .	Setaria italica, Kunth.
Khar jhara, ..	Andropogon intermedius, Br. *var*. genuinus.	Kore gadi, ..	Saccharum spontaneum, Linn.
		Korkol jodi, ..	Panicum sanguinale, Linn.
Khasil, ..	Triticum sativum, Lamk.	Korra gadi, ..	Andropogon gangeticus, Hack.
Khas khas, ..	Andropogon muricatus, Retz.	Kosa, ..	Saccharum spontaneum, Linn.
Khávi, ..	Andropogon laniger, Desf.	Kotu, ..	Setaria glauca, Beauv.
Khawi, ..	Andropogon laniger, Desf.	Kowain, ..	Panicum helopus, Trin.
Khawid, ..	Triticum sativum, Lamk.	Krer, ..	Pollinia argentea, Trin.
Khel, ..	Andropogon annulatus, Forsk.	Kudda jári, ..	Paspalum scrobiculatum, Linn.
Kheo, ..	Sporobolus orientalis, Kunth.	Kudpal, ..	Paspalum scrobiculatum, Linn.
Kher, ..	Heteropogon contortus, R. & S.	Kukar, ..	Cenchrus catharticus, Del.
Kher, ..	Setaria italica, Kunth.	Kukra, ..	Setaria glauca, Beauv.
Kheral, ..	Andropogon caricosus, Linn.	Kukri, ..	Zea Mays, Linn.
Khera madhána, .	Tetrapogon villosus, Desf.	Kuljud, ..	Avena fatua, Linn.
Khermakra, ..	Eleusine ægyptiaca, Pers.	Kullooa, ..	Saccharum officinarum, Linn.
Khet kapuri, ..	Elytrophorus articulatus, Beauv.	Kuluku, ..	Setaria glauca, Beauv.
		Kulus-nar, ..	Panicum paludosum, Roxb.
Khidi, ..	Chrysopogon cœruleus, Nees.	Kunch, ..	Coix Lachryma, Linn.
Khir, ..	Sporobolus indicus, R. Br.	Kunda buttam gadi, ..	Panicum Crus-Galli, Linn.
Khori, ..	Saccharum semidecumbens, Roxb.	Kundh, ..	Ischæmum pilosum, Hack.
Khurásh, ..	Panicum sanguinale, Linn.	Kungoo, ..	Setaria italica, Kunth.
Khuree, ..	Saccharum semidecumbens, Roxb.	Kunura, ..	Heteropogon contortus, R. & S.
		Kurankusha, ..	Andropogon Schœnanthus, Linn.
Khuree,	Miscanthus fuscus, Anders.		
Kilat, ..	Miscanthus fuscus, Anders.	Kura tuka gadi, ..	Panicum flavidum, Retz.
Killa, ..	Andropogon pertusus, Willd.	Kuri, ..	Panicum helopus, Trin.
Killa-machhar, ..	Andropogon caricosus, Linn.	Kuri chinke, ..	Eleusine verticillata, Roxb.
Kirma giláram gadi, ..	Chionachne barbata, R. Br.	Kuriya, ..	Panicum helopus, Trin.
		Kurkán, ..	Pennisetum cenchroides, Rich.
Koda, ..	Paspalum scrobiculatum, Linn.	Kurki, ..	Ophiurus lævis, Benth.
		Kuror, ..	Eleusine indica, Gærtn.
Koda, ..	Eleusine coracana, Gærtn.	Kús, ..	Eragrostis cynosuroides, R. & S.
Koda gadi, ..	Paspalum scrobiculatum, Linn.		
Koda johor, ..	Andropogon intermedius, *var*. punctatus.	Kusa, ..	Imperata arundinacea, Cyrill.
		Kusa, ..	Eragrostis cynosuroides, R. & S.
Kodda gadi, ..	Paspalum scrobiculatum, Linn.	Kusa, ..	Pennisetum cenchroides, Rich.
Kodda jari, ..	Paspalum scrobiculatum, Linn.	Kusal, ..	Heteropogon contortus, R. & S.
		Kusal, ..	Heteropogon contortus, R. & S.
Kode, ..	Eleusine coracana, Gærtn.	Kusáli, ..	Heteropogon contortus, R. & S.

Vernacular name.	Botanical name.
Kush, ..	Eragrostis cynosuroides, R. & S.
Kusha, ..	Eragrostis cynosuroides, R. & S.
Kusht, ..	Setaria italica, Kunth.
Kussab, ..	Dendrocalamus strictus, Nees.
Kutaki, ..	Eragrostis pilosa, Beauv.
Kutki, ..	Panicum miliare, Lamk.
Kutra, ..	Eleusine coracana, Gærtn.
Kutta, ..	Setaria verticillata, Beauv.
Kutta bari, ..	Setaria verticillata, Beauv.
Kutta choti, ..	Setaria glauca, Beauv.
Kutti pushli, ..	Eragrostis nutans, Nees.
L.	
Lahoria, ..	Eragrostis uniloides, Nees.
Lahra, ..	Pennisetum typhoideum, Rich.
Lál báli, ..	Eragrostis nutans, Nees.
Lál kusal, ..	Andropogon fastigiatus, Sw. *var.*
Lál rámpla, ..	Aristida, sp.
Lam, ..	Aristida depressa, Retz.
Lamb, ..	Aristida depressa, Retz.
Lamb, ..	Heteropogon contortus, R. & S.
Lamba, ..	Aristida depressa, Retz.
Lamchá, ..	Eragrostis nutans, Nees.
Lam'e, ..	Aristida depressa, Retz.
Lámp, ..	Aristida depressa, Retz.
Lámp, ..	Aristida hystrix, Linn. f.
Lamp, ..	Heteropogon contortus, R. & S.
Lampa, ..	Heteropogon contortus, R. & S.
Lámpla dhauli, ..	Aristida hystrix, Linn. f.
Lampor, ..	Heteropogon contortus, R. & S.
Lap, ..	Heteropogon contortus, R. & S.
Lápra dhaula, ..	Stipa, sp.
Lápri dhauli, ..	Aristida hystrix, Linn. f.
Lappa, ..	Aristida depressa, Retz.
Láppa, ..	Aristida hystrix, Linn. f.
Lapta, ..	Cenchrus catharticus, Del.
Laptáwa, ..	Setaria verticillata, Beauv.
Lapti, ..	Setaria verticillata, Beauv.
Laraiya, ..	Pennisetum holcoides, Schult.
Layo gundli, ..	Panicum antidotale, Retz.
Lendha, ..	Pennisetum typhoideum, Rich.
Lijhar, ..	Eleusine indica, Gærtn.
Liyum gadi, ..	Pollinia argentea, Trin.
Liyur gadi, ..	Andropogon fastigiatus, Sw.
Lodi gadi, ..	Panicum indicum, Linn.
Lohiya, ..	Leptochloa filiformis, R. & S.
Loidau sarpot, ..	Panicum erucæforme, Sibth.
Loidau siput, ..	Panicum erucæforme, Sibth.
Lonák, ..	Aristida plumosa, Linn.
Loniya, ..	Eragrostis uniloides, Nees.
Luinji, ..	Iseilema laxum, Hack.
Lukki, ..	Eragrostis tremula, Hochst.
Lukui, ..	Pogonatherum saccharoideum, Beauv.
Lumra, ..	Eragrostis nutans, Nees.
Lundi, ..	Setaria intermedia, R. & S.
M.	
Machauri, ..	Iseilema laxum, Hack.
Madanya, ..	Eleusine indica, Gærtn.
Madhána, ..	Eleusine ægyptiaca, Pers.
Magar báns, ..	Bambusa arundinacea, Retz.
Maggru gadi, ..	Ischæmum rugosum, Gærtn.
Majori, ..	Saccharum ciliare, Anders.
Makamakna, ..	Eleusine ægyptiaca, Pers.
Makaraila, ..	Eleusine indica, Gærtn.
Makai, ..	Zea Mays, Linn.
Makka, ..	Zea Mays, Linn.
Makki, ..	Zea Mays, Linn.
Makur-jalee, ..	Panicum ciliare, Retz.
Makur-jali, ..	Eleusine ægyptiaca, Pers.
Maknala, ..	Panicum prostratum, Lamk.
Makora, ..	Andropogon Schœnanthus, Linn.
Makra, ..	Eleusine coracana, Gærtn.
Makra, ..	Eleusine ægyptiaca, Gærtn.
Makrai, ..	Zea Mays, Linn.
Málakaya, ..	Adropogon pachyarthrus, Hack.
Mal-ankuri ..	Eleusine indica, Gærtn.
Male, ..	Panicum antidotale, Retz.
Malhar, ..	Polypogon monspeliensis, Desf.
Malhar, ..	Andropogon pertusus, Willd.
Malicha, ..	Eleusine ægyptiaca, Pers.
Máliyar, ..	Andropogon annulatus, Forsk.
Maljhanji, ..	Dinebra arabica, Beauv.
Málka phalka, ..	Andropogon pachyarthrus, Hack.
Malwa jari, G., ..	Iseilema laxum, Hack.
Manchi malwa gadi, ..	Iseilema laxum, Hack.
Mandal, ..	Eleusine coracana, Gærtn.
Mandiál jori, ..	Eleusine indica, Gærtn.
Mandiya, ..	Panicum ciliare, Retz.
Mandjiro, ..	Eleusine scindica, Duthie.
Mandua, ..	Eleusine coracana, Gærtn.
Mandusi, ..	Polypogon monspeliensis, Desf.
Mandwa, ..	Eleusine coracana, Gærtn.
Mandwa, ..	Eleusine indica, Gærtn.
Mangrur, ..	Panicum antidotale, Retz.
Mansa, ..	Eleusine ægyptiaca, Gærtn.
Maror, ..	Ischæmum rugosum, Gærtn.
Mársi, ..	Paspalum scrobiculatum, Linn.
Marua, ..	Eleusine coracana, Gærtn.
Marudi, ..	Ischæmum rugosum, Gærtn.
Masán, ..	Iseilema laxum, Hack.
Masán, ..	Iseilema laxum, Hack.
Mathaniya, ..	Chloris Roxburghiana, Edgew.
Mathna, ..	Eleusine ægyptiaca, Pers.
Mehat, ..	Ischæmum rugosum, Gærtn.
Mez, ..	Isachne australis, R. Br.
Mijhri, ..	Panicum miliare, Lamk.
Miniyár, ..	Andropogon annulatus, Forsk.
Mircha, ..	Andropogon Schœnanthus, Linn.
Mircha gand, ..	Andropogon laniger, Desf.
Mirchia, ..	Andropogon Schœnanthus, Linn.
Mirchia gand, ..	Andropogon Schœnanthus, Linn.
Mirchua, ..	Andropogon Schœnanthus, Linn.
Moi, ..	Eragrostis bifaria, W. & A.

Vernacular name.	Botanical name.
Moiya, ..	Pennisetum Alopecuros, Steud.
Moka, ..	Zea Mays, Linn.
Mondia jori, ..	Eragrostis tenella, Beauv.
Morbhaga ghás, ..	Chloris tenella, Roxb.
Mortham, ..	Pennisetum Alopecuros, Steud.
Mothi kabbal, ..	Panicum sanguinale, Linn.
Motia, ..	Panicum distachyum, Linn.
Motia, ..	Panicum helopus, Trin.
Mowa, ..	Pennisetum Alopecuros, Steud.
Mujna, ..	Andropogon foveolatus, Del.
Mukka, ..	Zea Mays, Linn.
Mular, ..	Andropogon intermedius, Br., *var.* genuinus.
Mulkas, ..	Bambusa arundinacea, Retz.
Mungil, ..	Bambusa arundinacea, Retz.
Munhák, ..	Andropogon foveolatus, Del.
Munj, ..	Saccharum ciliare, Anders.
Munji, ..	Pollinia eriopoda, Hance.
Munkil, ..	Bambusa arundinacea, Retz.
Munmona, ..	Apluda aristata, Linn.
Munmuna, ..	Ischæmum rugosum, Gærtn.
Murdi, ..	Ischæmum rugosum, Gærtn.
Murgai, ..	Andropogon foveolatus, Del.
Murha, ..	Eleusine coracana, Gærtn.
Murjaini, ..	Andropogon foveolatus, Del.
Murjnah, ..	Andropogon foveolatus, Del.
Murmuru, ..	Apluda aristata, Linn.
Musán, ..	Iseilema, Wightii.
Musán, ..	Iseilema laxum, Hack.
Musapunchi, ..	Panicum myosuroides, R. Br.
Musel, ..	Iseilema laxum, Hack.
Musel, ..	Anthistiria ciliata, Linn. f.
Musel, ..	Heteropogon contortus, R. & S.
Mushkani, ..	Andropogon muricatus, Retz.
Musiál, ..	Iseilema laxum, Hack.
N.	
Naga-sara maitantos, ..	Phragmites Roxburghii, Kunth.
Nai, ..	Hordeum vulgare, Linn.
Nai, ..	Phragmites Roxburghii, Kunth.
Nai-bindi, ..	Bambusa arundinacea, Retz.
Naka-kora, ..	Setaria glauca, Beauv.
Nakurnaral, ..	Eragrostis nutans, Nees.
Nal, ..	Phragmites Roxburghii, Kunth.
Nál báńs, ..	Bambusa arundinacea, Retz.
Nalli, ..	Phragmites Roxburghii, Kunth. (*var.* angustifolia).
Nallia, ..	Andropogon annulatus, Forsk.
Nalli-pootiki, ..	Aristida depressa, Retz.
Nalu, ..	Phragmites Roxburghii, Kunth.
Nar, ..	Phragmites Roxburghii, Kunth.
Naria, ..	Phragmites Roxburghii, Kunth.
Narkat, ..	Phragmites Roxburghii, Kunth.
Narkúl, ..	Phragmites Roxburghii, Kunth.
Narri, ..	Diplachne fusca, Beauv.
Narsal, ..	Phragmites Roxburghii, Kunth.
Ne, ..	Hordeum vulgare, Linn.
Neer, ..	Paspalum Kora, Linn.
Nella-shama, ..	Panicum miliare, Lamk.
Neori, ..	Setaria glauca, Beauv.
Newaree, ..	Oryza sativa, Linn.
Nika sáńwak, ..	Eragrostis pilosa, Beauv.
Nili dúb, ..	Cynodon Dactylon, Pers.
Nilon, ..	Andropogon annulatus, Forsk.
Nis, ..	Triticum sativum, Lamk.
Noktowa, ..	Setaria intermedia, R. & S.
Nonák, ..	Sporobolus diander, Beauv.
Nudar-nar, ..	Phragmites Roxburghii, Kunth.
Nulka gadi, ..	Pollinia eriopoda, Hance.
O.	
Oda, ..	Panicum flavidum, Retz.
Onei, ..	Andropogon muricatus, Retz.
Ooloo, ..	Imperata arundinacea, Cyrill.
Orai, ..	Andropogon muricatus, Retz.
Oyia, ..	Panicum colonum, Linn.
P.	
Paba, ..	Ischæmum ciliare, Retz.
Pachchian, ..	Saccharum officinarum, Linn.
Padar, ..	Saccharum spontaneum, Linn.
Padda jalla gadi,	Sorghum halepense, Pers.
Paddatunga gadi,	Panicum flavidum, Retz.
Paika gadi, ..	Phragmites Roxburghii, Kunth.
Palengi, ..	Sporobolus pallida, Nees.
Palichhi, ..	Eragrostis pilosa, Beauv.
Palinji, ..	Sporobolus, pallida, Nees.
Palinji, ..	Eragrostis plumosa, Link.
Pálla paggar gadi,	Chrysopogon cœruleus, Nees.
Palmaha, ..	Andropogon annulatus, Forsk.
Palmanega gadi,	Andropogon caricosus, Linn.
Pálon, ..	Panicum flavidum, Retz.
Paluah, ..	Chloris barbata, Swartz.
Palwa, ..	Andropogon pertusus, Willd.
Palwal, ..	Andropogon pertusus, Willd.
Palwal, ..	Andropogon Ischæmum, Linn.
Palwal, ..	Andropogon annulatus, Forsk.
Palwan, ..	Andropogon Ischæmum, Linn.
Palwán, ..	Andropogon annulatus, Forsk.
Palwán, ..	Andropogon annulatus, Forsk.
Palwán, ..	Andropogon Ischæmum, Linn.
Palwán, ..	Andropogon annulatus, Forsk.
Palwán, ..	Andropogon annulatus, Forsk.
Palwán, ..	Andropogon pertusus, Willd.
Palwánh, ..	Andropogon annulatus, Forsk.
Palwar, ..	Saccharum ciliare, Anders.
Panhawa, ..	Setaria glauca, Beauv.
Pankhágar, ..	Paspalum scrobiculatum, Linn.
Pánni, ..	Andropogon muricatus, Retz.
Panni, ..	Andropogon Schœnanthus, Linn.
Panni, ..	Andropogon muricatus, Retz.
Panni, ..	Erianthus Ravennæ, Beauv.
Panni, ..	Saccharum Sara, Roxb.
Panookoo, ..	Ophiurus lævis, Benth.
Pansheroo, ..	Hemarthria compressa, R. Br.

Vernacular name.	Botanical name.
Paraura,	Heteropogon contortus, R. & S.
Parba,	Heteropogon contortus, R. & S.
Parbi,	Heteropogon contortus, R. & S.
Pareba,	Heteropogon contortus, R. & S.
Parsál,	Hygrorhiza aristata, Nees.
Parwal,	Andropogon annulatus, Forsk.
Parwal,	Andropogon pertusus, Willd.
Passáhi,	Hygrorhiza aristata, Nees.
Passai,	Hygrorhiza aristata, Nees.
Passári,	Hygrorhiza aristata, Nees.
Pastál,	Hygrorhiza aristata, Nees.
Pata khuree,	Miscanthus fuscus, Anders.
Patáwar,	Saccharum ciliare, Anders.
Patoo-ederoo,	Phragmites Roxburghii, Kunth.
Paunda,	Saccharum officinarum, Linn.
Pedda,	Eleusine coracana, Gærtn, *var.* stricta.
Pedda-gantee,	Pennisetum typhoideum, Rich.
Pedda-panookoo,	Ophiurus corymbosus, Gærtn.
Pedda-woondoo,	Panicum Crus-Galli, Linn.
Peti-nar,	Panicum flavidum, Retz.
Phalwán,	Andropogon Ischæmum, Linn.
Phasáhi,	Hygrorhiza aristata, Nees.
Phikar,	Panicum miliaceum, Linn.
Phulaira,	Andropogon annulatus, Forsk.
Phularwa,	Eragrostis plumosa, Link.
Phulkia,	Chloris barbata, Swartz.
Phulkia,	Leptochloa filiformis, R. & S.
Phulni,	Tetrapogon villosus, Desf.
Phundi,	Chloris barbata, Swartz.
Phundra jadi,	Tetrapogon villosus, Desf.
Pingi,	Setaria italica, Kunth.
Pingi-natchi,	Setaria glauca, Beauv.
Pithi,	Eragrostis plumosa, Link.
Piyána koru gadi,	Ischæmum ciliare, Retz., *var.* villosum.
Pochati,	Heteropogon contortus, R. & S.
Pohwa,	Setaria glauca, Beauv., *var.*
Pona,	Saccharum officinarum, Linn.
Poori,	Saccharum officinarum, Linn.
Pootstrangali,	Apluda aristata, Linn.
Pulsú malwá gadi.	Iseilema Wightii.
Puniya	Perotis latifolia, Ait.
Punji,	Chloris barbata, Swartz.
Punya safed,	Eragrostis bifaria, W. & A.
Putti gadi,	Chrysopogon montanus, Trin.
R.	
Rad,	Panicum miliaceum, Linn.
Rági,	Eleusine coracana, Gærtn.
Ráha,	Panicum ciliare, Retz.
Ráli,	Panicum miliaceum, Linn.
Rám ghás,	Cynodon Dactylon, Pers.
Rámpla,	Aristida depressa, Retz.
Rara,	Saccharum spontaneum, Linn.
Rasaurah,	Eragrostis nutans, Nees.
Ratop,	Manisurus granularis, Swartz.
Ratua,	Sporobolus indicus, R. Br.
Rauṅs,	Andropogon Schœnanthus, Linn.
Relloo-gaddy,	Saccharum spontaneum, Linn.
Rhauṅsa,	Andropogon Schœnanthus, Linn.
Rhausa,	Andropogon Schœnanthus, Linn.
Riskawa,	Heteropogon contortus, R. & S.
Rohish,	Andropogon Schœnanthus, Linn.
Roiṅsa,	Andropogon Schœnanthus, Linn.
Ronák,	Aristida plumosa, Linn.
Rosa,	Andropogon Schœnanthus, Linn.
Roshegavat,	Andropogon Schœnanthus, Linn.
Rotka,	Eleusine coracana, Willd.
Rukab,	Andropogon pertusus, Willd.
Runa,	Andropogon laniger, Desf.
S.	
Sabe,	Pollinia eriopoda, Hance.
Saboi,	Pollinia eriopoda, Hance.
Sadanapa-vedroo,	Dendrocalamus strictus, Nees.
Safed bhurki,	Eragrostis plumosa, Link.
Saga,	Heteropogon contortus, R. & S.
Sager,	Tetrapogon villosus, Desf.
Sahri,	Panicum ciliare, Retz.
Sainad,	Ischæmum laxum, R. Br.
Sairan,	Ischæmum laxum, R. Br.
Sál,	Oryza sativa, Linn.
Sala kodam gadi,	Chloris Roxburghiana, Edgew.
Sálan,	Panicum miliaceum. Linn.
Sali,	Heteropogon contortus, R. & S.
Salla-woodoo,	Panicum helopus, Trin.
Samá,	Panicum frumentaceum, Roxb.
Sáma,	Panicum frumentaceum, Roxb.
Sáma,	Panicum Crus-Galli, Linn.
Samaghás,	Panicum colonum, Linn.
Sama jodi,	Panicum flavidum, Retz.
Sámak,	Panicum colonum, Linn.
Samei,	Panicum frumentaceum, Roxb.
Sámuka,	Panicum frumentaceum, Roxb.
Samwán,	Panicum helopus, Trin.
Sánka,	Panicum flavidum, Retz.
Sánklu,	Coix Lachryma, Linn.
Sankru,	Coix Lachryma. Linn.
Sántha,	Saccharum officinarum, Linn.
Santhran,	Apluda aristata, Linn.
Sáṅwak,	Panicum frumentaceum, Roxb.
Sáṅwak,	Panicum colonum, Linn.
Sáṅwak,	Panicum Crus-Galli, Linn.
Sáṅwan,	Panicum frumentaceum, Roxb.
Sar,	Phragmites Roxburghii, Kunth.
Sar,	Saccharum ciliare, Anders.
Sarahri,	Saccharum ciliare, Anders.
Sarála,	Heteropogon contortus, R. & S.
Sarári,	Heteropogon contortus, R. & S.
Sarghás	Saccharum Sara, Roxb.

Vernacular name.	Botanical name.	Vernacular name.	Botanical name.
Sariála, ..	Heteropogon contortus, R. & S.	Sirwala, ..	Andropogon foveolatus, Del.
		Sitiya, ..	Panicum flavidum, Retz.
Sarjbar, ..	Saccharum ciliare, Anders.	Siuri, ..	Panicum cimicinum, Retz.
Sarkanda, ..	Saccharum ciliare, Anders.	Siuri, ..	Panicum ciliare, Retz.
Sarkara, ..	Saccharum Sara, Roxb.	Sivaen, ..	Panicum colonum, Linn.
Sarkara, ..	Saccharum ciliare, Anders.	Siwan, ..	Elionurus hirsutus, Munro.
Sarmal, ..	Heteropogon contortus, R. & S.	Soa, ..	Hordeum vulgare, Linn.
		Soda, ..	Panicum paludosum, Roxb.
Sarpat, ..	Saccharum Sara, Roxb.	Sodee, ..	Eleusine coracana, Gærtn.
Sarpot, ..	Panicum erucæforme, Sibth.	Solára, ..	Andropogon laniger, Desf.
Sarpur, ..	Panicum prostratum, Lamk.	Som, ..	Pollinia eriopoda, Hance.
Sarput, ..	Panicum erucæforme, Sibth.	Soma, ..	Setaria glauca, Beauv.
Sarr, ..	Saccharum ciliare, Anders.	Sona, ..	Pollinia eriopoda, Hance.
Sarwála, ..	Heteropogon contortus, R. & S.	Sona-jhara, ..	Pollinia argentea, Trin.
		Sonthe, ..	Ophiurus corymbosa, Gærtn.
Sarwár, ..	Heteropogon contortus, R. & S.	Sukna, ..	Arundo Donax, Linn.
		Suntu bukrui, ..	Eleusine ægyptiaca, Pers.
Sarwára, ..	Ophiurus lævis, Benth.	Supedkar, ..	Panicum myosuroides, R. Br.
Satgathia, ..	Ophiurus lævis, Benth.	Sur, ..	Eragrostis nutans, Nees.
Satgattua, ..	Ophiurus lævis, Benth.	Surári, ..	Heteropogon contortus, R. & S.
Sathiya, ..	Panicum flavidum, Retz.	Suria, ..	Elytrophorus articulatus, Beauv.
Sauri ghás, ..	Heteropogon contortus, R. & S.		
Sawá, ..	Setaria intermedia, R. & S.	Suriála, ..	Heteropogon contortus, R. & S.
Sáwan, ..	Panicum frumentaceum, Roxb.	Surwál, ..	Heteropogon contortus, R. & S.
Sáwan bhedeha, ..	Panicum frumentaceum, Roxb.	Surwála, ..	Heteropogon contortus, R. & S.
Sáwan chaitwa, ..	Panicum miliaceum, Linn.	Surwár, ..	Heteropogon contortus, R. & S.
Sáwan dungarko,	Paspalum Kora, Linn.	Surwára, ..	Heteropogon contortus, R. & S.
Sáwan jethwa, ..	Panicum miliaceum, Linn.	Swati, ..	Pennisetum holcoides, Schult.
Sawánk, ..	Panicum colonum, Linn.		
Saweli, ..	Panicum colonum, Linn.	**T.**	
Sedwa, ..	Ischæmum laxum, R. Br.		
Sehri, ..	Panicum ciliare, Retz.	Tai, ..	Oryza sativa, Linn.
Semai, ..	Panicum helopus, Trin.	Takri, ..	Panicum sanguinale, Linn.
Send, ..	Apluda aristata, Linn.	Takriya, ..	Panicum sanguinale, Linn.
Sentha, ..	Saccharum ciliare, Anders.	Talaphetar, ..	Heleochloa schœnoides, Host.
Seran, ..	Ischæmum laxum, R. Br.	Talla, ..	Cynodon Dactylon, Pers.
Shak, ..	Setaria italica, Kunth.	Tám, ..	Pollinia argentea, Trin.
Sháli, ..	Setaria italica, Kunth.	Támbat, ..	Andropogon glaber, Roxb.
Shálian, ..	Oryza sativa, Linn.	Tandua, ..	Sporobolus orientalis, Kunth.
Shálu, ..	Setaria italica, Kunth.	Tángun, ..	Setaria italica, Kunth.
Shama, ..	Panicum frumentaceum, Roxb.	Táni, ..	Oryza sativa, Linn.
Shama, ..	Panicum colonum, Linn.	Tarar, ..	Panicum prostratum, Lamk.
Shamukha, ..	Panicum antidotale, Retz.	Tatiyán, ..	Themeda Forskalii, Hack.
Shangali-gaddi, ..	Panicum ciliare, Retz.	Taura, ..	Pennisetum cenchroides, Rich.
Shar, ..	Saccharum Sara, Roxb.	Tella, ..	Sorghum vulgare, Pers.
Shervoo, ..	Hemarthria compressa, R. Br.	Teng, ..	Saccharum procerum, Roxb.
Shilpuroo kalli, ..	Aristida hystrix, Linn.	Thanzatt, ..	Hordeum vulgare, Linn.
Shiroka, ..	Hordeum vulgare, Linn.	Thikhari, ..	Andropogon Schœnanthus, Linn.
Shiwan, ..	Elionurus hirsutus, Munro.		
Shrúk, ..	Hordeum vulgare, Linn.	Thontwa, ..	Setaria glauca, Beauv.
Shur, ..	Saccharum Sara, Roxb.	Thún, ..	Panicum helopus, Trin.
Sikka, ..	Panicum ciliare, Retz.	Tigri, ..	Chrysopogon cœruleus, Nees.
Sil, ..	Imperata arundinacea, Cyrill.	Tikhadi-moti, ..	Andropogon Schœnanthus, Linn.
Sin, ..	Elionurus hirsutus, Munro.		
Sink, ..	Andropogon muricatus, Retz.	Tikha lodan, ..	Iseilema laxum, Hack.
Sinka, ..	Aristida depressa, Retz.	Tikhari, ..	Andropogon Schœnanthus, Linn.
Sink-jháru, ..	Andropogon muricatus, Retz.		
Sipari gadi, ..	Eragrostis plumosa, Link.	Tikriya, ..	Andropogon pertusus, Willd.
Sir, ..	Imperata arundinacea, Cyrill.	Til, ..	Saccharum ciliare, Anders.
Sira, ..	Ischæmum laxum, R. Br.	Tilak, ..	Saccharum, sp.
Sir ghurai, ..	Andropogon laniger, Desf.	Tilchañwali, ..	Eragrostis ciliaris, Link., *var.*
Sirki, ..	Saccharum ciliare, Anders.	Tiliya, ..	Panicum erucæforme, Sibth.
Sirmakar, ..	Panicum colonum, Linn.	Tilla, ..	Cynodon Dactylon, Pers.
Sirom, ..	Andropogon muricatus, Retz.	Tilon, ..	Saccharum ciliare, Anders.
Siru, ..	Imperata arundinacea, Cyrill.	Tinni, .	Hygrorhiza aristata, Nees.

Vernacular name.	Botanical name.
Tipakia, ..	Eleusine ægyptiaca, Pers.
Titar, ..	Anthistiria scandens, Roxb.
Tokár, ..	Triticum sativum, Lamk.
Toli, ..	Ischæmum rugosum, Gærtn.
Tomar, ..	Triticum sativum, Lamk.
Torchandbol, ..	Eragrostis ciliaris, Link.
Tro, ..	Hordeum vulgare, Linn.
Tro, ..	Triticum sativum, Lamk.
Tsedze, ..	Panicum miliaceum, Linn.
Tudi, ..	Ischæmum rugosum, Gærtn.
Tur-murgah, ..	Andropogon Ischæmum, Linn.
U.	
Ukh, ..	Saccharum officinarum, Linn.
Ukhári, ..	Saccharum officinarum, Linn.
Ula, ..	Anthistiria arundinacea, Roxb.
Ula, ..	Imperata arundinacea, Cyrill.
Uṅdar gin, ..	Arthraxon ciliare, Beauv.
Uṅdar puchha, ..	Perotis latifolia, Ait.
Uṅdar punchha, ..	Setaria intermedia, R. & S.
Uṅdar punchho, ..	Eragrostis ciliaris, Link.
Undri, ..	Arthraxon ciliare, Beauv.
Urai, ..	Andropogon muricatus, Retz.
Urdiya, ..	Panicum humile, Nees.
Urenka, ..	Eragrostis nutans, Nees.
Uri dhán, ..	Oryza sativa, Linn.
Ursori, ..	Andropogon muricatus, Retz.
Usar ki ghás, ..	Sporobolus orientalis, Kunth.
Ushir, ..	Andropogon muricatus, Retz.
Usirh, ..	Imperata arundinacea, Cyrill.
Utaniya, ..	Oplismenus Burmanni, Linn.
Ute sirkun jári, ..	Eleusine ægyptiaca, Pers.
Ute sirla gadi, ..	Eleusine ægyptiaca, Pers.
V.	
Vál, ..	Andropogon muricatus, Retz.
Varágu, ..	Panicum miliaceum, Linn.
Várelu, ..	Andropogon muricatus, Retz.
Vedroo, ..	Bambusa arundinacea, Retz.
Vettiver, ..	Andropogon muricatus, Retz.
Vidar gucha gadi,	Andropogon pertusus, Willd.
W.	
Wadata-toka-gad-dee, ..	Dinebra arabica, Beauv.
Wanji jári, ..	Andropogon brevifolius, Sw.
Ware gadi, ..	Andropogon brevifolius, Sw.
Watániya, ..	Oplismenus Burmanni, Linn.
Woetiwear, ..	Andropogon muricatus, Retz.
Wooda-tallum, ..	Eragrostis bifaria, W. & A.
Woodoo-gaddi, ..	Panicum flavidum, Retz.
Woondoo-gaddi,	Panicum colonum, Linn.
Worga, ..	Panicum miliaceum, Linn.
Y.	
Yangma, ..	Hordeum vulgare, Linn.
Yava, ..	Hordeum vulgare, Linn.
Yeddi, ..	Heteropogon contortus, R. & S.
Yellika-tungoo-gadi, ..	Sporobolus coromandelianus, Roxb.
Yerwa, ..	Oplismenus Burmanni, Linn.
Z.	
Zad, ..	Triticum sativum, Lamk.

APPENDIX.

I AM indebted to Professor Hackel of St. Pölten for another valuable communication on Indian Grasses, which has fortunately reached me in time to enable me to include in this Appendix some important notes in the way of additions and corrections.

***Page* 2.** In addition to the Indian species of *Paspalum* already referred to, the following should be mentioned :—

P. costatum, *Hochst. Vern.*—RAJPUTANA: *Kuri* (Mount Abu). A very elegant little grass, growing in wet ground on Mount Abu.

P. minutiflorum, *Steud.*, of which I have specimens gathered in Dehra Dún.

The name **Eriochloa annulata,** *Kunth.*, should replace that of *E. polystachya*, H. B. & K.

***Page* 3.** The Rájputána vernacular name "*mez*" given under *Isachne australis*, R. Br., refers to another species called **I. dispar,** *Trin.*

***Page* 17.** The name **Pennisetum lanuginosum,** *Hochst.*, should replace that of *P. holcoides*, Schult.; and the name on *Plate* XLIX. should be similarly altered.

***Page* 21.** Allied to *Rhynchelytrum Wightii*, is an undescribed species, specimens of which, gathered at Ajmere, have been named **Tricholæna tuberculosa** by Professor Hackel.

***Page* 26.** A variety of *Erianthus Ravennæ*, Beauv., called **purpurascens,** (*Syn.*—*E. purpurascens*, Anders.,) occurs also in the plains.

***Page* 27.** Add **Pollinia ciliata,** *Trin. Syn.*—*P. lancea*, Nees. Ravines, Dehra Dún.

„ "*A. ciliare*" should be "*A. ciliaris.*"

***Page* 28.** The vernacular names given under *Arthraxon ciliaris*, Beauv., refer to *A. lanceolatus*, Hochst. (*Syn.—An-*

dropogon lanceolatus, Roxb.) I have, however, specimens of *A. ciliaris* from Mount Abu.

Page 28. Add to *Rottbœllia exaltata*, Linn. f. *Vern.*—RAJPUTANA: *Dábir* (Mount Abu).

Page 29. The name **Ophiurus perforatus**, *Trin.*, should replace that of *O. lævis*, Benth.

Page 30. Under *Ischæmum ciliare*, Retz., the vernacular name "*Kála*" should be omitted.

Page 31. After "*I. pilosum*, Hack.," read "*Monogr. ined.*"

Page 34. After "*A. gangeticus*, Hack.," read "*Monogr. ined.*"

Page 35. Add "**Andropogon Hügelii**, *Hack. Monogr. ined.* HABITAT: Mount Abu in Rájputána."

,, *Andropogon laniger*, Desf. Specimens collected at Ajmere are pronounced by Professor Hackel to be intermediate between this species and *A. Iwarancusa* (*A. Schœnanthus*, Linn.)

Page 36. Add "**Andropogon micranthus**, *Kunth.* *Var. villosulus*, Hack. Monogr. ined. *Vern.*—BUNDELKHAND: *Ballak* (Mount Abu)." See remarks on this species under *Chrysopogon montanus*, Trin., p. 40.

Page 37. Add **Andropogon Nardus**, *Linn.*; Sub-species *khasianus*, Hack. Monogr. ined. *Syn.*—*A. khasinus*, Munro. M. S. *Vern.*—*Tachla* or *chiriála* (Dehra Dun). A tall sweet-scented grass resembling *A. Schœnanthus.*

After "*Andropogon pachyarthrus*, Hack.," add "Monogr. ined."

Page 38. Add **Andropogon Pseudoischæmum**, *Nees.* Abundant in the plains of Northern India, and often confounded with *A. annulatus*, Forsk, and *A. Ischæmum*, Linn.; also *var. obtusnisculus*, Hack. Monogr. ined., which differs from the type by its blunter glumes.

Page 39. "*Chrysopogon cæruleus*, Nees." should be **Andropogon Trinii**, *Steud.* *Syn.*—*Chrysopogon serrulatus*, Trin.; *Rhaphis cærulea*, Nees.

,, The vernacular name "*tigri*" under *C. cæruleus*, Nees. refers to *C. montanus*, Trin., on p. 40.

Page 40. Under *Chrysopogon montanus*, Trin., add Vernacular names "*Tigri* (Bundelkhand)" and *Karmi* (Mount Abu). The other name "*ballak*" refers to *Andropogon mic-*

ranthus, Kunth, as also the remarks regarding its value as fodder.

Page 42. "*Anthisteria gigantea*, Cav.," is "**Themeda gigantea,** *Hack. Monogr. ined.*" *Var. caudata. Syn.—A. caudata*, Nees. and *A. Hookeri*, Griseb.

Page 43. After "*Themeda ciliata*, Hack." A. (*Themeda Forskallii* Hack.)" and "*I. laxum*, Hack.," add "*Monogr. ined.*"

Page 47. *Aristida hystricula*, Edgew., occurs in the Etáwah District, and is called "*lappa.*"

Page 49. Professor Hackel is of opinion that the specimens I have named *Sporobolus orientalis*, Kunth, and what is represented on *Plate* XXXII., should be referred to **S. pallidus,** *Nees*, or to a variety of that species. Only the name requires alteration, and the synonym *Vilfa orientalis* should disappear.

Page 54. The name **Chloris digitata,** *Steud.*, should replace that of *C. Roxburghiana*, Edgew.

Page 55. Add **Tetrapogon tetrastachys,** *Hack. Monogr. ined* (n. sp.), concerning which Professor Hackel remarks—"A very surprising new species, not only differing from *T. villosus* by its four spikes, but by a host of characters." It is this grass which is so especially characteristic of the reh soils of the Doab. The N.-W. Provinces Vernacular names under *T. villosus* should be referred here, also *Plate* LXVIII.

,, Line 14 from bottom, for "*Sporobolus orientalis*," read "*Sporobolus palludus*."

Page 64. Professor Hackel distinguishes a variety of *Eragrostis plumosa*, Link., with congested panicles, under the name of *densiflora*. This variety is plentiful in Northern India on sandy and saline soils.

Page 65. Add **Eragrostis stenophylla,** *Hochst.* Abundant in wet ground. I have specimens from the Doab, Bundelkhand, and from Mount Abu.

,, For *Eragrostis tremula*, Hochst., substitute the name **Eragrostis rachitricha,** Hochst., the true *E. tremula* being apparently confined to Nubia.

Add to Vernacular List—

Ballak = Andropogon micranthus, Kunth. *Var.* villosulus.

Chiriála = Andropogon Nardus, Linn. Subsp. khasianus, Hack.

Dábir = **Rottbœllia exaltata, Linn. f.**
Karmi = **Chrysopogon montanus, Trin.**
Kuri = **Paspalum costatum, Hochst.**
Lappa = **Aristida hystricula, Edgew.**
Mez = **Isachne dispar, Trin.**
Tachla = **Andropogon Nardus, Linn. Subsp. khasianus, Hack.**
Uñdar gin
Undri } = **Arthraxon lanceolatus, Hochst.**

INDEX OF LATIN AND ENGLISH NAMES.

R.

* See also in Appendix.